SYSTEMS
AND ACTORS
IN INTERNATIONAL
POLITICS

Chandler Publications in Political Science
Victor Jones, Editor

SYSTEMS
AND ACTORS
IN INTERNATIONAL
POLITICS

Edited by
LE ROY GRAYMER
University of California, Berkeley

CHANDLER PUBLISHING COMPANY
An Intext Publisher · Scranton / London / Toronto

CONTENTS

v

PREFACE

The purpose of this book is to provide an introduction to international relations which helps to bridge the distance between theoretical work being developed by scholars and the more topical materials needed by beginning students in this field. In this book, we have employed two broad conceptual approaches to the study of international relations as organizing tools for the discussion of historical materials and case studies. The first part of the book focuses on broad patterns of international relations. The historical materials selected for this part help to illustrate how "systems concepts" may be employed to understand general patterns of relations among nations and how these relationships change over time. This approach also helps students to gain some historical perspective for thinking about current international affairs.

In the second part of the book case studies are used to illustrate how "foreign-policy decision-making analysis" can be used in the study of international relations. The focus of analysis is on the characteristics of the countries and their foreign-policy decision makers. By using actual cases involving several different types of countries, this material also helps to provide students with some important factual information about foreign policy in the world today.

It is our hope that the students who use this book will learn how to think more systematically about international relations and at the same time acquire additional knowledge of recent trends and events in the international arena.

I wish to express appreciation to the Institute of International Studies at the University of Oregon, and the Ford Foundation for support in developing the materials which have been incorporated in this book.

LeRoy Graymer

THE CONTRIBUTORS

MICHAEL P. GEHLEN is the Chairman of the Political Science Department at the University of New Mexico. From 1965 to 1969 he was Professor of Political Science at Purdue University. His major fields of interest are comparative analysis of Soviet and East European politics, and international relations among Communist states. Some of his publications in these fields include: *The Politics of Coexistence,* 1967; *The Communist Party of the Soviet Union: A Functional Analysis,* 1969; "The Educational and Career Backgrounds of the Members of the Central Committee of the CPSU," *The American Behavioral Scientist,* April, 1966; "The Integrative Process in Eastern Europe: A Theoretical Framework," *The Journal of Politics,* February, 1968; "The Soviet Central Committee: An Elite Analysis" (with Michael McBride), *The American Political Science Review,* December, 1968; "Group Theory and the Study of Soviet Politics," in *Approaches to the Study of the Soviet Political System,* edited by Sidney I. Ploss.

LE ROY GRAYMER is Associate Dean of the Graduate School of Public Affairs at the University of California, Berkeley. Previously he was Assistant to the Chairman of the Political Science Department at Berkeley. From 1963 to 1966 he was a member of the staff of the Institute of International Studies at the University of Oregon, where he directed a program to improve understanding of International Relations in secondary schools. His publications include: "Violence, Conflict Management and the United Nations," *WAR*, Institute on World Affairs, San Diego, 1966; "Teaching International Relations: Three Systematic Approaches" (co-author), Spring 1966 issue of *The Michigan Journal of the Secondary School Principals' Association.* He has edited and co-authored several studies published by the Institute of International Studies at the University of Oregon including: "The United Nations," "Africa: A Crucible for Social and Political Change," "The Sino-Soviet Rift," and "European Integration and Atlantic Partnership."

RICHARD L. HAINES is currently on the faculty of the Department of Political Science at Purdue University. Previously he taught in the Political Science Department at the University of Calgary, Alberta, Canada. Professor Haines' fields of interest include systems approaches to the administrative process, and the role of ideology in local elite decision making. Most recently Professor Haines has been engaged in an investigation of the ideological antecedents of policy processes in the American Midwest. He has also taught courses in research methodology, Canadian parties and voting behavior, and organization theory.

OLE R. HOLSTI is Associate Professor of Political Science at the University of British Columbia. From 1962 to 1967 he was a member of the Political Science faculty at Stanford University. His major fields of interest are in foreign-policy decision making, international politics, and political theory. He has published numerous articles and contributed to several books in those fields. His books include: *Content Analysis for the Social Sciences and Humanities,* 1969; *Crises, Escalation and War,* 1971; *Enemies in Politics* (co-author), 1967; and *The Analysis of Communication Content: Developments in Scientific Theories and Computer Techniques,* 1969. Currently he is serving as associate editor of *Western Political Quarterly, Journal of Conflict Resolution,* and *International Studies Quarterly.* He is a past president of International Studies Association/West.

ROBERTA KOPLIN MAPP is Assistant Professor of Political Science at the University of Alberta, Canada. Her research interests and activities include a study of the relationship between education and national integration in Ghana and Kenya, participation in the multinational student survey co-sponsored by the Western Behavioral Sciences Institute (La Jolla, California) and the Institute for Peace and Conflict Resolution (Copenhagen), and a study of the phenomenon of political instability in sub-Saharan Africa. Her published work includes: "A Model of Student Politicization in Developing Nations," *Comparative Political Studies,* Vol. 1, October, 1968; "Ghana" (with David Finlay), in *Students and Politics in Developing Nations,* edited by Donald K. Emerson, 1968; and "Kenya University Students and Politics," in *African Students and Politics,* edited by William J. Hanna.

SYSTEMS
AND ACTORS
IN INTERNATIONAL
POLITICS

INTRODUCTION

Le Roy Graymer
University of California, Berkeley

For a great many reasons, Americans today are highly conscious of international affairs and the involvement of the United States in these events. The Vietnam war in particular has become a part of and has stimulated a host of domestic social, economic, and political issues in American society. The arguments over the appropriateness of United States policy in Southeast Asia have raised a great many questions about the nature of international politics and the domestic considerations that influence foreign-policy decisions. The debates on this issue have revealed a great number of conflicting assumptions about the general configuration of international politics. Supporters of United States intervention have argued that the revolutionary forces of the Viet Cong with the aid of the North Vietnamese are part of a generalized revolutionary scheme to expand communism throughout the world by force, subversion or any other means. In support of this argument, they point to public statements by Communist Chinese leaders, Marxist-Leninist ideology, and the fact that both China and the Soviet Union are supplying vast quantities of aid to these and other revolutionary groups.

Opponents of United States intervention have attacked the policy from many positions. Generally, most reject the assumption that the revolutionary forces in Vietnam constitute a threat to United States security. They argue that indigenous revolutions grow out of the conditions within these countries. The fact that they are communist doesn't necessarily make them subject to con-

1

trol and direction from the Soviet Union or Communist China. Furthermore, it is argued that by opposing "Communism" everywhere in the world, the United States has become the supporter of the status quo, thereby losing the confidence of many leaders of smaller nations who are seeking social change.

The major consideration in both of these arguments centers around different concepts of the "balance of forces" between major powers in the world and of the way specific events in areas like Southeast Asia affect that relationship.

This debate has also focused on how foreign policy is formulated in the United States. Questions have been raised about the appropriate foreign-policy roles of Congress and the President, about who controls the military, about the relative priorities between foreign and domestic affairs.

In attempting to develop some clear thinking on these vital questions, it is necessary to develop some analytical concepts that will enable us to sort out arguments on specific issues and see how they relate to broader questions of international politics and foreign policy. This is not the first time these questions have arisen. Questions about the basic factors that influence the way nations relate to one another have been discussed before, during, and after every war. The Concert of Europe following the Napoleonic wars, the League of Nations, and the United Nations created in 1945 to "save succeeding generations from the scourge of war . . ." were all based on assumptions about the factors that influenced how nations related to one another. The primary purpose of this book is to introduce some broad concepts which can be used to order and analyze information about international politics. Both historical material and cases in foreign policy will be used to show how these concepts can be applied in the analysis of international politics and foreign policy.

While historical perspective is very useful for understanding current developments, the "lessons of history" are not necessarily self-evident. Selecting from an array of historical "information" the items that can be applied to a subject such as international politics requires some organizing tools that will enable us to see broad patterns and trends. Two major conceptual frameworks provide the focus of this book. The first is designed to provide the broadest perspective by attempting to discover the patterns of relationships that exist between and among nations. In Part I (Chapters 1 and 2), we have approached international relations as a social system consisting of a number of actors who relate to one another in accordance with some regular and predictable patterns depending on how certain key variables function in the system.

Developing a list of these key variables and explaining their relationships require that we devise a method of examining these processes. Since we can't examine this subject under controlled laboratory conditions, we must resort to a much cruder type of study. For this purpose we have taken recorded history in the last 200 to 300 years and probed this literature to ascertain which key variables and relationships have been most important in the political relations between nations.

In this examination we have first tried to ascertain who the actors or participants were in this system. Beginning in the eighteenth century, the most important "actors" in the system were nation-states. Since politics at any level involves questions of who is exercising influence or power, we attempted to see how different actors (nation-states) are related to one another in these terms. The way in which power and influence are distributed among the actors is one of the primary factors determining how the system functions.

The actors having been identified, and their relative capabilities to influence one another assessed, this analysis then searches for regularities in the patterns of relationships between these actors. Do nations form alliances and, if so, with what other actors and with what degree of permanence or flexibility? Out of this examination, we sought to identify some recurring patterns of behavior that we can describe as the "rules of the system." We then attempted to see what factors promoted or detracted from stability or change in the system.

By examining history from this perspective, we should be prepared to describe at least tentatively the general framework within which international politics functions. We may also be able to recognize, or hopefully even to predict, broad trends in relations between nations. Stability, instability, and change are a part of the patterns and trends that we are interested in observing and analyzing. For example, if the number and relative capability of nations is undergoing change, we can expect that there will be some change in the "rules" by which the system functions. This same change process may also affect the stability of the relations between actors.

The obvious danger of relying solely on this level of analysis is that nations are not individual entities or people. They themselves are complex social systems. Internal factors will greatly influence the decisions made by governments on foreign-policy issues. The question of whether or not to sell arms or give other types of foreign aid to countries can be influenced by internal political, social, and economic considerations. For this reason, the second major section of this book focuses on the internal processes influencing foreign-policy decision making.

Part II of the book is devoted to an examination of the types of people who get involved in decision making, the political processes that operate within countries, the physical factors that set certain limits on choices, and the broader social setting which has salience for foreign-policy decisions. We are also interested in how and when these factors become important in decision making.

The historical and case materials used in this book have been selected both for the applications discussed above and to provide a source of information about political events and political systems that have important implications for international politics today. The historical periods discussed are those in which the nation-state has been the dominant political actor in the international system. Furthermore, the international system that began in the eighteenth century deteriorated by the later part of the nineteenth century and was followed by a period of great instability. The events following World War II have been exceedingly important in shaping the perceptions of foreign-policy decision makers in the past twenty years.

The foreign-policy cases have been selected to focus attention on several different political systems. For example, Chapter 3 examines two crucial decisions in United States foreign policy — President Kennedy s actions in the 1962 Cuban missile crisis and the decision by the United States Senate in 1919 *not* to ratify the Treaty of Versailles, thereby excluding the United States from membership in the League of Nations. These two decisions are compared primarily from the standpoint of the influences that internal political processes have on foreign-policy decision making.

In contrast, Chapter 4 examines the ways in which the backgrounds of the leaders influence their foreign-policy *orientations*. The two cases of the Soviet Union and Communist China are used to demonstrate contrasts in orientation based on the different backgrounds and experiences of the leaders in these two nations.

The fifth chapter discusses French and Ghanaian foreign policies in the light of a wide range of domestic factors such as a culture, geography, and national cohesion. These cases provide an opportunity to discuss factors that influence the attitudes of the general population as well as the outlook and actions of political leaders.

While the cases are designed to illustrate some of the different factors that should be examined to learn more about foreign policies, they also provide much information about different types of nations and international situations. One should use the information in the different cases to examine the concepts set forth in the other chapters. For example, the discussion of the leaders in the Soviet Union in Chapter 4 provides information on Soviet political processes that relates to the discussion of the Cuban missile crisis in Chapter 3.

Taken together, the two broad approaches to studying international relations discussed in this volume can provide a person with some valuable intellectual tools to make sense out of the vast array of disconnected information he receives daily. The fact that events which occur in areas geographically remote from us can have a profound effect on our personal lives and the future of nations and populations should provide us all with compelling reasons to cultivate these skills.

Part I

INTERNATIONAL SYSTEMS

Chapter 1

THE BALANCE-OF-POWER SYSTEM IN EUROPE

Richard L. Haines
Purdue University

This chapter is concerned with an international system that functioned in Europe during the two centuries before World War I. For this discussion, the term "balance of power" will be used to label this system. Careful consideration of the conditions that gave rise to this particular pattern of relationships among the European powers, and of the events that contributed to its eventual collapse in the first decades of the twentieth century, will add to our ability to analyze and make sense out of world politics today. As the discussion proceeds it will become clear, for instance, that much of present-day international conflict has very deep historical roots. Indeed, familiar patterns of conflict and cooperation among the major powers since World War II have been strongly conditioned by past events and time-honored diplomatic habits.

A second contribution of this chapter will be its introduction to the insights one may derive from employing a particular type of analytical approach to international relations — namely, "systems theory." This way of looking at world politics attempts to take into account a multitude of diverse factors affecting international behavior, but it highlights the characteristic responses of individual nations that are closely bound up in a complex system of interaction with other nations. Rather than specific foreign-policy decisions, long-term characteristic patterns of action and response in the arena of world politics become the focus of analysis.

THE CONCEPT OF "SYSTEM"

We are all aware of a multiplicity of systems operating in our world. There are computer systems, river-tributary systems, "systems" to beat the tables at Las Vegas, and many others. All such systems are composed of a number of interrelated or interacting elements. The operation or performance of these elements contributes to some larger and more important performance by the entire system; that is, each system does something, with its individual units acting together to fulfill this system function. For example, associated with the tributary system of the Mississippi River are many smaller rivers and streams (and not a few sewage systems) all of which contribute to moving water from the Middle West of the United States to the Gulf of Mexico. A good gambling system, on the other hand, is a set of interrelated rules for playing, each of which contributes to winning money. And a computer system is composed of a number of extremely elaborate electronic devices each having its own role in assuring that complex mathematical computations are performed rapidly and accurately.

What is most significant about the elements of these systems is not the fact that they may be in close proximity to one another or that they are somehow alike or operate in similar ways, but that each element in its own way contributes to the performance of some system function or process. In the study of international affairs a system can be seen as a group of nations engaged in an interactive process designed (they hope) to allow them to pursue their national goals while maximizing national security. From the perspective of systems theory, the function of this system is to maintain international stability within certain allowable limits. Central to the analysis of any system is an investigation of the internal and external conditions underlying system stability. As will become evident in the following discussion of international affairs, systems analysis focuses initially on regular patterns of interaction among system elements, while change or instability tends to be attributed to alterations in the conditions under which systems operate.

By definition, the elements of a system are in more or less continuous regular interaction. That is, in a system the elements interact with one another over a period of time and they do so in much the same manner throughout this period. Saying this about the behavior of the members of a system is the same as saying that they act according to a set of rules. If nations appear to interact with one another according to regular patterns, then we can learn a good deal about international relations by examining these recurrent patterns and specifying what kinds of rules seem to be influencing such recurrent international behavior.

It should be emphasized that the behavior of nations is in fact the behavior of national leaders in a social and political context. For this reason we would not expect such rigid conformity to system rules as we find in systems of physical objects like rivers or electronic devices. Nevertheless, the fact remains that nations and people do act in large part according to fairly regular patterns and for this reason it is often useful to analyze such phenomena from the perspective provided by the notion of "systems." In the following pages an attempt will be made to discuss the patterns of international behavior that seem to have emerged over the last two hundred or so years of world history. In this way it may be possible to demonstrate that there has been a certain amount of continuity in world affairs, even though pressures for instability, and thus system change, are always present to some degree. From the analytical approach emphasizing "systems" in international relations a great deal can be learned which helps explain present-day international problems.

THE BALANCE-OF-POWER SYSTEM

The familiar concept of "balance of power" has been a subject for intense argument among scholars and statesmen for many years. A dispute rages over just what this idea refers to in terms of the realities of international affairs. Is it a valid description of the real world of international relations either today or in the past? Is it a goal sought by all nations but hardly ever attained? Is balance of power an ideology that stresses hard-nosed realism rather than idealism in the conduct of foreign affairs? Or, is it simply an easy justification for any particular desired state of international affairs? Despite such ambiguities, the idea of balance of power has been usefully employed to describe the patterns of international politics among the major powers in Europe throughout the eighteenth century and much of the nineteenth. This type of international system is said to have developed early in this period as an answer to attempts by various individual rulers to create and maintain military and political domination over the whole of Europe. The present-day controversy over the exact meaning of "balance of power" is probably a symptom of the difficulties involved in sustaining such a system during the closing years of the nineteenth century. Indeed, by the time statesmen were fully convinced of the critical importance of the rules of this type of system, world social and political conditions had changed so much that the system was in the process of decay and transformation to a new kind of international system that emerged in the twentieth century.

Basically, what is referred to by the concept of balance of power is a system composed of several independent states possessing roughly equal military power. Each state is expected to act strictly according to its own national self-interest most of the time. However, in the event that one state decides that its national interest is to destroy or dominate others in the system, military alliances are quickly made to oppose such aggression with superior force. In this manner an equilibrium is maintained in the system, which ensures independence and freedom of action for all.

As with any kind of international system, the balance of power did not emerge overnight but developed over a long period of time through usage. As early as the sixteenth century, Cardinal Wolsey, a close adviser to King Henry VIII of England, is supposed to have launched a deliberate policy of maintaining a European balance of power by shifting England's support alternatively to the Bourbon monarchy of France and to the Hapsburg empire of Austria. French kings, until well into the eighteenth century, used alliances with the Turkish Empire to offset the power of the Austrian Hapsburgs. King Henri IV and his chief minister, Cardinal Richelieu, also exploited the division between Europe's Catholic and Protestant rulers to France's political advantage. The treaty of the Peace of Westphalia in 1648 ended the European religious conflict called the Thirty Years War by breaking up the Austrian-dominated Holy Roman Empire in Central Europe. By keeping Germany divided into numerous weak states for more than two hundred years, this treaty created both a political and a religious balance in Europe and assured France that no power in Central Europe could be great enough to threaten French security. In a similar manner England, after warding off the invasion of the Spanish Armada in 1588, was forced to meet Louis XIV's bid for French domination in Europe and attempted to mobilize Protestant European support. In the eighteenth century an alliance built around England, the Netherlands across the English Channel, and Austria in Central Europe, became the political and military instrument for bringing French expansion to a halt. In addition, from an English point of view, Russia's defeat of Sweden in the same century established an equilibrium of power in the Baltic Sea area which guaranteed English access to this vital source of supply. Russia's success against France's other ally, Turkey, was similarly applauded by England since it secured the British naval position in the Mediterranean.

Ironically, what might be called the "golden age" of the balance-of-power international system — the eighteenth century — was an era of continual warfare. And yet warfare itself was so different from what we know of war today that it seems almost ridiculous by modern standards. Battles between armies were slow, formal, elaborate, and almost always indecisive. Soldiers of all countries were professionals usually recruited from a common pool of international mercenaries rather than from useful, productive and tax-paying civilians at home. Soldiers were a class apart who enlisted for long terms, were paid regular wages, and dressed in an infinite variety of colorful and elaborate uniforms, even in battle. Generals hesitated to risk their troops because they took years to train and equip and were therefore very expensive. All-out battles to the death were judiciously avoided because for one thing soldiers could not always be relied upon to stand to the last man in an uneven fight. Strategy took the form, not of seeking out the enemy's main force to destroy it in battle, but of maneuvering for the best military position. In this way a clear view of the probable outcome of a battle might stimulate the withdrawal of the army left in a disadvantageous position. Weapons were limited to small arms, and because of the difficulties of transportation battles took place within a few miles of the base of supply.

Never has war been quite so harmless, certainly not in the religious wars prior to the Peace of Westphalia nor in the national wars of the last years of the nineteenth century. For these reasons, European governments went to war on what now seems the slightest provocation. On the other side of the coin, governments also withdrew from war much more readily than they do in the twentieth century, especially when national treasuries were exhausted or when casualties among the best-trained soldiers began to mount.

There was little nationalistic feeling in warfare during this period. War was between governments or between the ruling groups represented by governments, not between entire peoples. It was fought for power, prestige, or calculated practical interests, not for ideologies, world conquest, national survival, or ways of life. Hence peace was almost as easy to make as war.

Peace treaties during this period were negotiated between equals and not imposed by conquerors over the vanquished. Thus the eighteenth century saw a series of wars and treaties, more wars, treaties, and rearrangements of alliances, all arising over much the same issues and with exactly the same powers present at the end as at the beginning. Out of this kind of experience the idea arose that a balance-of-power system was the natural state of international politics. Throughout the nineteenth century the principles of this type of system were on various occasions adhered to, invoked as justification for policy, violated for expediency, and damned as unprincipled. At the same time, however, new military, economic, and ideological forces made such a system increasingly difficult to sustain. The beginnings of the nineteenth century saw the importance of the balance-of-power type of international system reach its apex. The last years of the same century saw a steady decline in its capacity to maintain international stability.

THE RULES OF BALANCE OF POWER

If one examines the patterns of international relations among the major European powers during the era of balance of power it is possible to argue that certain general rules of war and diplomacy were followed. These principles may not have been clearly understood by all the rulers in Europe but each ruler seems to have acted in a manner designed to implement them. International stability depended on adherence to the following three rules:

First, always act to increase your own nation's capabilities or power, or in your national interest. If possible, do so through diplomatic negotiations rather than war, for war is costly and can lead to unforeseen consequences which might threaten the stability of the system. Nevertheless, go to war rather than fail to pursue your own national interests. Unless you are capable of protecting them they are not likely to prevail. Each nation's primary obligation is to itself.

Second, always negotiate a peace before you completely destroy another important nation in the system. Allow every defeated nation to reenter the system as an acceptable alliance partner or at least bring in another from outside the system to reestablish the balance. Treat all nations as acceptable alliance partners for you never know when you will need them to advance your own interests or to protect yourself.

Finally, oppose with utmost vigor any nation or alliance of nations which threatens to hold a position of dominance over the entire system of nations. This rule provides protection against being prevented from pursuing your own national interests. For the same reason, discourage those nations which act to create an international organization to control this system.

The rules of balance of power rely for the maintenance of international equilibrium on the rationality of individual states rather than on an obligation to submit to international control or arbitration. There is no "international policeman" who acts to restore order if a nation violates the rules of the system. Each power automatically sees to it that the rules are enforced because the importance of doing so is clear. Deliberate or unconscious violations of these rules, for instance by destroying an important nation, lead to conditions under which the benefits of the balance of power can no longer be counted on. In the extreme case the balance of power can be expected to collapse.

VIOLATIONS OF THE RULES

The balance-of-power system, as it emerged through practice, provided the major European powers a set of general principles which made international politics more calculable. The principles made it possible for individual states to avoid unnecessary losses. They also prevented a single power from making overwhelming gains. But, as with many such standards for social behavior, their significance became clearest when divergences from them threatened the stability of the European system.

One serious violation of the principles which seemed to underlie the balance of power occurred in the late eighteenth century when several powerful European monarchs decided to take advantage of military weakness and political instability in Poland. In three quick moves the rulers of Russia, Austria, and Prussia divided among themselves Poland's territories and people. This partition was a clear violation of the second rule of the balance-of-power system, which argues against the complete subjugation and elimination of another nation. It might be asserted that Poland was so feeble at this time that its loss was not an important factor in affecting the European balance, but the partition did destroy a potential alliance partner. It also demonstrated that under a system of rules which were supposed to assure that any major nation would survive, even a very large country could be eliminated. Moreover, dividing up the spoils of Poland not only stimulated the appetite of Russia and Prussia for further expansion in the nineteenth century, but also created suspicions of unequal rewards between them which served to delay the building of an alliance to meet the French threat in the years soon after. Violation of the system rules in the case of Poland was a cause of continual unrest in the nineteenth century, especially for the Russian tsar who, because of nationalist resentment, could not rely on peaceful loyalty in his Polish territories when it was needed most.

There was a second set of circumstances which threatened successful operation of the balance-of-power system in the late years of the eighteenth century. For such a system to work effectively it is necessary that each participating nation pay extremely close attention to the actions and motives of all the others so that a balancing countermove can be made in time to prevent the breakdown of the system. But the preoccupations of the European powers — especially France and Britain — with their struggle over colonies made it much more difficult to maintain a cautious European policy. Britain was particularly guilty of this. Being embroiled with preserving her American colonies and desiring to disentangle herself from European obligations, she found herself with few friends in Europe as a result. The most notorious example of this lapse in policy was British desertion of the alliance with Prussia in the Seven Years War (1756-1765) against France, Austria, and Russia. This placed Frederick the Great of Prussia in mortal danger and made Prussia an implacable foe of Britain. In this manner Great Britain lost a powerful friend and potential alliance partner, and as a result her position during the Napoleonic Wars was made extremely difficult because an effective alliance against France could not be assembled rapidly enough. Except for a brief interval she was at war with France from 1792 to 1815, at times in various European coalitions, but for a number of years all by herself.

It seems clear, from the perspective of systems analysis, that deliberate violation of the maxims of balance-of-power diplomacy by the occupiers of Poland, in conjunction with Britain's policy of disengagement from European power politics so that she might deal more effectively with her colonial problems, created a situation in which effective implementation of military alliances to meet threats to system stability became extremely difficult. The most critical development, however, was that a key member of the European state system, France, underwent a violent revolution that totally reshaped its internal political system and altered drastically its character as an international actor. The French monarchy collapsed; then, after passing through several phases of violent internal upheaval, the French republic emerged as a powerful champion of the principles of government based on the popular will; there could be no greater danger to the legitimacy and survival of the remaining European monarchies. Having finally consolidated its military power in the 1790's, France became a force for the destruction of the balance-of-power system, and in the years following nearly succeeded in creating a new European equilibrium based on radically different principles.

Napoleon's attempt to create in Europe a unified monarchy under the leadership of the French nation, and himself, was a direct attack on the existing system's rules. The strategy of limited war, a legacy of the eighteenth century, was abandoned. Napoleon's aim was annihilation of the armed forces of his enemies and he almost always achieved it with what he termed "lightning speed" and at great risk and cost. He had at his disposal much greater manpower than the absolute monarchs had commanded and he never hesitated to use all of the human and physical resources of France and of any country he conquered in order to gain absolute decisions on the battlefield and dictate political terms to the defeated. Peace itself was not negotiated but imposed militarily. Conquered states did not regain their political independence; they were made satellites of France. On almost all counts, then, Napoleon violated the principles which seemed vital to the maintenance of the European balance of power. His victories stemmed from great military skill, the inability of the other powers to react effectively in this new kind of war, and the popular support he met in each of the areas he conquered. This ingredient of popular enthusiasm was totally lacking in former limited wars.

Napoleon's military success was often greeted as a welcome relief from the despotism of the Central European monarchs. He encouraged and symbolized what many felt were the liberal political reforms of the French Revolution. But in a manner similar to that of a more recent would-be conqueror, Adolf Hitler, Napoleon rapidly lost popular support as his actions were compared unfavorably with his initial promises. Eventually his plans grew overambitious and were finally wrecked by the inability to eliminate England as a European power and his fatal decision to try to conquer the inhospitable vastness of Russia. Being defeated by the Russian forces and by the harsh Russian winter destroyed the myth of French invincibility. As Napoleon retreated westward during the last weeks of 1812 his political influence crumbled even more rapidly than his military power. First Prussia, and then increasing numbers of the smaller German states joined with the Russian tsar to drive Napoleon back into France. In short order the addition of Austria's armies and financial backing by the English solidified the European alliance which ultimately destroyed Napoleon's power and brought his empire to an end. It remained then to reestablish system stability.

THE VIENNA SETTLEMENT

In 1815 the allies who had defeated Napoleon assembled in Vienna, the Austrian capital. Their intent was to build a European state system designed to assure that such a threat to international stability would not be repeated. Even with this common purpose, however, there were significant differences of opinion over what this international system should look like. Both Russia and Prussia had more in mind than a simple replication of the old arrangement.

Flushed with the unimagined success of his army, the Russian Tsar Alexander I expected that by emerging as the liberator of the European states he would gain a position as the general protector of reorganized Europe and the leader of a "holy alliance" against the evils of atheistic liberalism so recently manifested by the French Revolution. Prussia's renewed war aims had been the complete expulsion of the French from Central Europe and the rebuilding of a Germany even more fully united than it had been under the ancient Holy Roman Empire. This time, however, Germany was to be united under the aegis of Prussia rather than of Austria. The Austrians, for their part, could not help but be alarmed by this prospect.

Austria's leading statesman, Prince Metternich, felt that Napoleon's defeat had provided an opportunity for the revival of an independent Austrian state, but he knew also that such independence could not be secure so long as Prussia dominated Germany. His, therefore, was the foremost expression of the vital principles of balance of power at the Congress of Vienna. He argued diligently against the elimination of France as one of the great powers in Europe and diligently opposed the creation of a united German nation which might dominate Central Europe.

Austria's policy of restoring the European balance-of-power system would have failed had it not been in accord with the aims of Great Britain at the Congress. The British main concern after France's defeat was to limit Russian expansion and influence to the west. Russia's place among the powers of Europe was incontestable, but she too could not be left in a position to dominate the continent. Through the strenuous efforts of Britain and Austria in the late hours of the peace conference, France was readmitted as a major power in Europe and served to tip the scales in favor of the formal re-creation of the balance-of-power system.

The main problem at the Vienna Conference was how to relate the general interest of preventing aggression to the particular interest of each country. Great Britain and Austria wanted little for themselves except a period of tranquillity and security. Russia, however, claimed most of Poland for itself, including a part of what had been Prussian since the earlier partitions. This claim forced the weaker Prussia to look for compensation elsewhere, particularly toward Saxony in the west. Control of Saxony would have made Prussia the largest and most powerful of the German states and would have assured her dominance in this area. Russia's demand for Poland, which threatened the equilibrium of Europe, was Britain's main concern. Prussia's insistence on possession of Saxony threatened domination of Germany and was therefore opposed vigorously by the Austrian minister. The common front which Russia and Prussia presented at the Congress almost led to its breakdown and to a war between these two powers and Britain, Austria, and France. But compromise ended the serious crisis. Russia received a good part of Poland. Austria retained her own Polish possessions. Prussia was granted a band of Polish territories east of the Oder River, and certain principalities in the west along the Rhine River which were willingly ceded by Austria. Through this arrangement Russia's territories abutted those of Prussia's Polish possessions and in this way barriers were erected against further Russian expansion toward the west. Russia, then, was the first nation to feel the strength of the new European balance of power created at the Congress of Vienna. Prussian expansionism, however, was limited more by treaty than by force, and remained potentially troublesome.

In spite of uncertainties introduced by its Central European provisions, the Vienna settlement created a European political system whose foundations lasted a full century. The statesmen at Vienna came to agree on the overriding necessity of establishing an equilibrium among the five powers which dominated the political life of Europe. During the early part of the nineteenth century conflicts were mitigated by a shared sense of European responsibility, but the victorious powers felt no need to create international institutions which embodied these principles. The sovereignty of states remained unimpaired and the balance-of-power system in Europe was restored after its greatest challenge. Moreover, a "Concert of Europe" emerged on the basis of a gentleman's agreement among the major European powers to consult with one another whenever the status quo was endangered.

In effect, then, the system rules of the balance of power were formally recognized by the agreements reached at the Vienna Congress. Each nation was to be free to chart its own course, but provisions against disruption of the status quo were established, partly by means of power politics and partly through compromise. The principle of equilibrium among the five nations was accepted, and, while a formal alliance among the rulers of Europe was avoided, deep concern was shared that there be continual consultation among them to maintain system stability. This concern may have reflected a recognition (1) that the balance-of-power system could not rely solely on the self-interest of individual nations and

(2) that miscalculation of one's own and of others' national interest existed as a basic flaw in the balance-of-power system. More broadly, one might speculate that the necessity to formalize the balance-of-power arrangements indicated that some statesmen were becoming aware of shifting conditions of international relations in the European political arena.

THE DECLINE OF THE BALANCE OF POWER

The agreements made at Vienna in 1815 produced a minimum of resentment among French leaders. They were glad to accept the peace arrangements in return for restoration of their monarchy and reestablishment of France as an equal power in the European state system. Almost two centuries of colonial rivalry ended; for sixty or seventy years no colonial empire seriously challenged the British. In addition, two other causes of friction in the eighteenth century — the disposition of Polish territories and competition between Austria and Prussia in Germany — were smoothed over for fifty years. Thus the Congress of Vienna dealt effectively with past issues. What was not seen clearly enough at the time, however, was the significance of new forces for instability which arose in the remaining years of the nineteenth century.

Nationalism

Perhaps the most vital threat to European stability in the nineteenth century was the emergence of popular nationalism. Much more than mere patriotism, more than a feeling of solidarity with one's countrymen, nationalism is a political movement based on a doctrine that the interests of the nation, as interpreted by its spokesmen, take priority over parochial, class, or individual interests. Nationalist movements arise when a significant portion of a population defines its own needs and aspirations in terms of those of an abstraction called the "nation." The movements can be rooted in a battle for national independence, in a desire for revenge against erstwhile national enemies, or in the effort of nation building in a hostile world. Nationalism is not tied to any particular type of domestic political ideology. It can be liberal or conservative, republican or monarchist, communist or fascist. For purposes of this analysis the most essential characteristic of nationalism is that it is a dynamic and very often explosive force for international instability.

Nationalism emerged in protest against the idea of a European continent united by a uniform law and administrative system, with a continental economic system of its own, a single foreign policy, and all its armies combined under one command. Since this idea was Napoleon's, the nationalist movements were initially anti-French. Some nationalists, predominantly conservative in their views, feared that their own national customs and historic institutions might be destroyed under the Napoleonic system. Others insisted on national self-determination for all European peoples, increased popular participation in government, along with representative institutions, and more freedom for the individual against the bureaucratic interference of the state. Both groups united against the French emperor, defeated him, and continued to influence the course of European history in succeeding generations.

Nationalism in the nineteenth century appeared in different countries in different ways. It remained to plague Russia's Polish possessions for a hundred years. It was a moving force in the independence of Greece in 1830 and the unification of Italy at mid century. But by far the most significant nationalist movement arose in Germany. Baron vom Stein, Prussia's chief minister during the wars against Napoleon, had been convinced that a proclamation of truly national war aims directed toward all the peoples of Germany would set free additional fighting spirit needed for the French defeat. After a period in which this nationalism was suppressed by the postwar Prussian government because of its politically liberal overtones, Prussia was able after 1850 to mobilize the German peoples to fulfill Stein's vision of a great united Germany through just such a nationalist appeal. The Vienna treaty had made Prussia into the most important of the German states, for whoever guarded the Rhine River against France during the nineteenth century was inevitably viewed as the spokesman for a German national cause.

The years between 1815 and 1850 did see a strengthening of nationalism in Europe but the more liberal aspects of it were suppressed. An attempt in 1848 to create a liberal constitutional monarchy of all the Germanys came to nothing when the Austrian king refused to accept such radical proposals and to become its constitutional monarch. That same year a middle-class uprising in many parts of Europe was suppressed, partly through intervention by the Russian tsar and other Eastern European monarchist leaders. Having failed miserably, the German liberals after 1850 came to question the practical value of the liberal ideology of constitutional reform. Not ideas, but only power could bring German unification. They felt that they had to choose between unity or liberty if they did not wish to miss both forever.

The Prussian government was most effective in deflating the political aspirations of the German middle class by boldly putting into effect those liberal programs that were compatible with the continuation of an autocratic regime. In 1866, under the banner of German national unification, the Prussian Chancellor Otto von Bismarck eliminated by force Austria's remaining influence among the German states. In 1870, he regained certain areas along the French border to which there were historical claims, and unified most of Germany under the king of Prussia as German emperor. His military success against Austria and France, judicious social reforms, encouragement of industrial development, the creation of a great German army on the Prussian model, and an intricate alliance system which protected the German Empire's gains were the keys to Bismarck's success over domestic pressure for a liberalized constitutional regime. Thus nationalism became a major force for change affecting domestic no less than international political developments throughout the remainder of the nineteenth century in Europe. We shall see shortly how it helped to undermine the balance-of-power system so carefully reconstructed at the Congress of Vienna.

Industrialization

The second major force for instability that emerged during the nineteenth century was the rapid development in Europe of modern industrial capabilities and communications systems. This coexistence of nationalism and industrialization altered both the forms and the range of international behavior.

In an era of prosperity, growing populations, and nationalistic ideologies, the development of industrial capacity enabled the states of Europe to create bigger armies and navies than ever before. After mid century, peacetime armies grew even larger than those that had been in the field in 1815. Moreover, technological advances in the production of steel and the manufacture of complex machinery equipped these armies with ever deadlier weapons. The frightful casualties suffered during the Prussian actions against Austria and France showed how machines were multiplying man's destructive power, and the new massed forces and the increased firepower were made even more effective by modern telegraphic communication and rail transportation. Instability in international affairs resulted not simply from the rise of industrialization itself, but also from the fact that it emerged at an uneven rate in the various parts of Europe. Germany's drive for industrial greatness, for example, was at least partly a response to the technological head start that Britain had gained since the eighteenth century. In addition, the course of industrialization accentuated the differences in military capacity between Western Europe and tsarist Russia. This difference became especially clear at the time of the Crimean War (1853-1856), during which Russia was defeated on her own soil by a relative handful of British and allied soldiers. The key to Russia's defeat was her very primitive transportation system, which permitted the Russian generals to bring to the battlefield only a small proportion of the troops they had under arms. This disaster sparked great political unrest in Russia and led directly to sweeping social and economic reforms that made Russia a major industrial power by 1900. Looking at this period, then, it can be said that the uneven manner in which industrialization spread throughout Europe created conditions under which rough equality in military capacity, so vital for the preservation of the balance-of-power system, became impossible to maintain. Moreover, these rapid changes in relative power stimulated intense suspicions among nations and led to something of an arms race and to the militarization of the whole of Europe.

Not only had battle tactics become immeasurably more complex and murderous after the example set by Napoleon, but armies became large-scale organizations drawing manpower not from a small body of professionals as in the eighteenth century but rather from entire national populations. Prussia had adopted universal military service in the wars of liberation against Napoleon; this small and poor state could create a large army only through conscription. As a consequence of the German victories in 1866 and 1870, all the continental European states introduced universal military service as the most effective means for organizing a mass army. This innovation formed a common basis for the subsequent rapid expansion of European armies.

In the light of these developments it is not surprising that as the nineteenth century drew to a close a new relationship between war and peace emerged. Since the speed of war mobilization was vital, plans for mobilization had to be drawn up long beforehand. Every member of a nation liable for military duty had to know his place in the war machinery before war broke out. Thus, an ever growing part of the peacetime activities of governments was absorbed by war preparations. In addition, changes caused by this militarization of Europe laid the groundwork for treating national societies more and more as independent isolated entities. The

European states, for reasons of defense, grew more like medieval cities protected by fortified boundaries and passport regulations. In this regression we see the beginnings of social organization for total war which is now considered to be the natural state of the international system. Militarism, arms races, popular nationalism, and preparations for total rather than limited war profoundly affected the conduct of international diplomacy during the last decades of the nineteenth century. Clearly the judicious and flexible use of alliance systems and the calculated limitation of military aggressiveness which is required if a balance-of-power system is to be maintained were made extremely difficult under these changing conditions.

Colonialism

A third factor which made the conditions for a stable balance of power more difficult to sustain was the renewed incidence and popularity of foreign adventures in the non-Western world. Both nationalism and industrial development made colonialism more feasible for all the major powers of Europe. Previously, because of its naval supremacy, Britain had free rein in the establishment and exploitation of colonies. Her deep concern for many years in the nineteenth century was with Russian expansion in the areas of the Middle East; this was one British justification for the Crimean War. But even this threat to British interests was not decisive until Russian land transportation facilities were modernized in the last twenty years of the century.

By the turn of the twentieth century Germany coveted Turkey and its resources, and was extending a rail route in that direction. Russia, which had been badly defeated over its Middle Eastern expansionist policies in the Crimean War of the mid century, now had rail routes which would have made such a decisive defeat much less likely. Russia now extended itself through Siberia to the Pacific Ocean and was intruding on Asian sovereignty. In addition, both France and Germany began to threaten Britain's interests — France in North Africa and Germany in sub-Saharan Africa. No longer sole monarch of the seas because of rapid industrialization in other nations, Britain was forced to compete in colonial areas once again, and the attention of the major European powers was diverted to conflict on the peripheries of the political arena within which the balance-of-power system was designed to work.

This looking outward by European powers as a result of increased industrial capabilities and popular pressures for national expansion had several consequences accelerating the decline of the balance of power. The British, who had persistently supported the concept of balance in Europe so that stability in this area would allow their own concentration on overseas trade, were forced to reevaluate and contract their far-flung world interests. This necessity reflected not only the material cost of resisting increased competition, but also the increased instability in Europe as a result of German and Russian expansionism. Indeed, as a "balancer" Britain had been effective only sporadically; moreover, through preoccupation, she had allowed German power to advance well beyond what could reasonably be called a balance in Europe. Germany, in its effort to reach a position of power and influence commensurate with its nationalistic view of itself, never slackened its pace in military development after the Franco-Prussian war of 1870; especially with regard to naval forces, it was directly threatening the foundations of British power. For these reasons, mounting suspicion marked Anglo-German relations.

A final consequence of expansion into non-Western areas by European powers was the opening of the international system to include many more nations. The United States with its fleet intruded into East Asia by way of the Pacific, opened up Japan to Western influence, and conquered Spanish possessions in the Philippines. Russia expanded its military presence in northern Asia until defeated by an aroused Japan. All European nations, plus the United States, were found establishing spheres of military influence in a weakened and technologically backward China. The result was that the entire world became potentially significant in European rivalries. Perhaps more importantly, along with military and economic penetration of much of the non-Western world came European ideas and technology. Although the effects were uneven, the stimulus of nationalism and industrial development had a dramatic impact on the natives of these colonial areas, planting seeds of discontent which are yet bearing turmoil and instability for the Western-dominated international system.

THE END OF THE BALANCE

Imperial Germany has been held responsible for the eventual breakdown of the balance-of-power system in Europe. The first concern of its rulers was for unification of the diverse German territories and peoples under the king of Prussia; this was accomplished through military aggression. But even though the Germans did exact heavy indemnity payments from France after the war of 1870, they had no intention of destroying France or of incorporating her as a part of the new German Empire. This limitation was not entirely self-imposed, however, for other important European powers would probably have come to the assistance of France had not Prussian aims been limited to uniting the southern German states of Bavaria and Württemberg under the Empire. Clearly too, French nationalist sentiment would have created an effective resistance to permanent occupation. Indeed, weapons limitations and transportation problems would have made such occupation very difficult under the best of circumstances.

Chancellor Bismarck's policies might still have remained within the guidelines of the balance-of-power system's rules had he not decided to annex Alsace and Lorraine. Appropriating for the Empire these French border provinces was the major factor leading to a growing inflexibility in European alliance systems prior to the outbreak of war in 1914. The second rule for sustaining the balance of power was violated by this move. It so inflamed the French government and people that Germany and France could not have become alliance partners in the foreseeable future. Bismarck's fear of French revenge forced him to establish a complex and delicate system of alliances with Russia, Austria, and Italy in order to isolate France. This network of alliances and treaties was at best an unstable arrangement, given the fact that colonial rivalries in Africa and the Near East were being intensified during this period. Moreover, under the new German emperor, Wilhelm II, the architect of this security system was replaced by a less competent chancellor who made the mistake of taking Austria's side in her dispute with Russia over the troublesome Balkan states in southeastern Europe. Bismarck's alliance system was allowed to lapse, and while France and Russia developed ever stronger diplomatic and economic ties during the remainder of the century, Germany was drawn closer into a defensive alliance with Austria and Italy. As the continental European powers divided into two opposing camps, Great Britain saw herself as controlling the delicate balance between them, and the nerve center of European diplomacy shifted from Berlin to London.

The situation in Europe required that Britain contract her commitments throughout the British Empire. The original decision of the British government to ease the burdens of empire by compromising the major colonial conflicts was not made with any special reference to Germany. But the growing realization was that German naval policy was a threat to British security at home. The new German emperor's love of naval affairs enabled his admirals to construct and mobilize an ever larger German navy. For these reasons, in 1904 Britain began to concentrate the bulk of her naval forces in home waters. An alliance with Japan and an entente with France were helpful in the strategic shift. Britain also entered upon a shipbuilding program designed to maintain a safe margin of superiority over the German navy. Germany's naval expansion program, then, was the prime cause forcing Britain into close cooperation with France and her Russian ally. As a matter of fact, except for brief periods, Britain had never in her history been so closely integrated in the European political system as in the decade before the outbreak of World War I. Despite Britain's attempt to play the role of balancer, the balance-of-power system itself had in effect ceased to exist.

By forcing Britain to take sides in the alignment of the European powers, German naval policy completed the division of Europe into two political camps armed to the teeth and prepared to take up open hostilities. Any misunderstanding could seriously affect the precarious military stalemate on which the European nations had staked their security. Economic, industrial, and political changes in Europe and in the world during the nineteenth century had led gradually to a situation in which the alliance structure of Europe was rigid and brittle. It found itself unable to adapt to a new challenge rising out of nationalism.

The great powers of Europe were able to isolate the limited wars among the Balkan nationalist states in 1912, but two years later they found it impossible to localize a conflict in which a great power was directly involved. The assassination of the heir to the Hapsburg throne on June 28, 1914, set off an Austro-Serbian crisis that was used by the ruling groups of the Austrian Empire as an excuse to suppress once and for all the agitation for Yugoslav independence and unity. They wished to humiliate Serbia, the Balkan state that could likely become the active leader of a Yugoslav nationalist movement. The Austrian statesmen were fully aware that their policy could bring on war with Russia but they argued that such a war was bound to occur sooner or later and was not an absolute danger for the Hapsburg empire as long as German support was certain.

Europe had managed to live for a century without a general war. The impact of nationalism on the least-developed region of Europe and the desperate opposition of the older forces in that area produced a conflagration that enveloped the whole of Europe and eventually most of the world. Afraid of losing her most powerful ally, Germany backed Austria-Hungary to the hilt. France dreaded to be separated from Russia. Britain was fearful of alienating her French and Russian partners if she followed a too-independent policy. Thus when the Germans violated Belgian neutrality in their attack on France, the last support of the nineteenth-century order of Europe disintegrated and Europe was split into two powerful military alliances mobilized for total war.

Each of the two warring camps was confident that it could not only check but overwhelm the other. France, Britain, and Russia believed they could defeat Germany and Austria-Hungary, if not in the initial stages, then certainly as soon as Russia could throw her millions into the fray and the British shipping blockade began to take effect. Germany, on her part, had planned to use the time gained by the slow military mobilization of Russia to concentrate her might in the west and defeat the French army. Thereafter she had intended to turn eastward to stem the Russian tide. Although the French had to bear the brunt of the German attack, the Russian penetration into East Prussia and the presence of British troops at the western front were important elements in frustrating the German conquest of France. Events at the eastern front, however, prevented Britain and France from taking full advantage of their alliance with Russia. As long as Germany was sitting across the lines of communication between Russia and Western Europe, the German generals could select the place of their attack. Strategically isolated, her human and material resources badly depleted by the war effort, Russia found herself unable to respond effectively to the German challenge and her importance in assuring victory dwindled rapidly.

The year 1917 witnessed the abdication of the Russian tsar, a short-lived liberal regime, and the withdrawal of Russia from the war with the success of the Bolshevik revolution. Necessarily Britain and France began to look around for additional allies who might help break what had become a deadly stalemate in Western Europe. Although the entrance of Italy and Romania on the Allied side did delay the German timetable of operations, it was only after the United States sent military forces into the battle in 1917 that Germany and Austria were on the way to defeat. November of 1918 marked the end of World War I and the final collapse of the European state system as it had been known up to that time.

This final breakdown of the European balance of power during the war years of 1914 through 1917 could not fail to affect the entire world. Europe was the undisputed political, industrial, and financial center of the earth; but the European nations were locked in a bitter struggle, recklessly employing their rich resources for mutual destruction. The absence of the European states from other global scenes permitted a new nationalistic Japanese drive for expansion in the Pacific. The liberal revolution in China also was made possible by the European war. And, of more immediate importance, the war shifted the bases of United States security interests and made this country an active participant in the settling of World War I.

BALANCE OF POWER AND SYSTEM CHANGE

In the preceding pages we have been discussing the history of international politics in Europe prior to the twentieth century. This discussion has emphasized the patterns of interrelations which constituted a balance-of-power type of system. The rules of such a system were specified and illustrated by reference to what we know of this period of history and certain points were made in describing the increasing difficulties involved in maintaining it. In the next chapter our discussion will be about a new type of international system which emerged in the middle of the twentieth century. The events surrounding this transformation will be discussed and the system itself will be analyzed. But before proceeding to this topic one should be clear about what we have learned about modern conditions affecting international stability.

The members of an international system interact with one another and are mutually interdependent. Accordingly, the way one nation performs affects the performance of others and ultimately of the entire system. Hence, if the important members of such a system change their patterns of behavior significantly this change can cause either a major reorganization of the system or its complete breakdown. In either case war may be the symptom.

Most systems in the physical world are not very adaptable to changing conditions, but an international system is not a group of unthinking physical objects behaving like the works of a clock. The units of a social system have a capacity to learn, to perceive changes in their environment, and to adapt their behavior accordingly far beyond the capabilities of the units of the most complex system of computers. Thus social systems are among the most flexible and adaptable of all systems. Nevertheless, if deviance from the general rules of an international system on the part of an important actor is great enough, there is the danger that the entire arrangement will break down. It has always been the case with international systems that such major breakdowns are folowed by the establishment of an entirely new arrangement among all or most of the surviving elements of the former system. The international system takes a new form with new rules that take into account the new conditions under which the international actors must operate. In the course of the preceding discussion it has been suggested that one of the major reasons for the break-down of the balance of power, and the resulting world war, was that several of the essential actors violated one or more of the system rules for this kind of international arrangement.

Reasons for violating the rules of a balance-of-power system are numerous but can be categorized in a useful manner. For instance, a change of rulers in one nation, with a consequent change in the personalities responsible for policy, can be a force for instability. Napoleon Bonaparte, for instance, by reason of his immense skill and popular appeal was able to change the rules of war to his own advantage. He almost succeeded in destroying the old international system. For a time Tsar Alexander, the Russian monarch at the Vienna Congress, had in mind a "Holy Alliance" among Europe's monarchs, designed to maintain stability. If this idea had been taken more seriously it would have violated one of the cardinal tenets of balance of power by restricting the freedom of individual nations to pursue their own interests. Although the German Chancellor Bismarck was cautious in limiting the objectives and tactics of his drive to create a strong German Empire, the succeeding set of diplomats, representing a new emperor, lacked the skill or foresight to play the delicate game of balance. The immediate result was a breakdown of German-Russian relations which were vital to German security. From such illustrations we see that much of what happens in international politics can be accounted for in terms of the changing personalities involved in international statecraft.

Shifts in the domestic political conditions of the relevant nations in a balance-of-power system can be factors for instability as well. The most significant change in the nineteenth century was the rise of nationalism, especially in Germany. Before Napoleon's time, foreign affairs were the exclusive concern of a small group of ministers in each country. With the rise of nationalism, foreign affairs became a major topic of popular discussion and were increasingly important as a stimulus and support for aggressive expansionism. German nationalism succeeded in the unification of Central Europe under Prussian domination but it also outraged French national sentiments in the war of 1870, which in turn mobilized the French in an anti-German posture. Nationalism among the emergent leaders of small states in southeastern Europe challenged the supporters of the status quo in that area and precipitated Austria's reckless leap into war. Small-state nationalism in this case was not so much the major cause as it was the last straw which completed a breakdown of the system that had been developing over a long period.

It is clear that nationalism has been a major force in the modern world since Napoleon. Since the 1870's especially, this political phenomenon has repeatedly threatened international stability and on several very dramatic occasions has caused major disruption and rearrangement of the international political system. Nationalism in foreign policy is often directed toward changing the current patterns of international relations and thus the system rules. Typically, it reflects an aggressive intent by a nation to make for itself, or to recapture, a glorious place in the world. The effort often requires that the defenders of the status quo, seen as the "establishment," be elbowed aside to make room. Such international behavior is inconsistent with the system rules of balance of power. A nation pursuing an aggressive revisionist foreign policy is much less likely than the others in the system to respect the rules of limited war. The very high pitch of popular enthusiasm necessary to sustain the national integration and mobilization required for this kind of foreign policy often makes it domestically more feasible to fight than to negotiate and less possible to halt warfare at a specific point in time when practical interests are gained. There is intense popular hostility toward enemy oppressors—no matter that they are national actors necessary for international stability, or that they may be useful as alliance partners at some future time. Often, the nationalist state has no interest in maintaining the international status quo and has no compunctions about violating the principles that maintain international stability.

Aggressive nationalism as a part of foreign policy would not have been so critical had it not been for the development, throughout the nineteenth century, of the military and industrial capabilities which made it feasible. The growth of industry—resulting in advances in arms technology, transportation capabilities, and mobilization of material support for warfare—can be seen as an "environmental" change that created the potential for international instability. Such technological growth was not directly a political matter but in fact had political consequences. This relationship was made clear in the foregoing discussion of the development of modern warfare technology and the feasibility of prior economic and military planning for warfare. The late nineteenth century saw in Europe the rise of the "garrison state."

Contradictions arose during this period. As the capacity for rapid military mobilization was developed, nationalism made diplomacy much too rigid for success. Foreign policy was increasingly used for domestic purposes to stimulate loyalty and acquiescence to the rulers in the cause of national greatness or national survival. The growing rigidity of the European balance of power after the dramatic events of the Franco-Prussian war of 1870 produced a need for new kinds of actors in the system to replace the balancer role. One such new actor, and one symptom of the breakdown of the balance-of-power system, was the Hague Tribunal established in the Netherlands to decide disputes in international law; disputants resort to a court of law when other means for resolving conflict prove ineffective.

The period following 1870 was an era of colonialism by all of the major powers except Austria. Technology and nationalism in the last half of the nineteenth century were necessary conditions for pressure to expand European influence. Colonial conflict was an irritating factor in international affairs within Europe, but more importantly it expanded the scope of the international system. Japan was the earliest example of a non-Western nation emerging as an important factor in international calculations. Japan was followed by China. In recent years many new non-Western nations have made their influence felt. Expanding the international system in this way placed a strain on the resources of the European nations and severely disrupted any balance of capability which may have remained by the turn of the twentieth century. Competition in far-flung areas of Africa and Asia complicated greatly the estimate of national interests in Europe so that miscalculation, illustrated clearly by the naval armaments race between Germany and Britain, was made increasingly probable.

It is not at all clear that one factor and one factor alone was responsible for the system breakdown culminating in World War I. It was not a matter of economics or of personalities alone, nor was the rise of German nationalism the sole precipitating factor. Just as the conditions promoting stability in an international system such as balance of power are an intermeshed set of factors any one of which can be crucial at any point in time, so the developments which threatened the system were closely interrelated, indeed fed upon one another. Certain conditions within each national actor and other conditions external to them were in a process of rapid change by the end of the nineteenth century. These shifting conditions, singly and collectively, created a situation in which the rules of the balance-of-power system could not be adequately maintained. Whether such instability could have been controlled, whether in fact the breakdown could have been prevented, is a question that is without a simple and satisfying answer. All that can be said, based on the analytical discussion in this chapter, is that the balance-of-power system did finally collapse, and that the economic, ideological, and political developments which we have considered contributed mightily to its destruction.

Chapter 2

A CENTURY
OF SYSTEM CHANGE

Richard L. Haines
Purdue University

The balance of power had been a fairly effective international system for coping with relatively limited conflicts among a few neighboring European states of roughly equal power. But as changes in the conditions underlying international politics created imbalances in military capabilities and increased suspicion and rigidity in the system, the stage was set for a breakdown of the balance of power. The ensuing war was unprecedented in its brutality and in the material and human costs to both sides. When the long and bitter conflict finally ended, the victorious Allies assembled at Paris in January of 1919. Their task was not merely to conclude peace with Germany and her allies but to rebuild the European state system as well. They were not content, however, to reestablish a system according to the old blueprints of the balance-of-power model. For one thing, individual states were no longer to be trusted to act against aggression. Instead, an international organization, the League of Nations, was created to ensure peace and security in the world. Naturally the statesmen at the Paris conferences could not foresee that The Great War, as some called it, was to be only the beginning and not the end of an era of international turmoil and system change, and that the League of Nations would be merely the first experiment in the organization of international security.

THE COLLECTIVE-SECURITY SYSTEM

The underlying principle of the agreement signed by the founders of the League of Nations was that of "collective security." Each member of the new international organization agreed to consider any breach of world peace as a threat to its own security and to act jointly with other member nations to meet it. This concept of security was based on an expectation that any nation intending aggression would be deterred from it if all other nations were committed in advance to oppose such behavior. In a sense, the collective-security system was not greatly different from the balance-of-power system. The important distinction was that the obligation to meet aggression, previously dictated solely by self-interest, was made a formal commitment sanctioned by an international organization. In addition, the League of Nations was designed to replace the former military-alliance system by providing national security through continuous consultation and international mediation. The goal was to create an organization where statesmen would assemble to keep open the channels of communication whose blockage had been at least partially responsible for World War I.

The principles of collective security required that all nations act immediately and together to block aggression by any other nations. The assumption was that the prime interest of each nation could be prevention of aggression as it emerged anywhere in the world, even if there was no immediate threat at home. It is true that in the early years the League was able to resolve disputes between Britain and Turkey in the Middle East, between Finland and Sweden in the Baltic Sea area, and between Yugoslavia and Albania in southeastern Europe. But Poland's seizure of Vilna from Lithuania and Italy's bombing of the Greek island of Corfu in 1923 were not effectively opposed. The rather simple reasons for these failures to act were that the League of Nations had no military capabilities to enforce its decisions, and that the unanimous consent of the League Council, which was necessary for such decisions, was easily withheld. Unsatisfactory provisions to meet Japanese aggression in Manchuria in 1931, and failure of the League to act in the 1935 case of the Italian invasion of Ethiopia, demonstrated what might have been obvious from the start. Given the diversity of capabilities and national goals in a greatly extended international system such as this, not all nations had an equal interest in preventing military aggression, nor did they stand to gain equal advantage from general world peace.

The League of Nations was created to help prevent accidental wars such as the one which brought it into existence. But it was unable to prevent unprovoked wars of aggression. The peace arrangements arising out of the Paris Conference at the conclusion of World War I were inherently defective, and thus provided inadequate political conditions for the maintenance of stability in Europe. One problem was that the role of popular nationalism in determining foreign-policy goals and means was grossly misunderstood by some of the statesmen at the conference. Indeed, after World War I, uniquely nationalistic interests became even more compelling than before, at least partly as a result of the 1919 peace settlements.

THE PARIS PEACE SETTLEMENT

If we compare the final peace arrangements of Paris in 1919 with those of the Vienna Conference in 1815, it becomes clear that the Allies of World War I were unable to reach the same level of agreement achieved by the conquerors of Napoleon. Divergent views on what was required to ensure European stability remained almost uncompromised throughout the negotiations, and were never fully meshed together to form a solid foundation of agreement among France, Britain, and the United States.

The principal French minister at the treaty conferences spoke of restoring the balance of power in Europe by ensuring French military superiority over the defeated Germany. From his perspective, stability in Europe required large-scale amputation of German territory, guarantees against any possible unification of Germany and Austria, heavy German reparation payments, and French control of the west bank of the Rhine River. In the end France received no German territory other than the restored Alsace-Lorraine region. The Saar district, which had been the western seat of German industrial might during the war, was indeed separated from Germany, and France was given a preponderant position in its administration under the auspices of the newly formed League of Nations. A plebiscite was to take place after fifteen years to settle the final status of the region according to the wishes of its German inhabitants. In addition, although the Rhineland was demilitarized, its occupation by Allied troops was limited to a period of fifteen years. The French accepted these concessions in return for a British and United States promise of military assistance in the event Germany violated the treaty provisions.

Because the war was a military standoff between exhausted opponents when the United States entered in 1917, even her belated and somewhat limited contribution to the Western Allies gained her a leading role in the conclusion of the peace arrangements. President Woodrow Wilson wished a lasting world settlement, but he was little concerned with resurrecting the previous European system. He believed instead that the creation of popular liberal governments, in Germany especially but in the other states of Central and Eastern Europe as well, was the best guarantee of peace in the future. National self-determination of the European peoples, along with democratic institutions, would lay historical grievances to rest and would thus be a direct step towards a peaceful international society. In addition, creating a world security organization under whose auspices all the major governments of the world could consult on a continuing basis would prevent a breakdown in intergovernmental communications and the inevitable miscalculations which cause war. For assurance, any national threats to peace would be firmly met by the united military force of the new League of Nations members. The British had few illusions about the viability and good intentions of popular governments in Europe, but they were in agreement that rebuilding the Concert of Europe, which had worked effectively for the first half of the nineteenth century, was critical for a world settlement. The theme of British policy was not the French assertion that Germany and Austria were solely responsible for the war, but that international misunderstanding among European statesmen, resulting from inattention and inability to conciliate, had made the war inevitable. The League of Nations in the British view could provide a vital forum. Such an arrangement required no significant restructuring of the international system, and vanquished Germany would have to be reinstated just as France had been in 1815.

The tragedy of the Treaty of Versailles and other treaties negotiated at the Paris Conference was that none of these three programs was put fully into effect. At French insistence Germany was dealt a series of heavy blows to her territorial, economic, and military capabilities; yet France's security was never ensured by her allies. Alarmed by the British refusal to sign the mutual-guarantee pact that had been promised, France proceeded to build with the eastern European states a system of alliances which were of doubtful value. The newly independent states of eastern Europe, standing between a still large and potentially powerful Germany and an aggressive revolutionary Russian regime, provided poor guarantees for French security, and were of little use when in the 1930's a remilitarized Germany once again threatened Europe.

Another reason why the Paris treaties did not produce a stable world settlement was that the United States very shortly withdrew from her active role in European affairs. Many Americans had been reluctant to see the United States involved in the European war in the first place. The diplomacy of the European balance-of-power system had been considered totally unprincipled; it was characterized by petty national jealousies which resulted in permanent conflict over trivial issues. At least partly because of this suspicion about European power politics, the United States refused to become entangled, even though she had helped to design the collective-security system which was intended to replace the defunct balance of power. Thus one of the most powerful nations in the world did not feel obligated to respond to aggression as it emerged in the succeeding years, and the collective-security system was compromised as soon as it was created. It would have been desirable to have the United States join in the establishment of a world organization for the maintenance of peace, but an ironclad United States guarantee of the crucial Western European frontiers might have been equally decisive. After 1920, however, the United States felt that it should return to its nineteenth-century insularity and keep aloof from European power politics. This United States isolationism later became economic as well as diplomatic, and Europe was left alone to cope with her political problems, some of which stemmed directly from earlier intervention of the United States during the peace conferences.

When, in 1918, the German government had finally approached President Wilson with proposals for an armistice they were told firmly that there could be no peace unless the Allies had a democratic German government with which to deal. This demand from the United States, plus the fact that hunger and destitution among the German population had stimulated support for socialist and communist revolutionaries, contributed to the collapse of the German Empire and the creation of a new German republic. It was this democratic regime which concluded the armistice in November of 1918, then signed the Versailles Treaty seven months later. Allied refusal, at French insistence, to readmit the new German state as a full member in good standing of the rebuilt international system placed on its new liberal leaders a burden of responsibility which proved fatal to democracy in Germany. Even though the deposed imperial government had made great demands on the German people during the disastrous war period, the new "Weimar Republic" which signed the Versailles Treaty was forced to accept responsibility for the national humiliation and social and economic disorganization resulting from the harsh Versailles terms. Partly as a result of these circumstances, German politics in the 1920's developed into an uncompromising struggle between ideological extremists. The eventual winner, in 1933, was a nationalist movement substantially more virulent and expansionist than any before or since.

By the time the threat to world peace posed by Adolf Hitler's Nazi regime was fully recognized, the League of Nations had shown itself to be ineffective as a collective-security organization. Furthermore, the failure to conclude military alliances which would have guaranteed the Paris settlement against a renewed German threat kept Nazi Germany's offensive from being met in time. While Adolf Hitler was formulating his plans for domination of the whole of Europe, British statesmen still invoked the good faith of the German member of a mythical Concert of Europe—a strong and prosperous German state had always seemed necessary for stability in Europe. The United States had long since washed its hands of the whole affair.

GERMAN RADICAL NATIONALISM

Even before the Nazi dictator deposed the liberal Weimar regime in 1933, German diplomats had already gained some revisions of the Versailles Treaty. Hence just as international conditions for a more reasonable Central European settlement began to emerge, popular resentment in Germany was being mobilized by extreme nationalists. Hitler promised to erase the humiliation of 1919 and to rebuild a powerful German state in Europe, through force if need be. German remilitarization of the Rhineland in 1936 went unopposed at a time when counteraction against a relatively weak German army might still have been possible. Even though Germany was rearming rapidly, in violation of international agreements, neither the French nor the British leaders found it possible to take a firm stand against Hitler in the presence of what seemed to be plausible German grievances. The British trusted neither a resort to arms nor the League's problematical security arrangements. It was felt that satisfaction of Germany's legitimate complaints against the boundary provisions and armament restrictions of the Versailles Treaty would convince Hitler to accept less bellicose methods of European consultation and adjustment in the future.

The principle invoked to legitimize Hitler's policy of aggression was self-determination for the Germans then living beyond their homeland's borders as a result of the postwar boundary agreements. In March of 1938, Germany's annexation of Austria, after

it had fallen to a Nazi revolution from within, was effectively unopposed by the British and the French. During the last six months
of 1938 the new republic of Czechoslovakia was forced to cede to
Germany a large part of her territory in the west, including vital
military defense positions. German expansion was once again ex-
cused by Western statesmen as an attempt to consolidate under
one state the dispersed German population of Central Europe;
three million Germans were then living in Czechoslovakia. Only
in March of 1939, when Hitler's armies marched into the Czech
capital of Prague, did it become clear to Britain and France that
German national self-determination was not the sole Nazi goal in
Europe. Hitler's plan was to provide "living space" for the Germanic race on a radically reorganized European continent.

Then and too late it was perceived that the extreme form of nationalism which possessed the German government and people
was inherently and permanently expansionist, and that it could
not be inhibited by statesmanlike appeals to principles designed
for maintaining international stability. When, in 1939, it was
clear that Poland too was marked as German "living space" France
and Britain were still in the initial stages of war mobilization.

Soviet Russia, the only conceivable counterforce to German expansion in eastern Europe, was reluctant at this time to conclude
an alliance with the English and the French. Joseph Stalin, the
Soviet ruler, was suspicious of the Western powers' reliability and
good intentions in the light of their earlier desertion of Czechoslovakia. Moreover, the Russian army would probably have been
forced to bear the burden of the offensive war in its initial stages
while her slowly rearming allies followed a defensive holding
strategy on the peripheries of the conflict. The Soviet Union finally
struck a bargain with Hitler which permitted annexation of former Russian territories in Poland and the creation of a defensible
buffer between the German army and the Russian frontier. Thus
the invasion of Poland in September 1939 was a joint endeavor
from both the east and the west, and this unlucky country was
once again partitioned as she had been in the eighteenth century.
The following year Germany added Norway and Denmark to its
conquests, and a successful outflanking maneuver through Belgium forced France to give up her independence and much of her
land. By June 1941 Hitler's tank divisions breached the Russian
frontier and were advancing swiftly along the roads followed so
disastrously by Napoleon in 1812.

With the defeated nations of the European continent no longer a
significant factor, Russia and Britain, as in 1809, were forced to
stand alone. The critical difference in 1941 was that Hitler had a

prefabricated police-state apparatus ready to harness quickly for his own ends each occupied nation's people and industrial capability. A second difference was that twentieth-century warfare required highly sophisticated weapons, fast tanks and numerous aircraft, as well as highly mobile massed armies. These were beyond British capabilities in 1941. Whereas in 1810 Britain had fought with small armies buttressed by allied European forces, and during World War I was able to help checkmate the Germans on French soil with a large conscripted army, in 1940 after the Battle of France Britain was left without continental allies; hence an invasion of Europe by British and Commonwealth forces after 1940 could not have broken Hitler's iron grip. Even the mere defense of the British Isles and the Empire required financial and industrial support from the United States; actual defeat of Nazi Germany demanded United States war material and troops.

The German invasion of Russia in 1941, and Hitler's declaration of war against the United States after the Japanese attack on Pearl Harbor, forced the United States and the Soviet Union, together with Great Britain and other Commonwealth countries, into a coordinated allied effort aimed at the destruction of Nazi domination of Europe. But for three years the main burden of the anti-German war was borne by the Soviet Union, with losses of life and devastation on a scale unequaled in modern history. Although they did not win the war single-handedly, the Soviet armies, aided by the Russian winter, broke the offensive power of the German army at Stalingrad deep within their own borders. Thereafter the Russian westward advance occupied the bulk of the German armies and drew to the eastern war theater most of the German war production. Although acknowledging that United States and British supplies contributed to Soviet successes, Stalin insisted that what was most needed was a major allied military operation in Western Europe to alleviate some of the pressure on his forces. The seemingly overlong delay in the planned cross-Channel allied invasion produced increasing suspicion and fear that Britain and the United States were anticipating a separate peace settlement with Germany. Intense suspicion marked most of the interchanges among the allies during World War II. Not the least of the causes was Western uncertainty about the political motives of the Soviet Union in Europe.

THE EMERGENCE OF THE SOVIET UNION

Another reason why the peace settlement of 1919 had not become an effective system for maintaining international stability was the failure to integrate the revolutionary regime of Bolshevik Russia in some fashion into a European security system. During the first years of the war, tsarist Russia had been an ally of the Western European states. Having only a relatively low level of economic development, and internal difficulties partly caused by inept administration, Russia greatly overextended her material and human resources in the battle against the 1914 Imperial German army. Military and economic collapse in 1917 was followed by political and social revolution. The new rulers of Russia, Lenin and his communist cadres, withdrew as quickly as possible from the war effort and concluded an ignominious peace which permitted even greater German pressure on Britain and France in the western war theater. After 1919, there was a significant but poorly coordinated effort by tsarist loyalists and small military contingents from the western Allies to bring down the new Bolshevik government. This, and an abortive campaign by the Red Army to regain Russian territories in Poland and the Baltic states, resulted in an uneasy and hostile detente that left unresolved the problem of legitimacy and stability in eastern Europe. An additional vexation for the West was that the revolutionary communist ideology of Russia's new rulers eventually generated a style of foreign policy utterly without precedent in the experience of Western diplomats. A new type of national actor had entered the arena of world politics.

The modern world saw in the birth of the Soviet Union the creation of an aggressive new regime which fostered and sustained an international revolutionary movement designed specifically to instigate and exploit internal political cleavages in other nations. The ultimate goal, as expressed by Soviet spokesmen, was universal revolution against feudalism and capitalism to be followed by the emergence of a communist world utopia. The shorter-term practical objective of Soviet leaders at the end of World War II was to build in Europe a system of communist governments, directed from Moscow, that would serve to protect the Soviet regime. This type of international system would have been the direct opposite of a balance of power in Europe. Once a state was tied to such an international brotherhood of nations, independence in its foreign policy would be impossible. Fraternal communist governments would not be free to shift alliances according to national interests nor to cooperate with other noncommunist nations in a renewed collective-security arrangement. Hitler's much cruder blueprint for the domination of Europe had projected a forced union of Germanic peoples with the object of controlling and exploiting all other lesser peoples in Europe by means of a permanent system of police control. The Soviet policy, after an unavoidable period of suppression of "reactionary elements," counted on intense ideo-logical indoctrination and political control by native communists. This style of totalitarian domination turned out to be more sophis-ticated and successful.

The Soviet Union's success in at least partly carrying out its military and political design in Europe created a situation in which the patterns of international relations were altered in a funda-mental way. It was clear that to permit such an increase in capa-bilities by any one international actor would be critically dangerous to the national interests of any nation in the world, including the United States. A powerful bloc of nations tightly controlled by a government committed to international revolution and expansion-ism is in an excellent position to dominate its opponents individ-ually. Those faced with this kind of threat are forced to build for themselves a permanent counteralliance, or bloc, with at least equal capabilities. This is what occurred in Europe.

The concerted undertaking designed a century and a quarter before to defeat Napoleon stimulated social and political revolu-tions which gave rise to Prussian hegemony in Germany, enhanced Russia's position in European affairs, and produced conditions under which the old balance of power, even though augmented by the Concert of Europe, could not be maintained. The half-hearted attempt in 1919 to reconstruct in a more viable form this same type of international system, on the model of collective security, failed to cope effectively with forces stimulated by other dimensions of the Paris settlements. Thus the Potsdam Conference of World War II Allies, at the conclusion of hostilities in Europe in 1945, marked the end of a period of system transformation begun in the nine-teenth century and accelerated after 1914. Arising from the debris of the two world wars in this century was a new species of inter-national system which can be described as "bipolar." Before we consider this type of international system, it is useful to discuss the conditions of international-system transformation in the twen-tieth century.

MODERN CONDITIONS OF SYSTEM TRANSFORMATION

One of the persistent themes of the discussion thus far has been that patterns of international behavior are continually adapted to fundamental changes in the environmental conditions of the system. It is clear, for example, that advances in military tech-nology have forced nations to reassess their foreign-policy think-ing. In consequence of the development of long-range aircraft during World War II, Britain could no longer rely on her navy and geographic isolation to avoid being attacked on her home islands. The overwhelming air power of the Allies contributed a large share to Nazi Germany's defeat. Since World War II the development of nuclear bombs and missile delivery systems has placed the entire world in danger of destruction. Thus in the middle of the twentieth century, no corner of the world is immune from attack; indeed no nation can completely isolate itself from the world political arena.

The European balance of power and the expanded collective-security system of the League of Nations have been succeeded by a rearrangement of the international system in which many more national actors are taking an important role. From a Western perspective, nations outside Europe and North America were all but irrelevant in the international scheme of things until the twentieth century. But Western penetration during the period of colonial expansion in these areas planted the seeds of technological, social, and ideological innovation which are bearing fruit today. Non-Western peoples are creating nation-states on the European model and are claiming the right to independent foreign policy based on their own national interests. Starting with Japan, whose industrial modernization culminated in a resounding defeat of Russian forces at the turn of the century, increasing numbers of previously inconsequential countries and peoples have forced their way into the foreign-policy calculations of the major Western powers.

Together with the increased number of relevant nations in the international system, new types of international actors have emerged as well. In contrast to the essential equivalence of nations in the balance-of-power system, there are immense disparities in national capabilities among the various actors in the new system. Two "superpowers" have dominated the world since 1945 by virtue of their near monopoly on nuclear-weapons systems. During the 1950's a number of smaller states were clustered tightly around the United States and the Soviet Union, forming international "blocs." There has also been what might be called a "universal actor," the United Nations Organization. Like the League of Nations, this organization was established for collective security, yet like the League it lacks the military capabilities which would be required to perform this role. However, unlike the League, the United Nations includes in its membership all but one of the major powers in the world today. The fear of including mainland China in the United Nations may be a symptom of the fact that one environmental condition of international relations has not changed greatly since World War I—radical nationalism is still a factor which greatly affects international stability. Foreign policy based on radical nationalism, "radical" because it is directed against the international status quo, has taken on new strength and now disturbs the postwar international system as it threatened previous ones. The simple fact is that when nations perceive a diminished stake for themselves in the international status quo, those that are able will act to change it. The Congress of Vienna can be interpreted as an attempt to repair the great damage done to the balance of power by Napoleon. Bismarck developed a program of gaining for Germany what he felt was her rightful place as a strong unified nation dominating Central Europe. (There is some debate over whether the Prussian chancellor actually violated the rules for system stability or merely stretched them to the limit and left them to be broken later by less nimble strategists.) Hitler's Nazi regime, arising from the wreckage of Germany's first attempt at democracy, was bent on forceful reorganization of the European system of nations. As will be seen later in this chapter, the bloc leaders of the postwar bipolar system have been largely unsuccessful in preventing such radical nationalism from disrupting the international system to which they have adapted since 1945.

BIPOLARITY AT MID CENTURY

The "bipolar" type of international system which emerged in the 1950's can be sketched out in general terms. This system had been composed of two antagonistic superpowers each with a group of treaty-bound less powerful states formed into a "bloc" or an alliance with it. These associated states shared the fears and the foreign-policy goals of their bloc leader, and were mobilized for possible war with the rival bloc. The members of the two blocs in the bipolar system were dedicated to the elimination of the threat posed by the rival bloc, or at least hoped to contain its military power so that its domination of the system would be avoided. At the same time, because in the nuclear age each has had the capability to destroy the opponent, they found it convenient to negotiate rather than go to war, or to fight small wars rather than major ones. However, in order to maintain the credibility necessary for deterrence, each bloc had to convince the other that they would engage in all-out war rather than risk domination by the other. Making this a loose bipolar system has been a group of smaller powers, remaining largely independent and neutral, and the United Nations, whose primary role in the system has been to attempt to reduce the likelihood of major war between the two bloc leaders.

At the conclusion of World War II in 1945, the United States and the Soviet Union were the only two powerful and independent states that had survived relatively intact. The lines in Europe that separated them were held by United States and British military forces, but Poland and all of Eastern Europe had come under the influence of the Soviet Union as a result of the presence or direct threat of the Red Army. It may be that Western Europe as well would have been absorbed within the Soviet sphere if the United States had not been capable of making an absorption attempt too costly and if the Soviet leaders had not thought that communism would triumph in European elections as a result of the severe social and economic dislocation after the war. Western Europe would have been defended from Soviet aggression, but it is doubtful that Americans would have been willing to pay the cost of forcing the Soviet Union to relinquish control of Eastern Europe.

United States policy with regard to Eastern and Central Europe can be explained by several factors. There was grave doubt among United States leaders that the American people would be willing to assume long-range commitments in Europe beyond participation in the allied occupation of Germany and possibly of Austria. Furthermore, it was assumed that Britain and France would, after a period of recuperation, be able to resume something like their prewar position and act as a counterbalance to Russian power; but the problems of European reconstruction, and the terrible drain on British resources as a result of the war effort were grossly underestimated in Washington. With the nations of Central Europe destroyed and those of Western Europe weakened, there was no power in Europe that by its own strength or by alliance with all the other Western European states could have blocked Russian progress into Europe. Moreover, whatever the relative capabilities of the armies in Europe, the United States was greatly concerned about redeployment to the Pacific war zone, where many policy makers anticipated a much longer campaign than in fact took place. After Japan's unconditional surrender in August of 1945, domestic political forces in the United States insisted on a speedy and almost complete demobilization of the armed forces. Under these conditions it was several years before action was taken to offset Soviet influence.

Rejecting a United States plan for international supervision and control of atomic weapons, the Soviet Union preferred to rely for security on its own nuclear research, and by 1949 was equipped to conduct atomic warfare. In order to protect its interests in an international body where the majority was consistently against it, the Soviet Union made increasingly frequent use of its veto in the United Nations. The United Nations, without great-power agreement, was therefore unable to function as a collective-security organization in most major disputes. As this situation became patent, the United States began to develop a concerted national policy of its own to "contain" communist expansion. In 1947, on the basis of the "Truman Doctrine," it supplied military equipment and professional military advisers to Greece and Turkey. In addition, it announced a policy of assisting all peoples to prevent forcible capture of their governments by "minority radical parties."

The leaders of the Soviet Union vigorously denounced "the American warmongers." The United States had armed Greece and Turkey, had stationed its carrier fleets on all the sea approaches to the USSR, had occupied South Korea and Japan, and had demonstrated sufficiently the United States capacity for long-range bombing. Not unnaturally the Soviets felt encircled, and deep suspicion — stemming from as far back as the Allied intervention against the Bolsheviks in 1919 — was inflamed once again. From 1946 on, relations between the two superpowers deteriorated. The fundamental conflict over goals focused on Europe, where the Western Allies realized that the best interest of security from communist encroachment would be served by massive United States help in European reconstruction. Billions of dollars were poured into Western Europe and Germany especially under the Marshall Plan, which began in 1947. This program served only to increase Soviet agitation. One of the highlights of this period was the "battle of Berlin." In 1948 the Soviet Union cut off all rail, water, and highway routes to the sectors of Berlin under Western control. The United States responded with a massive "airlift" to supply the citizens of Berlin, and after eleven months the Soviet Union lifted the blockade. Meanwhile, the United States and the Western European powers proceeded with their plans to develop an alliance for the defense of Western Europe, while the USSR drew the nations of Eastern Europe into a closer and militarily more effective alliance system.

The step-by-step emergence of a bipolar system was completed by the mid 1950's. In the intervening years the establishment of a democratic regime in West Germany spurred the inauguration of East Germany as a communist satellite government. By these maneuvers the German nation was formally partitioned by the victors of World War II. Drastic reforms had reshaped the social and political structure of Eastern Europe, while Western Europe was being reindustrialized more or less on the United States model. By 1954 the German Federal Republic (West Germany) had regained all but complete sovereignty and independence. The Western powers retained only the right to station troops in Germany for their European military-defense structure, which the Germans were encouraged to join. By the terms of the 1949 North Atlantic Treaty, which created a military alliance between the United States and Western European nations, the United States had agreed to supply equipment for European rearmament, and guaranteed Western Europe against invasion. In 1955, after other plans for a European defense community had failed, partly because of French misgivings over rearming the Germans, the newly established Western European Union was enlarged to include West Germany, which was then authorized to create its own army under the over-all command of the North Atlantic Treaty Organization. In the East the Warsaw Pact served to formalize the military arrangement within the Soviet bloc, recently enlarged to accommodate East Germany. Polarization of the European area into Eastern and Western blocs was complete.

Japan, like Germany, profited from the tension between the Soviet Union and the United States. In the peace treaty of 1951, to which the Soviets were not a party, no war reparations were exacted. By 1954, in response to the Communist Chinese challenge in Asia, Japan, like Germany, was encouraged by United States leaders to take a place as an independent state within the Western alliance system. In the course of total war against the forces of aggression during World War II, it had been popularly understood in the United States that the vanquished would be disabled and controlled so that they would never again pose a threat to world security; but in less than ten years, their strategic power was deemed essential for stability in the bipolar confrontation between the anti-Communist Western bloc and the Communist Eastern bloc. Apparently, diplomatic necessity still overrules popular conviction; foreign-policy habits have not changed as drastically since the nineteenth century as some believe.

The reason for this change of policy during the 1950's was that the so-called Cold War between the United States and the Soviet Union shifted to open battle in Asia. In June of 1950 the North Korean government launched an attack against South Korea across a truce line established under the aegis of the United Nations. The attackers counted on a quick victory because of their superior forces and — partly on the basis of United States policy statements concerning that part of the world — they gambled that the West would do little more than lodge an outraged moral protest. But in response to this action, the United States intervened with military forces and succeeded in getting the United Nations to support the intervention; in turn, if not in consequence, Chinese forces entered the conflict on the North Korean side. Despite its then overwhelming superiority in such armament, the United States did not use its atomic weapons. There was some doubt about the effectiveness of nuclear weapons in this tactical situation, and there was the danger of nuclear confrontation with the Soviet Union. Facing a military stalemate in Korea, the United States accepted a truce which reestablished the truce line that had existed prior to the outbreak of hostilities.

Upon conclusion of the truce in 1953, the United States felt that a flagrant act of communist aggression had been checked. In the view of the communist nations, the greatest capitalist power, the United States, had been prevented from reasserting Western imperialist supremacy in Asia. The practical results of the Korean War were more complex than this. United States policy makers, under President Eisenhower, turned to a concerted program to contain communism throughout the world by relying on atomic weaponry rather than on more costly conventional capabilities. Communist aggression anywhere in the world was to be met by "massive retaliation" against the entire Soviet bloc. This new posture was quickly reflected in a rapid build-up of nuclear bombing aircraft and later of missile forces distributed under NATO agreements along the frontiers of the Soviet Union. Such was the situation in the middle 1950's.

Until the twentieth century, the world had normally had some half dozen or so truly great powers. The fact that there were only two left after World War II inevitably made a great difference in the conduct of international politics. One characteristic of the bipolar system, not found in a balance of power, was that each of the two antagonists knew positively in advance who its only dangerous enemy could be. In this situation, diplomatic delicacy broke down, since each measure that either power took for its own security seemed a provocation to the other. In a similar fashion each superpower tended to make allies of other less powerful states, and every move by these states, even if apparently spontaneous, was suspected by the other superpower of being instigated by its rival as a hostile act. Under such conditions it was natural that noncommitted nations in the world would judiciously avoid being entangled in an alliance which threatened them with nuclear destruction. There arose in the 1950's a group of neutralist or nonaligned nations which both the United States and the Soviet Union tried to win over for their respective causes.

THE NONALIGNED ACTORS

Coincident with the rising power of the Soviet Union was the increase in the number of nationalist revolutionary and anti-colonial movements in the non-Western world, many of whom drew support from the Soviet Union. For many Americans in the 1950's, these movements revived the specter of Communist world revolution. Certainly from the Soviet point of view, conditions for such a revolution had never been so favorable. The victory of Chinese Communist forces over the United States ally Chiang Kai-shek, in 1949, was seen by both sides in the bipolar conflict as a harbinger of further communist successes. Even with the multiplying tensions of the Cold War, however, neither a conventional nor a nuclear war has as yet broken out between the two bloc leaders.

On the Soviet side of the picture there has been good reason for refraining from outright war. The first years of the communist regime in Russia might well have seen an all-out war against the capitalist nations of Europe if Lenin, and later Stalin, had not understood the lesson of the outclassed Red Army's failure in Poland after the Russian Civil War in 1920. It was decided then to accept a temporary detente with the West to allow time for the military and industrial capabilities of the new revolutionary regime to grow and mature. Soviet policy reverted to the building of "socialism in one country," to be loyally supported by the communist brotherhood throughout the world. Even after having consolidated its domestic power and survived a mortal challenge during World War II, the Soviet Union found itself with a good deal to lose in the event of an all-out nuclear war with the capitalist powers of the West. Domestic necessities and international realities prevented the Soviet leaders, explicitly committed though they were to the expansion of the communist world revolution, from taking action that would risk such a nuclear holocaust. The most feasible alternatives under these conditions were to engage in "third-party" small wars such as in Korea, to support revolutionary movements wherever they might be found, and to court the favor of the new leaders of the emergent non-Western nations. Hence, strong ties with nationalist movements and newly independent governments in the non-Western world became a major goal for the Soviets and were correspondingly of great concern to the United States.

The course of the Korean War had brought a new understanding on the part of the United States leaders that there was little enthusiasm for the projected anticommunist crusade among the larger noncommunist nations in Asia, especially India, Burma, Indonesia, and Ceylon. These may have feared communism, but they refused to become involved in a direct confrontation between the two superpowers. Just as important, in their fresh independence from colonial domination, many distrusted the West. And by virtue of its predominance among the European powers, the United States became for some a symbol of renewed Western oppression and exploitation. The Soviet Union did its best to reinforce this impression.

One of the most profound effects of World War II had been the weakening of European control over local nationalist movements in the Asian and African colonies. The relationship between nineteenth-century nationalism which led to colonial expansion and the nationalism which arose in the non-Western colonial areas is necessarily very close. The appeal of national integration, independence, and aggrandizement to the Western-educated native leaders of these areas has been so compelling that the two superpowers could gain influence only by attempting to outbid each other in supporting these aspirations. Nevertheless, even massive United States foreign-aid appropriations and Soviet military- and technical-assistance programs did not prevent the formation of a loosely organized third bloc of avowedly neutral non-Western nations. In most cases the anticolonialist forces achieved their goal of national independence without having to commit themselves to either the Eastern or the Western bloc.

The maturing emergent nations benefited from their more or less nonaligned position between East and West, extracting economic and military aid from both sides. For a time, United States and Soviet desire for their favor gave these neutrals a high degree of bargaining leverage which helped moderate the Cold War. As an example, United States support for Egypt on the occasion of French and British attempts to reclaim the Suez Canal in 1956 strained Western unity for a time. In a similar example, Soviet moral and material support for India in its boundary dispute with China in the early 1960's did little for cohesiveness within the communist bloc. Most importantly, from the point of view of many of these new nonaligned nations, survival in the nuclear age rested on the ability to prevent small-power conflicts from becoming the initial battlefields of an East-West war. This risk was increasingly the concern expressed within the United Nations organization.

The emergence of the United Nations as a "universal actor" in the international political system was a symptom of the belief that nations could not be relied upon to act against or to limit aggression. Weapons developments during World War II, and the bloody excesses of that conflict, once again stimulated among nearly all the world's leaders a desire to avoid war at almost any cost. Thus the Security Council of the United Nations was organized to include all the big powers, and they were expected to act immediately against aggression anywhere in the world. As in 1919, there may have been faulty assumptions about the instinctive good-will and reasonableness of the great powers in the postwar world, but at least all of them, including the United States, were included as full and active members. In spite of this presence, initial expectations were not fulfilled. The provisions for a regular United Nations peace force under the direction of the Security Council have never been put into effect. The Council itself was organized so that any permanent member could veto any decision. To the dismay of many, the United Nations as an effective collective-security organization was stalemated from the first.

An alternative evaluation of the effectiveness of the United Nations to prevent war might argue that the inability of the Security Council to act in cases of apparent threats to peace actually has prevented either of the superpowers from drawing the whole membership into the Cold War. Despite the General Assembly's hasty self-authorization to recommend military action over the heads of the Security Council, since the Korean War the United Nations has been extremely reluctant to take stands involving the East-West conflict. Peacekeeping in the Middle East for a period of ten years after the 1956 Suez crisis, and action in the Belgian Congo in the early 1960's and in Cyprus more recently, have been part of the United Nations Secretary General's design to prevent direct United States or Soviet intervention in local disputes wherever possible. Exhortation against Cold War and arms-race policies has been within the power of the Secretary General, but exhortation has had little impact on bipolar maneuverings. The non-Western neutralist world is the Secretary General's true constituency, and both he and his supporters in this "third world" have judiciously avoided direct interference.

The existence of a third loosely organized but independent grouping of nations has prevented the emergence of a tightly bound bipolar system in which all nations are lined up on either one side or the other. World War I broke out when just such a situation developed. The two opposing alliances contained all the relevant nations in the system, and thus there was no balancer and no possibility for new alliances within Europe which might have discouraged the rapid moves towards war. Since 1945, war has been avoided partly because each side in the bipolar conflict has expected the neutrals to gravitate to it. It is true that neither this third force nor the United Nations possessed the military capabilities to alter the relative weight of the major blocs in the bipolar system. They gained leverage to the extent that the United States and the Soviet Union sought world support against each other.

Hence the influence which the nonaligned nations and the United Nations were able to bring to bear stemmed only from the perceived needs of the superpowers for moral and political support, not from the ability of these weaker powers to give or withhold material assistance. Whatever the case, the international system which grew out of World War II was transformed into a loose bipolar arrangement when the dangers of direct nuclear confrontation between the United States and the Soviet Union were fully appreciated by the leaders of the nonaligned nations.

In spite of the inability of the United Nations to take direct action in reducing the tensions of the Cold War, its vital role has been to prevent East-West conflict from involving nations other than the bloc members. More and more frequently attempts by either the United States or the Soviet delegation to enlist support for political attacks on its rival have been met with small-power abstentions in General Assembly voting. A loose bipolar system maintains a certain amount of stability to the extent that the non-bloc and universal actors are aware of their integrative roles and neither become overcommitted to one side nor decide to withdraw altogether. However, because of neutralist perplexities over Soviet policy during the Cuban missile crisis, and United States policy in Vietnam, there has been a tendency to avoid this integrative role and to become less ready to support either bloc leader. Another way of saying this is that there has been something of a shift in great-power policy away from catering to neutralist sensibilities in recent years, and a corresponding decline in small-power influence. This shift may signal that the loose bipolar international system is itself in the process of change. There are additional factors which point in this direction.

THE DECLINE OF THE BIPOLAR SYSTEM

In the bipolar type of international system each bloc considers the other as the greatest single threat to its security. With this threat in mind the bloc members are integrated within the military, and sometimes the political, organization of the bloc leader. So long as nuclear destruction remains imminent, both blocs in the bipolar system continue to be cohesive and tightly controlled, for any move toward independence on the part of a bloc member entails the risk of a reduction in national capabilities and defense facilities. On the other hand, any reduction of bipolar tensions could very well lead to a loosening of the controls within the contending blocs. Such a situation may develop out of an apparent stabilization of the nuclear race between the two bloc leaders. This description seems to fit the situation which developed in the 1960's.

In recent years it has appeared to some members of the Western bloc that the possibility of nuclear war over the East-West conflict in Europe has been greatly reduced. What is feared now is that the United States may be drawn into an accidental nuclear war as a result of her vigorous crusade against the expansion of communism in the non-Western world. United States leaders have had difficulty in trying to convince European skeptics that the menace of Soviet power in Europe still requires strong United States leadership, and, at the same time, that the containment of communism anywhere in the world is as much a concern of the West as the direct threat to Western Europe.

From the Truman Doctrine of 1948 to the Nixon Doctrine of 1969, one of the most striking characteristics of United States foreign policy has been its continuity. For more than twenty years the basic strategy of the United States government has been to maintain a standoff with the Soviet Union by the threat of nuclear war, while at the same time containing the spread of communism throughout the world by means of direct or indirect intervention. Debate among government leaders throughout this period has centered primarily on tactics; whether to intervene against suspected communist encroachment directly with conventional forces, or to focus on the threat of Soviet nuclear force while relying on military-assistance programs to ward off the communists elsewhere in the world. Experience with the Korean War led to a period of bipolar confrontation based on the threat of massive nuclear retaliation. Under Presidents Kennedy and Johnson, direct intervention in Latin America, and, more critically, in Southeast Asia, was accompanied by concerted attempts to reduce tensions arising from the extreme danger of nuclear war with the Soviet Union. The Nixon Doctrine, on its face, shifted emphasis once again to indirect containment of communism by means of aid to beleaguered governments, and assertion of United States determination to protect the West against Soviet domination by means of a more effective nuclear deterrent capability.

The bipolar international system has been accepted as a basic fact dominating all other foreign-policy considerations. Attention remains focused on the actions and intentions of the rival superpower; the main change is that less concern is felt over the approval or disapproval of nonaligned nations, and this change has been accompanied by an increased willingness to engage in bilateral negotiations to resolve common problems. Thus, the political confrontation between the United States and Soviet blocs may have been stabilized. However, the broader conflict between what is termed "the free world" and "world communist revolution" remains to plague both the Soviet Union and the United States.

United States foreign policy since 1948 has been to intervene quickly and forcefully in each case of rebellion or other internal strife in which communists were known or even suspected of being a leading force. For instance, a communist-tainted Guatemalan government had hardly been elected in 1954 before it was overthrown with clandestine United States backing; in that same year, after the French withdrawal from Indochina, the United States helped prevent the revolutionary forces of Ho Chi Minh from uniting the country of Vietnam under a communist regime. These moves, along with United States economic and political isolation of the revolutionary Cuban government in 1958, military intervention in the Dominican Republic a few years later, more recent massive armed conflict against communist-led forces in South Vietnam, the subsequent bombing of North Vietnam, and even the attempt to deescalate the Vietnam War itself, are all totally consistent with the official United States policy of *containing* the spread of communism, wherever it appears and whatever form it takes.

Unfortunately for United States policy makers, the distinction between communist-dominated and other less threatening types of nationalist or progressive movements in the non-Western world, has been a difficult one to make; in the eyes of many foreign and domestic critics it has rarely been made with sufficient care by United States leaders. A rather more critical view is that the communist vs. noncommunist distinction is itself irrelevant because indigenous revolutionary movements in the non-Western world are, in fact, much more nationalistic than communist, and their success or failure bears little on the relative capabilities of the communist bloc. Communist expansion, from this perspective, is no longer the threat to world security it once was, and therefore should not be dealt with as a threat to the security of the United States. The real danger, according to these critics of United States foreign policy, is that United States misunderstanding may lead to war with China over Vietnam, or to an eventual nuclear confrontation with the Soviet Union, or to both.

The fact that some communists have been able to identify their movement with the legitimate aspirations of nationalist and reform leaders in the non-Western world has, in the eyes of some, transformed the United States into the sole defender of the international status quo in a revolutionary age. This development has alienated many of the country's supporters, both at home and among opinion leaders abroad, and threatens to loosen ties within the Western bloc. In a similar manner, the leader of the Soviet bloc has been engaged in a bitter dispute with China, whose leaders feel that Moscow has grown timid and is ready to give up the communist world revolution in return for the security of a nuclear detente with the United States.

Since 1958, Western eyes have been focused on what is called the Sino-Soviet rift. It appears that this nationalistic confrontation, although contrary to everything the founders of international communism taught, has been a source of strain between the Soviet Union and Communist China for some years. Territorial disputes over Central Asia and Siberia, which go back as far as the days of the Russian tsars, are still sources of hostility. The Korean War, supported largely by the Soviet Union, drew a United States military challenge against China at a time when she had yet to consolidate her revolutionary gains. The Soviet Union's deemphasis of world revolution after the death of Stalin, and her failure to back up Communist China against the pro-Western Chinese Nationalists during the Formosa Straits crisis in 1958, were clear signals to the mainland Chinese that the Soviets were at best unreliable allies and, at worst, traitors to world communism. Later, in 1960, Soviet scientific assistance was withdrawn from China's nuclear-arms-development scheme, and despite urgent requests, no nuclear weapons have been proffered by the Soviet Union to her fraternal communist ally. By the end of the 1960's armed conflict was a recurrent fact of life along the Sino-Soviet border.

Chinese policy seems to reflect an attempt to force the Soviet Union back toward a militant direct confrontation with the West. A clear conflict of interest seems to have emerged between the two great powers of the communist world, and there is currently a vigorous contest over who is to become the bloc leader.

What seem to be decentralizing tendencies in communist relations may be one factor in the apparent reduction of United States influence over the leading members of its own bloc. After twenty years, some of the NATO allies in Western Europe have begun to question the likelihood that the Soviet Union would take direct action against Western Europe. However, United States policy with regard to the Soviet Union continues to rely heavily on NATO as a symbol of Western unity and determination, even though its actual military value may be questioned. The refusal of United States leaders to allow coequal status to its European allies in designing NATO policy, especially as to the disposition and use of nuclear weapons, led former French President de Gaulle to remove his forces from NATO command and to move toward the development of an independent nuclear-weapons system. The effect of this shift in policy on the Western bloc has been similar to that of Chinese policy among the communist states. The Franco-American dispute has placed other members of the NATO alliance, most notably West Germany, in a position of cross pressure between an American-style "Atlantic" approach to European defense and a French-style "European" approach. In the meantime, the French government has been establishing ties of its own with the Soviet leaders. France has also established diplomatic relations with Communist China. Moreover, the French have disowned United States Vietnam policy. Accidental nuclear war between the two superpowers appears to the French, and to many other Europeans, to be a greater threat than a communist world revolution. The result of this viewpoint is a foreign policy substantially more nationalistic than was possible in the early 1950's when a Soviet attack on Western Europe seemed imminent and the deterrent of United States nuclear retaliation more credible.

From the point of view of systems analysis, both China and France are challenging the strategy of their two bloc leaders. In terms of the politics of bloc leadership, the United States and the Soviet Union have, in a sense, become conservative status-quo nations. It is ironic that in terms of adherence to system rules, if not public policy pronouncements, it may be that each of these superpowers has found a stake in the loose bipolar system to which they have accommodated themselves since 1945. Even though ultimate goals may not have changed a great deal in succeeding years, the prospect of nuclear war seems to have forced the rival bloc leaders into a posture of moderation and international responsibility whenever direct military confrontation has threatened. And even more significantly, neither seems to desire any basic changes in the bipolar system as it exists which might disrupt what they see as a delicate balance between them. The consequences of foreseeable system transformations in the future, from both the United States and the Soviet point of view, are either undesirable or too unpredictable and risky.

POSSIBLE FUTURE SYSTEMS[1]

The question of whether the international system is being transformed in any fundamental way is always a matter of some controversy, just as is the true nature of any existing system. For

---

[1]The terms and concepts employed in this discussion of systems originate from the works of Morton Kaplan and Richard Rosecrance cited in the bibliography at the end of Part I.

instance, the world might well appear bipolar to policy makers in both Moscow and Washington even though the Chinese leaders in Peking have come to believe that there is a secret agreement amounting to an alliance between the two supposedly antagonistic superpowers, designed to compromise the battle between Western imperialism and world communism. Similarly, France may claim that basic changes in the international situation call for a reassessment of NATO alliance policy, while the United States maintains firmly that for the foreseeable future there is little likelihood of genuine change in Soviet goals, and that therefore necessity dictates continued strong United States leadership of the Western bloc. Thus recognition of system change, when it comes, is largely a matter of one's preconceptions. From the perspective of systems theory, the only position that can be taken is that the international system has changed fundamentally in the past and is likely to do so again in the future. There seems to be nothing inevitable about the timing of this change, nor about its actual direction, but it is true that certain trends in world politics are becoming clearer, and that new patterns of international relations are emerging. It is necessary to speculate on what the future may have in store.

Tight Bipolarity

If the direction of system change is neither clear nor inevitable, then there is no *theoretical* reason why there should not be a shift back to a previous state of affairs similar to that during the early stages of the Cold War, say from 1947 to 1955. Such a tight bipolar system would be much like the one existing today, with the exception that there would be no nonaligned nations or other significant actors who could operate independently of either major bloc leader. This tightening need not mean that every nation in the world would be tied to one or the other of the rival blocs, but rather that those not tied would be considered irrelevant in the foreign-policy calculations of the superpowers.

It may be argued that such a system, requiring direct and continual confrontation between the United States and the Soviet Union, would assure stability in the world by permanently deferring nuclear war. Certainly the bloc leaders would be forced to devote all their attention and energy to a policy of countering quickly each slight advantage of their opponents, and in this way confusion and miscalculation which might lead to war would be greatly diminished. Moreover, the continual menace of possible nuclear annihilation would probably force each bloc leader to avoid sudden unexpected tactical moves for fear of drawing nuclear retaliation. The hope might be that a need to meet frequent but limited crisis situations is likely to produce over time a pattern of mutual accommodation between the two superpowers in the form of a genuine détente, making nuclear war even less likely.

Contrary views on this subject hold that frequent crises between two hostile nuclear-armed superpowers, however limited in scope they might be, cannot but help increase world tension and escalate the arms race between them. Furthermore, it may be a valid assumption that Soviet expansionism would be redirected to other areas of the world peripheral to the main contest. This kind of shift is what occurred in the early 1950's. Reduction of the opportunity for communist expansion would require that most or all of the world be mobilized in support of one or the other of the contending blocs. In view of apparent trends, however, this alignment would be substantially more difficult than it might have been at the start of the Cold War.

Whatever the feasibility and probable viability of a tight bipolar international system, world conditions do not seem ripe for it now, especially when the strength of nationalism throughout the world is taken into account. Clearly whatever nuclear stalemate which has been established since 1947 has produced a loosening of the bloc controls in the bipolar system rather than their strengthening. Policy makers of both sides have been encouraging insubordination within the rival bloc while at the same time attempting to maintain rigid control of their own. Neither the United States nor the Soviet Union has been fully successful on either score. An additional perplexity for the two superpowers is that they may lose their monopoly on the capability to conduct large-scale nuclear war.

Unit-Veto System

It is conceivable that if the current bipolar system became any looser than it is, then large numbers of nations in Europe and in the non-Western world would find an increased opportunity to maintain complete independence from the two major world powers. If, as one might expect, industrial modernization brings some of the emerging nations to a point at which they could compete with the industrialized West, both politically and economically, then possibly a new balance-of-power system would develop, encompassing most of the world this time. As was described in the previous chapter, this type of international system is composed of a number of equally endowed states which are expected to pursue their own national goals by means of flexible alliance policies and limited rational wars. Even if it were not the case, however, that easy shifts in the alliances and small-scale "rational" wars have gone out of style in the twentieth century, in all likelihood both the United States and the Soviet Union will remain economically and politically dominant, and will continue to intervene at any place in the world whenever national interest requires. The balance-of-power system would be almost impossible to maintain in a world where there were such disparities of power among the relevant nation-actors. A more realistic prospect for the future is a system in which numerous middling and small nations have acquired their own independent nuclear-weapons systems. Each nation possessing one of these "equalizers" would be in a position to exert a good deal of influence in the world political arena, to impose a "unit veto."

No small nuclear power in such a unit-veto system could actually hope to defeat or deter United States and Soviet military power. Clearly there is more to being a superpower than having "the bomb" and a few missiles. Extremely elaborate delivery systems as well as an effective second-strike deterrent capability would be needed, and these are so costly that only the wealthiest and most advanced of nations could possibly afford to develop and maintain them. On the other hand, even the possession of a few hydrogen bombs would make it relatively easy for a small nation to spark an "accidental" war that might drive the superpowers precipitously into a nuclear holocaust. This fearful possibility has obsessed policy makers in both Washington and Moscow, and a nuclear nonproliferation treaty took easy precedence over more leisurely concern with consultation on mutual arms limitation.

Both the United States and the Soviet Union have guarded jealously their own nuclear-weapons stockpiles, even from their closest allies, in order to avoid being drawn into a war they did not intend. The fact that Great Britain has already developed the capacity to produce the hydrogen bomb, and that France is push-ing ahead with her own delivery system, was deemed less of a menace than having China reach this threshold as well. With more felt grievances against the international status quo, and supposedly less to lose in the event of nuclear war, the possibility of China using her new nuclear power irresponsibly in order to blackmail both the Soviets and the United States is a fearful one. With the prospect of other nations – like Germany, Egypt, Israel, Indonesia, South Africa, or India – developing their own nuclear arsenals, it is little wonder that Soviet-American cooperation on a nuclear nonproliferation treaty was the first order of business on the diplomatic front of the Cold War during the late 1950's and early 1960's. Both powers are at present engaged in the construction of costly antimissile defense systems which they avow are at least partly in response to China's surprisingly rapid advances in developing both a hydrogen bomb and a missile delivery system of her own.

Bipolar and Multibloc Systems

The conditions of world politics in the last half of the twentieth century are so complex that any predictions about future international systems must be made with extreme care. Surely there are many more short- and long-term possibilities than it would be possible to discuss here. It is just as sure that future patterns of international behavior will be substantially more intricate and complicated than any of the systems discussed so far. The prospect of more than a dozen or so nations in the world gaining some minimal nuclear capability is exceedingly slim, especially when one takes into account the great cost, and the fear and hostility this would stimulate among larger and more powerful nations directly threatened. But even with a limited number of nuclear armed nations in the world, life would not be simple. It has been suggested, for example, that the next configuration of international affairs will see a modified bipolar arrangement overlapping and interacting with a system which might be called "multibloc."

As the bipolar system has become even looser, states are drawing away from the influence of the two superpowers, but there are now the beginnings of regional alliances among them. Several unsatisfactory conferences among the Asian and African neutrals have demonstrated that a broad third-world compact is unfeasible at this time. The new African states tried and failed to come to some kind of general agreement on a united policy. The Arab states have for some time been grouped into a somewhat loosely integrated alliance directed primarily against the state of Israel. Europe gives some promise of emerging as an independent bloc of substantial power in its own right. Development of some fledgling efforts at common markets in Latin America suggest that some subgroups similar to the European Common Market may develop in other regions.

An international structure in which most nations were assembled into a half dozen or more independent blocs would assume some of the characteristics of a balance-of-power system. As members of regional blocs, the lesser states of the world might be able to offset some of the power disadvantage which has worked against them in the past. Blocs would be in a position to pursue their own bloc interests and yet be unable to threaten domination over the system as a whole. And finally, although such a system would probably increase the number of crisis situations, most could be settled at the regional level, perhaps through intervention by the United Nations or a regional organization, and fewer would become entangled in the bipolar struggle. Such a system might well be flexible enough to ensure against a third world war.

There are doubts about the efficacy of the multibloc system as a key to international stability. For one thing it is obvious that the old balance-of-power system became increasingly unstable with the development of industrial modernization and radical nationalism. Limited war because of limited means is one thing, but continual military confrontations which threaten the use of nuclear weapons is quite another. Not only would such a system increase the number of hostile encounters, but the increased variety of interactions would probably result in a great deal more uncertainty and confusion over appropriate diplomatic and military responses. In a bipolar world, threatening moves by one bloc are recognized quickly and the necessary adjustments can be made relatively easily. The complexity of a large number of limited interactions in a multibloc system would likely make it more difficult to perceive clearly the dangers involved in each or all of the various international encounters, and therefore foreign-policy reactions could be expected to be inadequate and ill-timed. Surely some kind of refurbished Concert of Europe, a collective-security system, or an enhanced role for the United Nations in interbloc peacekeeping would be necessary to prevent what might be a swiftly spreading nuclear war sparked in some remote corner of the earth. Another possible moderating force would be the intervention of the two superpowers.

It must be kept in mind that even if a multibloc system were to emerge among nonaligned nations in the world, for the foreseeable future the bipolar system in which the United States and the Soviet Union are so deeply involved will probably remain much the same as it is today. In this event two international systems are bound to become intermeshed, the dynamics of one affecting radically the patterns of the other. It is possible that the dangers of the bipolar arms race and the menace of a unit-veto system born out of the multibloc arrangement gone awry could be reduced because of this interpenetration of systems. There are some reasonable grounds for this hope.

The first point is that even though hostilities among the lesser blocs would remain localized so long as they did not involve one or the other of the principals in the bipolar struggle, the fact of Soviet support for social and political revolution and United States defense of the status quo will continue to push the superpowers toward intervention in the affairs of nonaligned nations whenever intervention seems to the respective advantage of either. The opportunity to exploit such situations, however, can be limited to the extent that the United Nations or other international organizations are able to take an expanded role in peacekeeping operations. Moreover, too great a concern with winning or influencing the non-aligned blocs will entail the risk of alienating the nonleading members of the allied blocs in the Cold War. With increased opportunity for independence, these allies may be in a position to demand more influence in bloc policy. In this situation involvement in the affairs of nonaligned blocs would be at the expense of control over a superpower's bloc allies. Alternatively the energy required to maintain unity of purpose in both the Soviet and Western blocs would draw away from the capacity to control events in the nonaligned world. In this manner it might be hoped that conflict in both systems would be moderated.

There is another way in which the probability of general nuclear war might be lessened. The fact that leaders of the nonaligned blocs would have available to them nuclear weapons would be enough to prevent either of the superpowers from coercing them into passive conformity. However, a real threat that the multi-bloc system was verging on a unit-veto situation would provide sufficient motivation for cooperation between the United States and the Soviet Union. Not just their combined military force, but their economic and political influence could be employed, perhaps in a "carrot and stick" fashion, to limit or broaden the policy alternatives of those who threatened the indiscriminate use of nuclear weapons. Such an international structure, in which a bipolar and a multibloc system overlap and influence each other, may be one of the more likely possibilities for the immediate future. On the other hand, the fantastic complexity of international affairs under these conditions would require an exceptionally high degree of sensitivity to world conditions and an unusual level of responsibility on the part of policy makers in Washington and Moscow.

In recent years, the major trends in the international system have included a loosening of the bipolar system so that neither the United States nor the Soviet Union has the influence over the "allies" that existed in the 1950's. This loosening has in part been attributable to the growth in the independent capabilities of some of these allies (among them France, West Germany, China, and Japan). Also, there has been a decline in the fear that either of the major powers will directly attack these countries. The number of actors who are not members in either bloc has increased substantially. While they do not constitute a third bloc, they nevertheless have been important in the efforts of the two superpowers to extend their influences. A projection of current trends in the world today would seem to make something like a bipolar multibloc system a likely outcome. Relationships between actors in such a system are complicated and delicate. There are more actors whose actions can affect a larger number of other actors in the system. Stability in such a system will depend on each actor developing a multitude of strategies that can be adapted to many different situations. It may be that stability will depend on the development of an effective system of third parties to mediate disputes. This need may lead to a more significant role for international organizations.

In efforts to make predictions about the trends in international systems, we need to explore more fully the characteristics of the actors in the international system. Before further pursuing the discussion of the possible future trends, we should turn our attention to the internal considerations influencing the actors' behavior. This is the focus of Part II.

Part I

Additional Reading

Claude, Inis L., Jr. *Power and International Relations*. New York: Random House, 1962.

Holborn, Hajo. *The Political Collapse of Europe*. New York: Knopf, 1959.

Kaplan, Morton A. *System and Process in International Politics*. New York: Wiley, 1957.

Kaplan, Morton A. (ed.) *The Revolution in World Politics*. New York: Wiley, 1962.

Kissinger, Henry A. *American Foreign Policy*. New York: Norton, 1969.

Lerche, Charles O., Jr. *The Cold War . . . And After*. Englewood Cliffs: Prentice-Hall, 1965.

Luard, Evan. *Conflict and Peace in the Modern International System*. Boston: Little, Brown, 1968.

McClelland, Charles A. *Theory and the International System*. New York: Macmillan, 1966.

Rosencrance, Richard N. *Action and Reaction in World Politics*. Boston: Little, Brown, 1963.

Rosencrance, Richard N. "Bipolarity, Multipolarity, and the Future." *Journal of Conflict Resolution*, X, September 1966, pp. 314-327.

Waltz, Kenneth N. "The Stability of a Bipolar World," *Daedalus*, XCIII, Summer 1964, pp. 881-909.

Part II

FOREIGN POLICY

Chapter 3

POLITICAL PROCESSES AND FOREIGN POLICY: DECISION MAKING IN CRISIS AND NONCRISIS SITUATIONS

Ole R. Holsti
University of British Columbia

When we want to understand foreign-policy decision making, we are in fact seeking the answers to two related questions. First, who makes the decisions? And second, what factors influence the persons who make the decisions?

The first question is deceptively simple. We can be almost certain that those holding important offices related to foreign policy will be included in the decision-making process. Thus, in the United States the President, the Secretary of State, and White House foreign-policy advisers are almost certain to participate. But we usually need to look further if we are to get a satisfactory answer to our question. For example, formal titles alone do not explain why Colonel Edward House, President Woodrow Wilson's personal adviser, had a great deal of influence, whereas Robert Lansing, the Secretary of State during Wilson's presidency had almost none, or why President Richard Nixon relies more heavily on Henry Kissinger (Special Assistant to the President for National Security) than on Secretary of State William Rogers. Conversely, Secretary of State John Foster Dulles's views cast a large shadow on United States policy during the 1950's almost totally eclipsing those of White House foreign-policy aides Harold Stassen, Nelson Rockefeller, William Jackson, and C. D. Jackson. In fact, Dulles's influence on United States foreign policy often exceeded that of the President. Winston Churchill, British Prime Minister during the early years of the Eisenhower administration, complained, "I cannot make it out. I am bewildered. It seems everything is left to Dulles. It appears the President (Eisenhower) is no more than a ventriloquist's doll." Nor can title alone explain why two successive Secretaries of State under the same President — such as James F. Byrnes and George C. Marshall, or Dulles and Christian Herter — should have such disparate influence on United States foreign policy.

We may, therefore, also need to consider the possible influence of those who hold no formal foreign-policy office. "Kitchen cabinets" and unofficial advisers are an old tradition in the United States, as well as elsewhere. For example, Presidents Eisenhower and Kennedy often relied upon their brothers for advice, although neither held a position associated with foreign policy: Milton Eisenhower was president of The Johns Hopkins University, and Robert Kennedy was Attorney General. In summary, then, the question "who makes the decisions?" is one which can rarely be answered adequately merely by looking at the formal organization of the government.

The answer to our second question is even more complex. Among the factors which may influence those who make the decisions (but not necessarily the only ones), are: the personalities of the decision makers; the organizations to which the decision makers belong; and the type of situation or problems for which policy must be formulated.

Although a decision maker brings with him into office his personal values and attitudes, even a high-ranking official such as a President or Secretary of State is not free from limitations on his actions and policies. These range from the constitutional and legal requirements of his office to informal, but nevertheless real, limitations imposed by the expectations of his colleagues and subordinates. The Secretary of State of the United States is formally accountable only to the President once his appointment has received Senate confirmation. But should he fail to establish and maintain good working relations with key members of the Senate, he will find himself severely hampered in the conduct of foreign policy.

A large and complex organization such as the State Department also has established goals and working procedures which cannot be completely disregarded by the head of the Department — or even by the President. A change of administration in Washington may bring new persons into high office, but changes in decision-making processes or in the substance of foreign policy, if any, are likely to come more gradually.

Finally, the nature of the situation which calls for a decision may be important in determining who has the opportunity to influence policy making. A new situation often creates demands for new types of expertise. A crisis in Africa may require the participation of persons or organizations who would not have the opportunity to influence a decision regarding Vietnam. In some situations, such as consideration of a foreign-trade law, Congress, the press, pressure groups, and others may have a significant impact on the final policy. On the other hand, in a crisis requiring an immediate response, a small handful of leaders may make all the important decisions because time or the requirements for secrecy may not permit consultation with even such important groups as the Senate Foreign Relations Committee. Such was the case during the Cuban missile crisis, in the crises over Korea in 1950 and Indo-China in 1954, and in many others. The remainder of this chapter will consider how the nature of the situation affects decision making. We shall compare the process by which United States leaders formulated policies on the League of Nations issue in 1919 with the process during the Cuban missile crisis in 1962.

THE LEAGUE OF NATIONS DEBATE (1919)

The "war to end all wars" had ended in November, 1918, with a military victory for France, England, the United States and their Allies. In order to insure that the bloody four-year war just ended would not be repeated—that the world had indeed been made "safe for democracy"—a League of Nations was established at the peace conference in Versailles, France. As a result, the United States government was faced with an issue of great importance: should the United States join the League? On July 8, 1919, President Wilson formally presented the Senate with the Treaty of Versailles, within which the Covenant of the League of Nations was embedded. Ratification by the Senate was the last remaining step in the process of deciding whether the United States would join the other nations of the world in the international organization that had emerged from the peace conference. Before examining the process by which a decision on American entry into the League of Nations was made, let us consider briefly the background of the issue.

The War as a "European" Affair
On June 28, 1914, a young Serbian nationalist assassinated

the heir to the Austro-Hungarian throne. Within five weeks this incident at Sarajevo in the Balkans had set off a chain of events which culminated in a general European war—France, Russia and England against Germany and Austria-Hungary. Many other European nations were drawn into the war in subsequent months.

The initial reaction of most people in the United States to the outbreak of war was one of relief that their country was far removed from the great battlefields of Europe. By the beginning of the twentieth century, many knowledgeable persons had come to believe that the increasing destructiveness of military weapons, the benefits of international trade, and the progress of Western civilization had made any general war unprofitable and senseless —and therefore impossible. The outbreak of war in Europe shattered such optimistic beliefs, and the reaction of many Americans was to counsel withdrawal from foreign entanglements. The apparent folly by which the nations of Europe had permitted themselves to be drawn into war over a royal murder reinforced the popular belief that a policy of isolation from the traditional rivalries of Europe was in the national interest of the United States. A popular song, "I Didn't Raise My Boy to Be a Soldier," reflected the prevailing mood of this period.

Neutrality was also the official policy of the government. Within days after the outbreak of war, President Woodrow Wilson called for Americans to be "impartial in thought as well as action." Despite the tenacity with which most of them clung to the idea of isolation, it was impossible for the United States to remain completely aloof from events in Europe. As an important industrial power, the United States had developed an extensive international trade with the nations of Europe. The outbreak of war increased the demand abroad for the products of United States agriculture and industry, and as the nation's exports rose, so did the desire of the belligerents to keep those products from reaching the enemy. Both sides came to regard the claim of a neutral nation for freedom of trade as a threat to their war effort. Before long British control of the high seas had effectively cut off German access to United States goods. A blockade was established around Germany, and the North Sea was heavily mined to prevent war materials from reaching German ports.

Germany, unable to match the mighty British fleet, turned to a new weapon of war—the submarine—to prevent the flow of United States goods to the Allies. Whereas the British navy could conduct leisurely searches for war materials in cargoes destined for Germany, submarines had no corresponding option except to sink vessels suspected of aiding the British. Both British and German actions violated the rights of neutral nations, but the British could act without endangering the lives of crews and passengers. In May, 1915, a German submarine sank the passenger ship *Lusitania* off the coast of Ireland with a heavy loss of life, including 128 Americans. To a public outcry for strong action, Wilson replied that "there is such a thing as a man being too proud to fight." Strong public protests apparently convinced German leaders that it was unwise to continue a policy of submarine warfare against noncombatant vessels. Continued interference with United States rights as a neutral was not limited to Germany. In 1916, the British government produced a "blacklist" of individuals and business firms in the United States suspected of dealing with the Central Powers.

President Wilson was faced with demands from a vocal minority who wanted the United States to take stronger action; in the words of their leading spokesman, ex-President Theodore Roosevelt, they advocated a "big stick" policy. Pressure from the isolationists was also strong. The President, aware of the dangers of leading a disunited nation into war, rather effectively resisted the demands of both sides.

The war and the state of United States preparedness became issues in the 1916 presidential election. The Democratic Party renominated Wilson. His supporters campaigned largely on the theme that "He kept us out of war," but Wilson was careful to refrain from any promises about the future. The Republican nominee, Supreme Court Justice Charles Evans Hughes, took an equivocal position on the issues of preparedness and war. Wilson defeated Hughes in an extremely close election.

Throughout the winter of 1916-1917, there were numerous official and unofficial attempts to end the bloody, stalemated war. In an address to Congress on January 22, 1917, the President declared that a peace dictated by the victors would not endure: "It must be a peace without victory. Only a peace between equals can last."

The United States Enters the War

Nine days later the German government answered Wilson's pleas with the announcement that unrestricted submarine warfare in the Atlantic and the Mediterranean would be resumed the following day, and during the next two months German submarines inflicted a mounting toll on United States shipping. In the meanwhile, a note from the German foreign minister to the President of Mexico was intercepted by the British, who revealed its content to Wilson. The "Zimmermann Note" proposed an alliance against the United States, in return for which Mexico would receive New Mexico, Arizona, and Texas. In April Wilson called a special session of Congress to consider a declaration of war against Germany. In his war message the President distinguished between British and German violations of United States neutral rights: "Property can be paid for: the lives of peaceful and innocent people cannot be." He added that the United States was entering the war because "The world must be made safe for democracy." The Senate and House of Representatives approved the declaration of war on April 6, 1917.

United States participation in the war went beyond mobilizing the armed forces. Rationing, war-bond drives, and home-front propaganda stimulated civilians to contribute to the war effort. On the eve of his war message to Congress, Wilson had told a newsman that, "Once lead this people into war, and they'll forget there was ever such a thing as tolerance. . . . A nation couldn't put its strength into a war and keep its head level."[1] Yet he supported a massive drive, skillfully organized by George Creel, head of a newly established Committee on Public Information, to mobilize the nation's spirit as well as its arms. Before the war had ended, some 150,000 lecturers, writers, actors, and scholars were engaged in the most extensive propaganda campaign in United States history. On the one hand, American participation in the war was characterized as an idealistic crusade for freedom and democracy throughout the world. The President himself gave impetus to this aspect of the campaign with his eloquent pleas for an enduring peace based on justice. The other side of the campaign was designed to stir up hatred for Germany and all aspects of German culture. Through newspapers, magazines, books, speeches, and even movies, the public was aroused to hate all things German, and especially the spike-helmeted, mustachioed Kaiser, the "beast of Berlin." Hamburger and sauerkraut were renamed "Liberty steak" and "Liberty cabbage." Among the victims of the emotionally aroused public were Americans persecuted for the "crime" of having German-sounding names.

The immediate result of this propaganda drive was a nation united for the massive effort required to win the war. The longer-term consequences were less desirable. The United States public was led to believe that German autocracy was responsible for all international problems, and that a military victory over the Central Powers would almost automatically solve all of them. Once

---

[1] Samuel Eliot Morison, *The Oxford History of the American People* (New York: Oxford University Press, 1965), p. 858.

such unrealistic hopes for the future had been aroused, an emotional letdown was almost inevitable as it became more evident that new international problems had emerged from the war.

Plans for a Permanent Peace

After the United States entered the war on the side of the Allies, President Wilson proposed a plan to end the war without retribution and punishment, and to remove the causes of future wars. His program, which became known as the "Fourteen Points," included a proposal for "A general association of nations . . . formed under specific covenants for the purpose of affording mutual guarantees of political independence and territorial integrity to great and small states alike." The idea of an international organization to secure peace was not an original one. For centuries philosophers and reformers had produced various plans, but it took the catastrophe of a world war to convince many statesmen of the practical need for such an organization. Throughout the war, concerned Americans had urged that plans for the postwar world include the development of an organization to prevent the outbreak of war in the future. A "League to Enforce Peace," dedicated to the promotion of postwar planning for a peaceful world, was organized by prominent citizens. In May, 1916, members of the League heard Senator Henry Cabot Lodge of Massachusetts argue that George Washington's warning against "entangling alliances" was not meant to preclude United States membership in an organization intended to "diminish war and encourage peace."[2]

The President Leads the United States Delegation to Paris

In Wilson's view, there were two primary tasks before the peace conference which met at Paris in January, 1919, two months after the armistice. First, the terms to be imposed on the defeated Central Powers should be just rather than punitive. If the treaty were drawn up to gain revenge, the defeated nations would eventually seek to change the settlement by force. The second, and even more important task was the establishment of a League of Nations; fulfilling this solemn obligation was a necessary step toward making "the world safe for democracy." So strongly did the President feel about the League of Nations that he broke all precedent by announcing, a week after the armistice, that he would attend the peace conference in person. He thus became the first United States President to visit Europe while still in office. Other members of the peace commission chosen were: Colonel Edward House, Wil-

---

[2] Morison, *The Oxford History*, p. 881.

son's closest personal adviser; Secretary of State Robert Lansing; General Tasker H. Bliss; and Henry White. Wilson's selection of this delegation created the first controversy on the League of Nations issue. No member of the United States Senate was chosen, although the Senate's approval of the treaty would later be required. Moreover, the Democratic President had chosen only one Republican, and not a very prominent one at that (Henry White). Many Republicans felt that ex-President William Howard Taft, ex-Secretary of State Elihu Root, or Senator Henry Cabot Lodge should have been included. During the war, all three had urged the establishment of an international organization, and each was considered a leading figure in the Republican Party.

Terms of the Peace

After his arrival in Paris, it became apparent to Wilson that other Allied statesmen were less willing to regard the Fourteen Points as the basis of a peace treaty. France and England, represented at the conference by Georges Clemenceau and Lloyd George, were determined to punish Germany. France wanted territorial concessions and reparations, as well as permanent military security against Germany. Clemenceau was less optimistic than Wilson that the proposed League of Nations would prevent war. Different views of the League were exemplified in the following conversation, which reportedly took place during the Conference.

Wilson: My one object in promoting the League of Nations is to prevent future wars.

Clemenceau: You can never prevent war by no matter what scheme or organization unless we can all agree on three fundamental principles.

Wilson: What are they?

Clemenceau: First, to declare and enforce racial equality. Japan already has a resolution to that effect before the Conference. She demands that it be incorporated in the Treaty. Do you accept?

Wilson: No, I'm afraid not. The race question is very touchy in the United States, and the Southern and West Coast senators would defeat any treaty containing such a clause.

Clemenceau: The second thing we must do is to establish freedom of immigration; no country to close her borders to foreigners wishing to come to live there. Do you agree?

Wilson: No; my country is determined to exclude Orientals absolutely, and Congress is already considering restrictions to European immigration.

Clemenceau: The third condition of an enduring peace is free trade throughout the world. How would you like that?

Wilson: I personally would like to see it, and my party has lowered the American tariff; but I could never get Congress to agree to a customs union with Europe, Asia, and Africa.

Clemenceau: Very well, then; the only way to maintain peace is to remain strong ourselves and keep our past and potential enemies weak.
No conceivable League of Nations can do that.[3]

Many other nations also wanted territorial adjustments, some
of which ran directly counter to Wilson's ideal of "self-determination"; that is, national boundaries which coincide with the desires
of the people. Satisfaction of some of the territorial demands had
been pledged in wartime treaties between various Allied nations.
Despite the disagreements on many issues, a covenant or charter
of a League of Nations was written and included as part of the
Treaty of Versailles. Among its twenty-six articles, which covered
such diverse subjects as arms reduction, a Permanent Court of
International Justice, and promotion of the Red Cross, two were
particularly important for the maintenance of peace. According to
Article X, League members pledged themselves to "respect and
preserve as against external aggression the territorial integrity
and existing political independence of all Members of the League."
Should aggression take place, the League Council was to decide
on the means to carry out this obligation. Among the means was
that outlined in Article XVI: "It shall be the duty of the Council
in such case [of aggression] to recommend to the several Governments concerned what effective military, naval or air force the
Members of the League shall severally contribute to the armed
forces to be used to protect the covenants of the League." Thus
the collective-security provisions of the League might require
member nations to contribute military units to aid the victims
of aggression.

The Domestic Political Process:
The Treaty Goes before the Senate

When he sailed back to the United States in February, 1919,
Wilson's immediate problem was to obtain approval by the Senate
of the Treaty of Versailles, of which the League of Nations Covenant was a part. According to Article II, Section 2 of the Constitution, the President "shall have the power, by and with the advice
and consent of the Senate, to make treaties, provided that two-
thirds of the Senators present shall concur." He appeared confident of winning the necessary support. As President and leader
of the Democratic Party, he could use persuasion, as well as the
power of patronage, to insure support of the Democratic Senators.
Wilson was equally certain that he could use the immense prestige

---

[3]Morison, *The Oxford History,* p. 877.

of his office to gain the support of Republican Senators for his position. He believed that not even his political enemies would dare fly in the face of public opinion, which he considered to be the ultimate source of political power. Public-opinion polls were relatively crude at that time, but they revealed widespread support for United States entry into the League of Nations. The same polls revealed, however, that only one voter in 25 had read the Covenant.[4] Like Thomas Jefferson, Wilson firmly believed that the public was able and willing to make decisions on moral issues— and to Wilson, entry of the United States into the League was a moral issue. To repudiate this "solemn obligation" would be to repudiate not only those who had lost their lives during World War I, but also those of future generations who would be forced to fight other wars.

The press was also strongly in favor of the treaty. A poll of 1377 daily newspapers in April, 1919, revealed that 52 percent supported the League unconditionally, 35 percent gave conditional support, and only 13 percent were opposed. During the early stages of the battle over the League, even Wilson's opponents thought he would win. One of them stated: "What are you going to do? It's hopeless. All the newspapers in my state are for it [the League]."[5]

The Political Battle Takes Form

Despite Wilson's optimism that the treaty would be approved without revision, there were indications as early as March, 1919, that a major political battle was developing on the issue of the League. In part, it would be a test of strength between the executive and legislative branches of government. During wartime the President, as Commander-in-Chief, often exercises almost dictatorial powers; it had been true of Lincoln during the Civil War and it was true of Wilson during World War I. During periods of national emergency the legislative branch is often reduced to a rubber stamp on many vital issues. Because it was virtually certain that the Senate would seek to restore a balance between the two branches of government once the war ended, Wilson's failure to appoint a single member of the Senate to the peace delegation was considered by many as a major political error; others regarded it as a deliberate insult.

The treaty was also becoming a partisan political issue, divid-

---

[4]Thomas A. Bailey, *Woodrow Wilson and the Great Betrayal* (New York: The Macmillan Co., 1945), p. 16.

[5]Bailey, *Woodrow Wilson,* p. 64.

ing Democrats and Republicans. Polls indicated strong public support for the treaty, but they also revealed that support was related to other political views. Pro-League sentiment was strongest in traditionally Democratic areas, and somewhat weaker in Republican areas of the country. For example, 73 percent of the daily newspapers in the South supported the League unconditionally, compared to only 47 percent in the traditionally Republican states of the Middle West. One newspaper made the point clearly: "The South is heart and soul for the Treaty. It hasn't read it, but it has read some of the speeches of them darned Republicans."[6] The opposing position was presented by the Columbus *Ohio State Journal,* "The attitude of most of us thoughtful Republicans seems to be that we're unalterably opposed to Article X, whether we know what's in it or not."[7]

The division along partisan lines was partly of Wilson's own making. During the war, the two parties had more or less agreed to refrain from seeking partisan advantage. But the President was anxious that his position at the peace conference be strengthened by a vote of confidence from the electorate in the Congressional elections which were to be held on November 5, 1918. A few days before the election he had issued an appeal to the voters to elect Democrat majorities in both the House of Representatives and the Senate: "The return of a Republican majority to either House of Congress would . . . certainly be interpreted on the other side of the water as a repudiation of my leadership."[8] The Republicans charged that the wartime truce on partisan politics had thus been broken. The election resulted in Republican majorities in both Houses of Congress, the first time since Wilson had taken office in 1913 that the Republicans had won a majority in either the House or the Senate. In the Senate, which would consider the peace treaty, the Republicans held 49 seats to 47 for the Democrats. The absence of a leading Republican on the peace delegation led many Republicans to believe that the President wanted the Democrats to get credit for the League of Nations; ex-President Taft charged him with a desire to "hog the whole show."[9] Some Republicans also feared that Wilson planned to run for a third term in 1920, capitalizing on popular support for the League. In short, the treaty and the League of Nations were so closely bound

---

[6] Bailey, *Woodrow Wilson,* p. 48.

[7] Bailey, *Woodrow Wilson,* p. 42.

[8] Arthur S. Link, *American Epoch* (New York: Alfred A. Knopf, 1955), p. 222.

[9] Thomas A. Bailey, *The American Pageant* (Boston: Little, Brown and Co., 1956), p. 749.

up with the President and the Democratic Party that a partisan political battle was nearly inevitable. In the absence of vigorous efforts by Wilson to keep the treaty from becoming a partisan issue, the Republicans saw only two alternative policies open to themselves. They could support the treaty as drafted, but would thereby add to Wilson's prestige. Or, they could try to amend the Covenant so that the Republicans could at least share in the credit for the League of Nations.

By the time Wilson returned to the United States from Paris in February, 1919, opposition to the Covenant was already forming in the Senate. Thirty-nine Republican Senators, two more than were required to prevent a two-thirds affirmative vote of the Senate, signed a "Senatorial Round Robin" which rejected the League of Nations in its existing form. Among those who had helped prepare this statement of opposition was Senator Lodge, Chairman of the Senate Foreign Relations Committee and a bitter personal enemy of the President. Wilson's reply to the Round Robin stressed that it would be impossible to amend the Covenant, and that rejection of the Covenant would be rejection of the entire peace treaty. "When the treaty comes back, gentlemen on this side will find the covenant not only in it, but so many threads of the treaty tied to the covenant that you cannot dissect the covenant from the treaty without destroying the whole vital structure. The structure of peace will not be vital without the League of Nations."[10] Wilson apparently felt that the Senate would not dare reject the entire treaty.

When Wilson returned to Paris in March, 1919, he did obtain some amendments to the League Covenant which were designed to overcome opposition in the Senate. In return he was forced to make some concessions on the insistent territorial demands by French, Italian, and Japanese leaders. Although some of these territorial compromises violated the "self-determination" principle of the Fourteen Points, Wilson felt that this was a necessary price to pay for his main objective — the League of Nations. And once established, the League would provide the machinery to redress grievances without resort to violence.

Four Factions in the Senate

When Wilson returned from Paris with the amended treaty, he presented it for ratification with a reminder to the Senators that: "Our isolation was ended twenty years ago. . . . There can be no question of our ceasing to be a world power. The only ques-

---

[10]Thomas A. Bailey, *A Diplomatic History of the American People,* 4th ed. (New York: Appleton-Century-Crofts, Inc., 1950), p. 661.

tion is whether we can refuse the moral leadership that is offered, whether we shall accept or reject the confidence of the world."[11] By this time the Senate had become divided into four factions on the issue of the League of Nations. The largest single group consisted of those Democrats who supported Wilson's position that the treaty must be ratified without amendments or reservations. Three other factions, composed mostly of Republicans, had also formed. The "mild reservationists" were strong supporters of the League of Nations, but wanted certain changes made before ratification. Nearly two dozen "strong reservationists," led by Senator Lodge, would support the League of Nations only if rather extensive changes were made in the Covenant. Finally, fourteen "irreconcilables" were opposed to United States entry into the League of Nations under any circumstances. The latter group was largely made up of isolationist Senators from the Middle West. It included such distinguished liberals as William Borah, Robert La Follette, and George Norris, as well as the notorious Albert Fall, who ended his career in a federal penitentiary. Perhaps equally important, this group included some of the ablest political debaters in the Senate: Senator James A. Reed, the only Democrat with oratorical skills to match those of the Republicans, was also one of the most outspoken "irreconcilables."

The Senate Foreign Relations Committee

Before the entire Senate votes on a treaty, it is sent to the Foreign Relations Committee. Owing to the Republican majority in the Senate, the committee was composed of ten Republicans—including the Chairman, Senator Lodge—and seven Democrats. The Foreign Relations Committee did not, however, accurately reflect the strength of various Senate factions. Senator Lodge had filled four vacancies on the Committee with opponents of the League, and he denied a seat to Senator (later Secretary of State) Frank B. Kellogg when the latter refused to guarantee in advance that he would always vote with Lodge. Of the seventeen Senators on the Committee, six were "irreconcilables."

Opponents of the treaty, aware of the public support for the League, adopted a strategy of delay. They felt that time was on their side, that the public would soon lose interest in the matter. In contrast to Wilson's theory of public opinion, someone suggested that: "The President proposes, the Senate disposes, while the country dozes."[12] Senator Lodge used the first two weeks of the Com-

---

[11] Link, *American Epoch,* p. 228.
[12] Bailey, *Woodrow Wilson,* p. 51.

mittee hearings to read the entire 268-page text of the treaty aloud, often to a completely empty room. For six weeks some witnesses testifying for the treaty – and more who were opposed to it – were called to testify. Many represented ethnic groups which were strongly opposed to various aspects of the treaty. German-Americans were anti-Wilson because of the United States part in the defeat of Germany. Irish-Americans, Italian-Americans, and other national groups were angry because territorial demands of their native countries had not been met at Paris. At one point in the hearings the committee heard a woman with an Irish name urge the claim of Italy to Yugoslavia's port of Fiume.[13] Closely allied with these groups were the Anglophobes, who regarded the League of Nations as a British plot for domination of the postwar world.

Other witnesses opposed United States participation in the League on historical grounds; they asserted that the United States should remain free of "entangling alliances" as Washington had advised in his Farewell Address. They inaccurately portrayed the League as a "superstate" to which the United States would be forced to surrender its sovereignty. Many opponents of the League concentrated their verbal fire on Article X of the Covenant, according to which League members pledged themselves to "respect and preserve as against external aggression the territorial integrity and existing political independence of all Members of the League." They raised the spectre of United States armed forces constantly sent to fight distant wars which were no concern of the United States. An advertisement for an anti-League meeting summarized the slogans of the isolationists.

AMERICANS, AWAKE!

Shall we bind ourselves to the War Breeding
    Covenant?
It Impairs American Sovereignty!
Surrenders the Monroe Doctrine!
Flouts Washington's Warning!
Entangles us in European and Asiatic Intrigues!
Sends our Boys to Fight Throughout the World
    by Order of a League!
"The Evil thing with a holy name."[14]

Ironically, many of those opposed to United States involvement in world affairs were also most vocal in urging that the United

---

[13] Bailey, *Woodrow Wilson*, p. 82.
[14] Bailey, *A Diplomatic History of the American People*, p. 668.

States take a stand on such "foreign" issues as Irish independence from Great Britain.

The case for the treaty was also weakened by the testimony of Secretary of State Lansing and William C. Bullitt, a minor official with the United States delegation at Paris; both suggested that some mistakes had been made in the negotiations at Paris. Such admissions added to the belief of some that the United States should not further involve itself in the affairs of "greedy" Europeans.

The President's Response to the Senate

During the summer Wilson was frequently advised to insure ratification of the treaty by accepting a compromise with Senator Lodge. His answer was always a clear rejection: "Accept the Treaty with the *Lodge* reservations? Never! Never! I'll never consent to adopt any policy with which that impossible name is so prominently identified."[15] The bitterness of feeling between Lodge and the President was a formidable barrier to compromise. On August 19, at a conference with the Committee on Foreign Relations, Wilson did agree to accept some interpretive reservations not requiring consent of the other parties to the treaty. This concession failed to satisfy the irreconcilables, who then launched a nationwide campaign against ratification, financed by Andrew Mellon and Henry C. Frick.

By early September, 1919, the President, convinced that the Senate would add crippling amendments to the Treaty of Versailles, decided that the only way to insure its ratification was to tour the country, arousing public opinion against his opponents in the Senate. His doctors advised against the trip, which would tax the energies of even a young man. Other advisers urged him to stay in Washington during this crucial period of the treaty fight. They also pointed out that even if every Republican Senator up for reelection in 1920 were defeated, the Democrats would still be short of the two-thirds majority required to ratify the treaty. Thus any strategy which failed to win the support of at least some Republican Senators was certain to fail.

During the 9500-mile train trip, Wilson delivered thirty-seven major speeches to enthusiastic crowds. Following behind him, on a tour in opposition to the Covenant, were two of the ablest orators among the irreconcilables, Senators Borah and Johnson. In the fourth week of the tour, after a speech in Pueblo, Colorado, the President collapsed and the remainder of his trip was canceled. On October 2 he suffered a stroke from which he never fully re-

---

[15] Bailey, *Woodrow Wilson*, p. 76.

covered. During the remainder of the fight over the League of Nations, even his closest advisers had only limited access to the President.

The Senate Votes

In early November, 1919, the treaty was finally reported out of the Foreign Relations Committee, accompanied by fourteen reservations. In a letter to the Democratic leader in the Senate, Wilson wrote that "I sincerely hope that the friends and supporters of the treaty will vote against the Lodge resolution of ratification."[16] To those who urged compromise he said, "Better a thousand times to go down fighting than to dip your colors to dishonorable compromise."[17] Instead, he hoped for a deadlock which public opinion would break in his favor. As a result of Wilson's appeal, 42 Democrats who remained loyal to the President and 13 irreconcilable Republicans joined to outvote 35 Republicans and 4 Democrats who supported the Lodge reservations. Ironically, had the Wilson Democrats voted for the Lodge resolution, the treaty would have obtained a 81-13 majority.

Public indignation with this result led to one more attempt to ratify the treaty. A bipartisan approach to ratification was wrecked in January, 1920, when Lodge yielded to threats by the irreconcilables against modifying his original reservations. Wilson was equally unwilling to compromise; rather, he urged giving the 1920 election "the form of a great and solemn referendum" in which the people of the nation could indicate their support for the League of Nations.

The treaty was again reported out of the Foreign Relations Committee with the Lodge reservations intact. In the final vote on March 19, twenty-one Democratic Senators deserted the President and joined twenty-eight Republicans to vote for the treaty with the Lodge reservations. But 35 Senators—12 irreconcilables and 23 Democrats—voted against the treaty. Thus, although the treaty won a 49-35 majority, it failed by seven votes to gain the necessary two-thirds support. The issue was never again considered by the Senate, and it was not until 1921 that a joint resolution of the House and Senate officially ended the war with Germany and Austria-Hungary.

Wilson considered Senate rejection of the treaty, as amended by the Lodge reservations, a victory. He remained confident that his position on the League of Nations would be vindicated by the peo-

---

[16] Bailey, *Woodrow Wilson*, p. 185.
[17] Bailey, *Woodrow Wilson*, p. 184.

ple. He urged the Democratic presidential nominating convention, which met in San Francisco in June, 1920, to endorse his views on the League. The Democratic platform and the Presidential nominee, Governor James M. Cox of Ohio, pledged unequivocal ratification of the Treaty of Versailles.

The Republican Party remained divided on the issue. A strong faction within the party remained unalterably opposed to United States entry into the League; on the other hand, such leading Republicans as Herbert Hoover, William Howard Taft, and Charles Evans Hughes urged the United States to join. This division of opinion was reflected in the platform. Senator Warren G. Harding was nominated by the convention. He effectively straddled the issue in his campaign; both supporters and opponents of entry into the League of Nations could find support for their views in his speeches. Harding was elected President by a landslide, but on issues which seemed to have little to do with the League of Nations; the election supported Harding's diagnosis of the desire of the American people for "normalcy" rather than idealism. Wilson's "solemn referendum" on the League issue never took place.

Some Conclusions

What generalizations might we draw from the League of Nations case? In one sense history proved Woodrow Wilson an accurate prophet. The outbreak of World War II less than twenty years after the United States rejected the Treaty of Versailles seemed to support Wilson's prediction that refusal of the United States to join the League would cripple that organization, and failure of the League would doom the world to another catastrophic war. Whether United States entry into the League would have prevented World War II is, of course, a point which cannot be proved.

More relevant for our purposes are generalizations about domestic politics and foreign-policy decision making. Whatever the international significance of United States entry into the League, this was one situation in which domestic considerations were almost certain to assert themselves. The constitutional procedures for ratification of treaties were clearly spelled out, and these established channels within which a President would have to work if he were to be successful. Wilson seemingly felt that the justness of his cause would by itself overcome any obstacles in the Senate.

Wilson appeared equally insensitive to the fact that an issue as important as the League was virtually certain to engage partisan political loyalties unless extraordinary efforts were taken to insure that the opposition Republican Party could share in the credit for the treaty. Instead, Wilson by his unyielding behavior made it considerably easier for Republican leaders to oppose the treaty than to support it. In many respects Wilson acted as if the Democrats rather than the Republicans controlled the Senate and its Foreign Relations Committee. A willingness to compromise with those who wished modification of the treaty would almost certainly have insured its passage. The President chose instead to avoid compromise, in part because he was sure that his position was correct, in part because of a deep personal hatred for the leader of the Republican Senators, Henry Cabot Lodge.

Finally, Wilson staked his case on public support of the treaty. Public opinion is not irrelevant to foreign-policy decision making, for it can set general boundaries of policy within which political leaders must operate. It does not follow, however, that public opinion can easily be mobilized in support of specific foreign-policy issues in a general election, as Wilson had assumed would happen in 1920. By the time of the 1920 elections, other concerns were more important to the majority of the electorate.

In summary, then, the League of Nations case is a classic example of the importance of domestic politics in shaping foreign policy, and the significance of internal political processes was in no small part related to the type of issue being resolved, a point to which we shall return after considering decision making during the Cuban missile crisis.

THE CUBAN MISSILE CRISIS (1962)

In October, 1962, the first nuclear confrontation in history was precipitated by the establishment of Soviet missile sites in Cuba. For a period of approximately one week, the likelihood of a full-scale nuclear exchange between the United States and the Soviet Union was exceedingly high. Recalling the events of the week of October 22, Attorney General Robert Kennedy stated: "We all agreed in the end that if the Russians were ready to go to nuclear war over Cuba, they were ready to go to nuclear war, and that was that. So we might as well have the showdown then as six months later." [18]

At various times during the past century and a quarter, Cuba has been an issue in the foreign and domestic politics of the United States. Prior to the Civil War, Southern politicians sought to extend slavery by purchasing Cuba, or failing purchase, wresting

---

[18] Stewart Alsop and Charles Bartlett, "In Time of Crisis," *The Saturday Evening Post,* Dec. 8, 1962, p. 16.

it from Spain by force. The Southern Democratic Platform in the 1860 presidential campaign, the last election before the Civil War, explicitly called for annexation of Cuba. During the years between the Civil War and the end of the nineteenth century, Cuba seethed with internal unrest aimed at the island's Spanish rulers. A mysterious explosion on the United States battleship *Maine* in Havana harbor led directly to war between the United States and Spain in 1898. As a result of Spain's defeat, Cuba gained nominal independence, although the United States retained until 1934 the right to intervene in Cuban affairs to maintain internal order.

On January 1, 1959, the Cuban regime of Fulgencio Batista was overthrown by rebels under the leadership of Fidel Castro. Initially American sympathies tended to be with Castro, in part because of the dictatorial nature of the Batista regime, in part because Castro's small band of rebels seemed to be underdogs fighting for freedom against prohibitive odds. But soon after the Castro government came into power, executions of former Batista supporters, the absence of free elections, expropriations of United States nationals' investments, and hints of Cuban links to the Soviet Union turned many Americans against Castro. Before the 1960 presidential campaign in the United States, diplomatic relations between Washington and Havana had been severed, and the two countries were engaged in an economic and verbal war.

In the televised debates between the two presidential candidates, Vice President Richard M. Nixon and Senator John F. Kennedy, the latter took the position that force should be used to remove the Castro government from Cuba. Nixon strongly dissented although he was aware that a military operation against Cuba was being planned at the highest levels of the United States government. When Kennedy took office as President in January, 1961, despite doubts about the wisdom of the operation and the effectiveness of the military force of Cuban refugees, he permitted the operation to proceed as scheduled. The result of the invasion at the Bay of Pigs in April, 1961, was a disaster for United States policy. Not only was the invasion force soon routed by Castro's army and air force, but United States involvement in the plan became apparent and was publicly acknowledged by the President.

Relations between the United States and Cuba continued to deteriorate as Cuban alignment with the Soviet Union became more obvious. At the same time, increasingly vocal demands that the Kennedy administration act against Cuba came from the public, the press, and many Congressmen. By 1962, in addition to attacks on administration policy by Senators Capehart, Bush, Goldwater, Keating, and others, the Republican Senatorial and

Congressional campaign committees had announced that Cuba
would be "the dominant issue of the 1962 campaign." Public-
opinion polls also revealed an increasing impatience with United
States policy toward Communist influence in the Caribbean. When
the President arrived at Yale University on a campaign tour in
mid-October, one "welcoming" sign said: "Less Profile – More
Courage."[19]

There had been a number of rumors regarding the emplacement
of Soviet missiles and troops in Cuba, but "hard" evidence was
lacking; those most critical of administration policy were not, in
fact, willing to reveal their sources of information, making it impossible for intelligence experts to determine the accuracy of these
reports. Eight U-2 reconnaissance missions, flown between August
29 and October 7, 1962, revealed the build-up of short-range defensive missiles in several locations in Cuba. No sites capable of
launching missiles at other countries were in evidence in any of
these photographs. On October 14, however, two sites for medium-
range ballistic missiles (MRBM) were discovered in areas previously photographed and found to be empty; overflights on October
17 confirmed these reports and revealed additional sites in various
states of readiness. The consensus among Congressmen in subsequent investigations was that construction on the offensive
missile emplacements was begun, and in some instances completed, between October 7 and 14.

Secret Deliberations in Washington

The first phase of the crisis, from October 14 to October 21, began
with the development of photographic evidence that Soviet missiles had indeed been located in Cuba. It was during this period
that, according to President Kennedy, "15 people, more or less,
who were directly consulted" developed "a general consensus"
regarding appropriate response to the missiles in Cuba.[20] The
rest of the world remained unaware of the ominous situation that
was developing.

Six alternative responses emerged from the initial discussions
between the President's advisers. The United States could: (1) do
nothing; (2) rely on diplomatic pressure against the Soviet Union;
(3) attempt to split Castro from the Soviets; (4) initiate a blockade
of Cuba; (5) undertake an air strike against military targets in
Cuba; (6) or launch an invasion to overthrow the Castro government. The decision to undertake a limited blockade rather than,

---

[19] Elie Abel, *The Missile Crisis* (New York: J. B. Lippincott Co., 1966), p. 36.
[20] CBS News, "A Conversation with President Kennedy," Dec. 17, 1962 (mimeographed transcript), p. 2.

as some strongly urged, an air strike or invasion was the result of a very deep concern for action at the very lowest level of violence or potential violence necessary to achieve the goals. According to Kennedy, the decision to impose a naval quarantine was based on the reasoning that:

. . . the course we finally adopted had the advantage of permitting other steps, if this one was unsuccessful. In other words, we were starting, in a sense, at a minimum place. Then, if that were unsuccessful, we would have gradually stepped it up until we had gone into a much more massive action which might have become necessary if the first step had been unsuccessful.[21]

By this step no irrevocable decisions had been made, and the Soviet leadership was thus given the time and the opportunity to reassess its position.

The concern of the President and his advisers with keeping open a number of options was based at least in part on a distinction between threats and acts. The use of threats had become a more or less accepted tool of international politics during the nearly two decades of the Cold War. The United States and the Soviet Union, on the other hand, had consistently abstained from direct violent action against each other. The desire to avoid killing Soviet troops was an important factor in the decision to refrain from an air strike against Cuba.[22] Instead, the quarantine shifted the immediate burden of decision concerning the use of violence to Premier Khrushchev. Even if Soviet ships refused to honor the blockade, the plan was to have United States forces disable the rudders of the vessels, rather than sink them.[23]

United States decision makers also displayed considerable sensitivity for the position and perspective of the adversary in the development of the crisis. Theodore Sorensen, special counsel to the President, described the deliberations regarding the United States response to the missiles in Cuba as follows: "We discussed what the Soviet reaction would be to any possible move by the United States, what our reaction with them would have to be to that Soviet reaction, and so on, trying to follow each of those roads to their ultimate conclusion."[24] President Kennedy and others were aware of the possibility of misperceptions by their counter-

---

[21]CBS News, "A Conversation," p. 4.

[22]NBC, "Cuba: The Missile Crisis," Feb. 9, 1964 (mimeographed transcript), p. 22.

[23]Theodore Sorensen, *Kennedy* (New York: Harper & Row, 1965), p. 698.

[24]NBC, "Cuba: The Missile Crisis," p. 17.

parts in the Kremlin. "Well, now, if you look at the history of this century where World War I really came through a series of mis-judgments of the intentions of others . . . it's very difficult to always make judgments here about what the effect will be of our decision on other countries."[25]

This sensitivity for the position of the adversary was apparent in a number of important decisions. There was a concern that Premier Khrushchev not be rushed into an irrevocable decision; it was agreed among members of the decision group that "we should slow down the escalation of the crisis to give Khrushchev time to consider his next move."[26] An interesting example of the Presi-dent's concern emerges from his management of the naval quaran-tine: "The President ordered the Navy screen not to intercept a Soviet ship until absolutely necessary – and had the order trans-mitted in the clear" (that is, not in code).[27] In addition, every ef-fort was taken not to reduce the alternatives of either side to two – total surrender or total war. According to one participant, "Pres-ident Kennedy, aware of the enormous hazards in the confronta-tion with the Soviets over Cuba in October, 1962, made certain that his first move did not close out either all his options or all of theirs."[28] Sorensen added that:

The air strike or an invasion automatically meant a military attack upon a communist power and required almost certainly either a military re-sponse to the Soviet Union, or an even more humiliating surrender. . . . The blockade on the other hand had the advantage of giving Mr. Khrush-chev a choice, an option, so to speak; he did not have to have his ships approach the blockade and be stopped and searched. He could turn them around. So that was the first obvious advantage it had. It left a way open to Mr. Khrushchev.[29]

The World Learns of the Crisis

The second phase of the crisis began with President Kennedy's television address on October 22. He started by revealing recent developments in Cuba.

Within the past week unmistakable evidence has established the fact that a series of offensive missile sites is now in preparation on the im-

---

[25] CBS News, "A Conversation," p. 3.

[26] NBC, "Cuba: The Missile Crisis," p. 19.

[27] Roger Hilsman, "The Cuban Crisis: How Close We Were To War," *Look*, Aug. 25, 1964, p. 19.

[28] Theodore Sorensen, *Decision Making in the White House* (New York: Columbia University Press, 1963), pp. 20-21.

[29] NBC, "Cuba: The Missile Crisis," p. 22.

prisoned island. The purpose of these bases can be none other than to provide a nuclear strike capability against the Western Hemisphere. . . . This urgent transformation of Cuba into an important strategic base — by the presence of these large, long-range and clearly offensive weapons of mass destruction — constitutes an explicit threat to the peace and security of all the Americas.[30]

The United States would, according to Kennedy: (1) impose a "strict quarantine" around Cuba to halt the offensive Soviet build-up; (2) continue and increase the close surveillance of Cuba; (3) answer any nuclear-missile attack launched from Cuba against any nation in the Western Hemisphere with "a full retaliatory response upon the Soviet Union"; (4) reinforce the naval base at Guantanamo; (5) call for a meeting of the Organization of American States to invoke the Rio Treaty; and (6) call for an emergency meeting of the United Nations. At the same time he stated that additional military forces had been alerted for "any eventuality." It was reported "on highest authority" that, "ships carrying additional offensive weapons to Cuba must either turn back or submit to search and seizure, or fight. If they try to run the blockade, a warning shot will be fired across their bows; if they still do not submit, they will be attacked." In accordance with the Joint Congressional Resolution passed three weeks earlier, the President signed an Executive Order on October 23 mobilizing reserves.

The military steps the United States had taken before the President broke the news of the crisis to the nation attested to the severity of the situation. The Strategic Air Command increased its alert forces; more B-52's were placed on constant airborne status, and a plan to disperse military forces to reduce their vulnerability in the event of nuclear war was put into operation. Navy, Marine, and Air Force aircraft flew a total of 26 million miles during the crisis period.[31] Of 180 naval vessels directly involved at the height of the Cuban operation, ninety warships were engaged in the blockade and the other ninety (including eight aircraft carriers) were deployed in the Atlantic Ocean. Ten battalions of Marines were afloat in the vicinity of Cuba and two additional battalions were sent to the Guantanamo naval base in Cuba.

The United States Army was prepared for the largest invasion

---

[30] All quotations from Soviet and United States messages during the missile crisis were found in *The New York Times*, special supplement entitled, "The Cuban Crisis, 14 Days That Shook The World."

[31] Henry M. Pachter, *Collision Course: The Cuban Missile Crisis and Co-Existence* (New York: Frederick A. Praeger, 1963), p. 56.

operation since World War II. According to General Earle Wheeler, "100,000 Army troops would have gone ashore in Cuba, plus an additional 10,000 to 20,000 that would have been in support in the base area back in the United States." Five of the eight divisions of the Army Strategic Reserve (100,000 men), members of the Air Force (100,000 men), Navy personnel (85,000 men), and Marines (12,000 men) were alerted, and United States troops overseas were put "on the ready." Finally, United States retaliatory forces which were alerted included over one thousand missiles of varying sizes and ranges but all capable of hitting the Soviet Union, 1600 long-range bombers, and 37 aircraft carriers.

It was hoped that such actions would convince Soviet leaders not only of the severity of the situation but also of the United States resolve to force withdrawal of the offensive missiles. As one official put it, United States intentions were signaled to Premier Khrushchev in large part through actions "by moving troops around in a slightly more visible way."[32]

In its initial response to the United States actions, the Soviet government denied the offensive character of the weapons, condemned the quarantine as "piracy," and warned that Soviet ships would not honor it. William Knox, Chairman of Westinghouse Electric International, was told by Premier Khrushchev on October 24 — the day the blockade went into effect — that "as the Soviet vessels were not armed the United States could undoubtedly stop one or two or more but then he, Chairman Khrushchev, would give instructions to the Soviet submarines to sink the American vessels."[33] It was also reported that Defense Minister Malinovski had been instructed to postpone planned demobilization, to cancel furloughs, and to alert all troops. Although the issue was immediately brought before the United Nations and the Organization of American States, the events of October 22-25 pointed to a possible violent showdown in the Atlantic, in Cuba, or perhaps in other areas of the world. President Kennedy apparently expected some form of retaliation in Berlin. In his October 22 address he specifically warned the Soviet Union against any such move: "Any hostile move anywhere in the world against the safety and freedom of people to whom we are committed — including in particular the brave people of West Berlin — will be met by whatever action is needed."

The blockade, postponed one day on the advice of United Nations Ambassador Adlai Stevenson to permit the Organization of Amer-

---

32 Pachter, *Collision Course*, p. 56.
33 NBC, "Cuba: The Missile Crisis," p. 36.

ican States to sanction it, went into effect at 10 a.m. Eastern Standard Time on October 24. At that time a fleet of 25 Soviet ships nearing Cuba was expected to test the United States policy within hours. Statements from Moscow and Washington gave no immediate evidence that either side would retreat, although the Soviet Premier dispatched a letter to Bertrand Russell in which he called for a summit conference. The next day rumors of a United States attack or invasion of Cuba were strengthened by the announcement by Representative Hale Boggs that, "if these missiles are not dismantled, the United States has the power to destroy them, and I assure you that this will be done." At the same time, United States intelligence sources revealed that work on the erection of missile sites was proceeding at full speed.

The first real break in the chain of events leading to an apparently imminent confrontation came on October 25 when twelve Soviet vessels turned back in mid-Atlantic. It was at this point that Secretary of State Dean Rusk remarked, "We're eyeball to eyeball, and I think the other fellow just blinked." [34] Shortly thereafter the first Soviet ship to reach the patrol area—the tanker *Bucharest*—was allowed to proceed to Cuba without boarding and search.

By the following day the crisis appeared to be receding somewhat from its most dangerous level. The Soviet-chartered freighter *Marucla* (ironically, a former United States Liberty ship now under Lebanese registry), was searched without incident, and when no contraband was discovered, allowed to proceed to Cuba. In answer to an appeal from Secretary General U Thant, Soviet Premier Khrushchev had agreed to keep Soviet ships away from the patrol area for the time being. President Kennedy's reply to the Secretary General stated that he would try to avoid any direct confrontation at sea "in the next few days." At the same time however, the White House issued a statement which said: "The development of ballistic missile sites in Cuba continues at a rapid pace. . . . The activity at these sites apparently is directed at achieving a full operational capability as soon as possible." The State Department added that "further action would be justified" if work on the missile sites continued. Photographic evidence revealed that such work was continuing at an increased rate and that the missile sites would be operational in five days.

Washington and Moscow Bargain over the Missiles

The "bargaining phase" of the crisis opened later in the evening

---

[34]Alsop and Bartlett, "In Time of Crisis," p. 16.

of October 26. A secret letter from Premier Khrushchev for the first time acknowledged the presence of Soviet missiles in Cuba.[35] He is reported to have argued they were defensive in nature, but he understood the President's feeling about them. According to one source, "Never explicitly stated, but embedded in the letter was an offer to withdraw the offensive weapons under United Nations supervision in return for a guarantee that the United States would not invade Cuba." It was also on October 26 that Aleksandr S. Fomin, a counselor at the Soviet embassy in Washington, approached John Scali of ABC News with essentially the same terms for a settlement.[36] A second message from Premier Khrushchev, dispatched twelve hours later, proposed a trade of Soviet missiles in Cuba for NATO missile bases in Turkey; the United Nations Security Council was to verify fulfillment of both operations, contingent upon approval of the Cuban and Turkish governments.

In his reply to Khrushchev's secret letter of Friday evening (October 26), the President all but ignored the proposal to trade bases in Turkey for those in Cuba. At the Attorney General's suggestion, the President simply interpreted Premier Khrushchev's letter as a bid for an acceptable settlement — as if the message regarding bases in Turkey had never been received. Replying to the Soviet leader, President Kennedy stated:

As I read your letter, the key elements of your proposal — which seems generally acceptable as I understand them — are as follows:

(1) You would agree to remove these weapons systems from Cuba under appropriate United Nations observation and supervision; and undertake, with suitable safeguards, to halt the further introduction of such weapons systems into Cuba.

(2) We, on our part, would agree — upon the establishment of adequate arrangements through the United Nations to ensure the carrying out and continuation of these commitments — (a) to remove promptly the quarantine measures now in effect and (b) to give assurance against an invasion of Cuba.

Kennedy added, however, that,

. . . the first ingredient, let me emphasize, . . . is the cessation of work on missile sites in Cuba and measures to render such weapons inoperable, under effective international guarantees. The continuation of this threat, or a prolonging of this discussion concerning Cuba by linking these prob-

---

[35]This is the only written message between the United States and the USSR during the crisis period which has not been made public. The letter is paraphrased in Abel, *The Missile Crisis,* pp. 179-183.

[36]ABC News, "John Scali, ABC News," Aug. 13, 1964 (mimeographed transcript).

lems to the broader questions of European and world security, would surely lead to an intensification of the Cuban crisis and a grave risk to the peace of the world.

In responding to Khrushchev's proposal to trade missile bases in Turkey for those in Cuba, a White House statement rejected that offer, stating that, "Several inconsistent and conflicting proposals have been made by the USSR within the last 24 hours, including the one just made public in Moscow. . . . The first imperative must be to deal with this immediate threat, under which no sensible negotiation can proceed."

Despite the beginning of negotiations, the situation was still dangerous. On October 27 an American U-2 reconnaissance plane had been shot down over Cuba, and several other planes had been fired upon. The Defense Department warned that measures would be taken to "insure that such missions are effective and protected." At the same time it announced that twenty-four troop-carrier squadrons — 14,000 men — were being recalled to active duty. The continued construction on the Cuban missile sites, which, it was believed, would become operational by October 30, was of even more concern than attacks on the U-2's. Theodore Sorensen, recalling the events of October 27, said, "Obviously these developments could not be tolerated very long, and we were preparing for a meeting on Sunday [October 28] which would have been the most serious meeting ever to take place at the White House."[37]

The Crisis Is Resolved

On Sunday morning, however, Radio Moscow stated that the Soviet Premier would shortly make an important announcement. The message was broadcast in the clear (that is, not in code) to shortcut the time required by normal channels of communication. Premier Khrushchev declared:

I regard with great understanding your concern and the concern of the United States people in connection with the fact that the weapons you describe as offensive are formidable indeed. . . . The Soviet Government, in addition to earlier instruction on the discontinuation of further work on weapons construction sites, has given a new order to dismantle the arms which you describe as offensive, and to crate and return them to the Soviet Union.

---

[37]NBC, "Cuba: The Missile Crisis," p. 42. For further details see Sorensen, *Kennedy,* p. 714; and Robert F. Kennedy, "Thirteen Days: The Story about How the World Almost Ended," *McCall's,* Nov., 1968, pp. 152, 167.

The statement made no reference to the withdrawal of United States missiles from Turkey.

In reply, President Kennedy issued a statement welcoming Premier Khrushchev's "statesmanlike decision." He added that the Cuban blockade would be removed as soon as the United Nations had taken "necessary measures," and further, that the United States would not invade Cuba. Kennedy said that he attached great importance to a rapid settlement of the Cuban crisis, because "developments were approaching a point where events could have become unmanageable."

Although Khrushchev stated that the Soviet Union was prepared to reach an agreement on United Nations verification of the dismantling operation in Cuba, Fidel Castro announced on the same day that Cuba would not accept the Kennedy-Khrushchev agreement unless the United States accepted further conditions, including the abandonment of the naval base at Guantanamo. But the critical phases of the Soviet-American confrontation seemed to be over. Despite the inability to carry out on-site inspection, photographic surveillance of Cuba confirmed the dismantling of the missile sites. The quarantine was lifted on November 21, at which time the Pentagon announced that the missiles had indeed left Cuba aboard Soviet ships.

DECISION MAKING IN CRISIS AND NONCRISIS SITUATIONS

These brief narratives suggest two closely related questions. First, how did the decision-making process during the Cuban missile crisis differ from that regarding the Versailles Treaty? And second, to what extent can these differences in decision making be attributed to the nature of the situation?

At this point it may be useful to define more precisely a term which has been used with some regularity in this chapter—*crisis*. According to one definition, a crisis is an unanticipated situation in which important values are threatened and in which the time for making a decision is short.[38] If these three criteria are applied

---

[38] Charles F. Hermann, "Some Consequences of Crisis Which Limit the Viability of Organizations," *Administrative Science Quarterly*, VIII (1963), pp. 61-82. See also Charles F. Hermann, *Crises in Foreign Policy* (Indianapolis: Bobbs-Merrill, 1969), and Charles F. Hermann (ed.), *Contemporary Research in International Crisis* (New York: Free Press, 1971).

to the Cuban and Versailles cases, we have a way of comparing them by asking, which of the situations was more unanticipated? Which presented a greater threat to important values? Which required a decision within a shorter time? We can then try to assess the impact of these characteristics of the situation on the decision-making processes.

There is little doubt that the Cuban situation was unanticipated. Rumors and unsubstantiated reports about Soviet activities in Cuba had been circulating throughout the summer of 1962, but even the United States intelligence community tended to dismiss as highly improbable the notion that Premier Khrushchev would permit volatile Cuban leaders to have modern Soviet weapons denied to more reliable allies in Eastern Europe. While surveillance of Cuba had been going on for some time, the photographic evidence of missile sites caught nearly all United States leaders by surprise.

As an unanticipated and unprecedented situation, there were few guidelines as to the procedure to be followed in formulating a response to the Soviet missiles in Cuba. In the short run—that is, during the crisis period—President Kennedy was relatively free to use his judgment as to the process by which a response to the Soviet missiles would be formulated. It was up to him to determine who would take part in the discussions leading up to a decision and, ultimately, to choose among the alternative courses of action.

The President called together a group of his most trusted advisers, who in many cases held high-level foreign-policy positions (as Secretary of State Dean Rusk, Secretary of Defense Robert McNamara), but in other cases did not. Robert Kennedy, who played a key role during the crisis, was Attorney General, a position usually associated more closely with domestic than foreign policy. And Dean Acheson, Secretary of State under Harry S. Truman but a private citizen since 1953, was asked to participate in some of the crucial sessions of the group which formulated United States policy during the missile crisis.

Notably absent from these deliberations were members of the House or Senate, many of whom later expressed considerable impatience with Kennedy's policy of using force with restraint. Democratic Senators J. William Fulbright and Richard B. Russell were among those who were later to urge an immediate invasion of Cuba, a suggestion against which the President stood firm.[39] While some long-range political risks might have been involved

---

[39] NBC, "Cuba: The Missile Crisis," p. 30.

in excluding Congressional leaders from the decision group, in the short run President Kennedy could almost surely rely on the general tendency of the public, newspapers, and even the opposition party in Congress to support the President during a crisis. For example, Charles Halleck, a Republican leader in the House, wanted the record to indicate that he had only been informed, not consulted, about the Cuban situation, but he promised to support the President.

President Kennedy's decision to rely on an informal group of trusted advisers rather than on an established institution such as the Cabinet or the National Security Council also appears to have significantly affected the process by which a decision was formulated. According to Theodore Sorensen:

> . . . one of the remarkable aspects of those meetings was a sense of complete equality. Protocol mattered little when the nation's life was at stake. Experience mattered little in a crisis which had no precedent. We were fifteen individuals on our own, representing the President and not different departments. Assistant Secretaries differed vigorously with the Secretaries; I participated much more freely than I ever had in an NSC [National Security Council] meeting.[40]

In contrast, the decision on whether or not to join the League of Nations in 1919 was anything but a surprise. Indeed, we have already seen that much planning took place during World War I, both within and outside the government, for the creation of a general international organization once the war had ended. The resulting political process in the League of Nations case was markedly different from that of the Cuban crisis. Because joining the League involved ratifying a treaty, there existed well-established procedures to be followed, and even under the best of circumstances the entire process would take considerable time.

That the United States would, from time to time, enter into treaties and agreements had been anticipated by the framers of the Constitution, who spelled out the requirements for the Senate to "advise and consent" in the process of treaty ratification. Some of the bitterest conflicts between the executive and legislature have centered on the requirement that all treaties must receive the approval of two-thirds of the Senate. John Hay, Secretary of

---

[40] Sorensen, *Kennedy,* p. 679. A different viewpoint had been expressed by Dean Acheson, who has charged that these "uninhibited" and "leaderless" meetings were a waste of time. Acheson was among those who advocated bombing Cuba to remove the missiles. "Dean Acheson's Version of Robert Kennedy's Version of the Cuban Missile Affair," *Esquire,* Feb., 1969, pp. 76-77+.

State under President Theodore Roosevelt, once commented that, "A treaty entering the Senate is like a bull going into the arena. No one can say just how and when the final blow will fall. But one thing is certain – it will never leave the arena alive."[41] While Hay's remark is something of an exaggeration, it is true that historically the Senate has actively exercised its power: about one-sixth of all treaties submitted by the Presidents have been amended or had reservations added to them, and a number of others have been rejected outright. Moreover, during the century and a quarter preceding 1919, the Senate had also established both formal and informal working rules which would govern the Versailles Treaty's course through the Senate. Thus President Wilson was constrained by both the formal requirements spelled out in the Constitution and by the customary operating procedures of the Senate.

Compared to the situation in October, 1962, Wilson's ability to include or exclude those who would participate in deciding the fate of the Treaty of Versailles was much more restricted. To be sure, he was free to select members of his delegation to the Paris Peace Conference, but he could neither avoid active Senate participation in the decision-making process, nor exclude those Senators – notably Henry Cabot Lodge of the Foreign Relations Committee – who might oppose the treaty. If for no other reason, exclusion of both Senators and Republican leaders from the delegation to the Paris Peace Conference was a political blunder of major proportions.

The Cuban and League of Nations episodes also differed in the degree of threat to important values inherent in the situation. The presence of Soviet missiles in Cuba was, at least in the view of those responsible for making policy during October, 1962, an immense threat to the security of the United States. Only Secretary of Defense Robert McNamara took the position that the weapons in Cuba added little to the already awesome power of nuclear-armed missiles based in the Soviet Union.[42]

A direct consequence of the nature of the Cuban threat was the need to maintain secrecy until a United States policy was formulated. Premature public discussion would return the initiative to Soviet leaders. This need for secrecy made it important to limit the decision group in size. Many high-ranking officials and close advisers of the President, who would normally be consulted about

---

[41] Hans J. Morgenthau, "The American Tradition in Foreign Policy," in Roy C. Macridis (ed.), *Foreign Policy in World Politics,* 2nd ed. (Englewood Cliffs, N.J.: Prentice-Hall, 1962), p. 219.

[42] Abel, *The Missile Crisis,* p. 51.

any major foreign-policy issue, were not even informed about the presence of Soviet missiles in Cuba, much less consulted about the appropriate United States response. According to Dean Rusk, "Some of my own basic papers were done in my own handwriting in order to limit the possibility of further spread" of information.[43]

More generally, the crisis characteristics of the Cuban situation ruled out the possibility of broad consultation on the proper course of action. Beyond awareness of a general public unease about developments in Cuba, there was, of course, no direct effect of public opinion on the decision to establish a blockade around Cuba. Nor was there any Congressional participation in the decision-making process. Indeed, it was not until an hour before the President's television address to the nation on October 22 that a few leading members of the Senate Foreign Relations and House Foreign Affairs Committees were informed about the events of the preceding week. Nor was there any change in this respect during the week that followed the President's address. The basic decisions continued to be made by the small group of advisers.

Until he chose to make public the existence of the Soviet missiles in Cuba, President Kennedy and his advisers had a monopoly on the precise and verified information about the situation. After the crisis had ended, both interested publics and Congress could evaluate United States policy; Congressional elections in November might serve to reflect public attitudes toward the handling of the missile crisis, Congress might hold hearings on the general conduct of foreign policy in later months, and so on. Yet, even during the most intense period of the crisis, considerations of partisan politics were not totally absent. That is, while the primary problem was that of removing the Soviet missiles without triggering World War III, calculations of the domestic political consequences of the crisis remained as background factors in the decision-making process. In anticipation of a public reaction against the President's Democratic Party should the missiles be allowed to remain in Cuba, one of the advocates of an air strike against Cuba passed a note to Theodore Sorensen reading: "Ted — Have you considered the very real possibility that if we allow Cuba to complete installation and operational readiness of missile bases, the next House of Representatives [to be elected in three weeks] is likely to have a Republican majority?"[44] The House Republican Campaign Committee charged that the President's policy was false and ineffective and others maintained that the entire crisis was manufactured to

---

[43] Abel, *The Missile Crisis*, p. 49.
[44] Sorensen, *Kennedy*, p. 688.

gain political advantage for the Democratic Party. But on the whole, leaders of both parties pledged complete support for the President's policy. Thus, during the immediate crisis period, President Kennedy was able to operate with considerably more freedom from constraints of domestic political processes than had President Wilson.

The situation with respect to the Treaty of Versailles was quite different. Many agreed with President Wilson that United States failure to join the League of Nations would ultimately undermine the League's effectiveness and therefore doom the world to suffer future wars. But this type of threat to United States security was neither immediate nor concrete. Moreover, at least a sizeable minority of both the United States public and the Senate were sincerely convinced that an unamended treaty was an even greater and more immediate threat to United States security and prosperity, because under provisions of Article X, the Unites States might become involved in settling conflicts in which it had no direct interest. Wilson's efforts to appeal to a purpose higher than partisan politics met with little success. In part, the difficulty can be attributed to serious errors in Wilson's political strategy. Equally important, the issue of the Versailles Treaty was inherently one which did not permit the President to dominate the decision-making process to the degree possible in a crisis situation.

Perhaps the clearest distinction between the League of Nations and Cuban cases appears with respect to the time within which a decision was required. In October, 1962, the estimate that Soviet missile sites would be operational within ten days after the quarantine was put into operation placed a clear deadline on United States decision makers. Once the missile sites had been completed, an entirely different set of alternatives might have to be considered.

Time pressure was woven inextricably into the entire crisis situation. First, there was the pressure created by the presence of the Soviet missile sites in Cuba, vividly described by Theodore Sorensen: "For all of us know that, once the missile sites under construction became operational, and capable of responding to any apparent threat or command with a nuclear volley, the President's options would be dramatically changed."[45] Second, there was the countervailing force created by the President and his advisers, who sought to minimize the probability that either side would respond by a "spasm reaction."

Despite the pressures to develop a policy before Soviet missiles were operational, Kennedy was fully aware that a premature de-

---

[45] Sorensen, *Decision Making in the White House*, p. 31.

cision based on inadequate information or hasty consideration of alternatives might precipitate World War III. Hence, United States decision making in regard to the missiles in Cuba was character-ized by a concern for action based on adequate information, in spite of public and Congressional pressures from many quarters for direct action against the Castro government. The resistance of the Administration against action until photographic evidence of the missile sites was available has already been noted. McGeorge Bundy recalled that upon receiving the first news of the photo-graphic evidence, "his [President Kennedy's] first reaction was that we must make sure, and were we making sure? And would there be evidence on which he could decide that this was in fact really the case?"[46] As late as Thursday, October 18, a series of alternatives was being considered pending more accurate infor-mation, and while the decision to institute a blockade was being hammered out, open discussion of the alternatives was encouraged. The President recalled that "though at the beginning there was a much sharper division . . . this was very valuable, because the people involved had particular responsibilities of their own."[47] Another participant in the decision making at the highest level wrote: "President Kennedy, learning on his return from a mid-week trip in October, 1962, that the deliberation of the NSC [National Security Council] executive committee had been more spirited and frank in his absence, asked the committee to hold other prelimi-nary sessions without him."[48] Thus, despite the very real pressure of time—the missile sites were to become operational by the end of the month—the eventual decision was reached by relatively open discussion.

It was not until Saturday, October 20, almost a week after the photographic evidence became available, that the general consen-sus developed. The President himself acknowledged that the in-terim period was crucial to the content of the final decision: "If we had had to act on Wednesday [October 17] in the first 24 hours, I don't think probably we would have chosen as prudently as we finally did, the quarantine against the use of offensive weapons."[49]

On the other hand, no deadline existed with respect to the League of Nations decision. Naturally President Wilson was eager to have Senate approval of the Treaty as soon as possible but, owing to the

---

[46]NBC, "Cuba: The Missile Crisis," p. 14.
[47]CBS News, "A Conversation," p. 4.
[48]Sorensen, *Decision Making in the White House,* p. 60.
[49]CBS News, "A Conversation," pp. 2-3.

nature of the situation, there was little he could do to prevent delaying tactics by the Senate Foreign Relations Committee. Senator Lodge and others opposing the unamended version of the Treaty seemed aware that their chances for victory depended in part on being able to delay a vote as long as possible. Lodge's strategy of stalling committee hearings contributed toward defeat of the Treaty in two important respects. First, it permitted the obvious public support for United States entry into the League of Nations to be dissipated. Perhaps more importantly, the delaying tactics apparently goaded President Wilson into the tour around the nation which ended with his physical collapse. This is not to say, of course, that an earlier vote would have assured passage of the Treaty in its original form, nor is it certain that a healthy President would have been more willing to compromise with Senator Lodge. But it does seem clear that the absence of time pressure was a factor which eroded the initial advantage enjoyed by supporters of the League Covenant.

President Kennedy correctly perceived that the unprecedented nature of the Cuban missile crisis permitted him a large measure of freedom from normal constraints of the political process in molding the decision-making process to meet the situation. On the other hand, President Wilson's perceptions of the situation were much less accurate. He was correct in believing that public opinion supported United States entry into the League of Nations, but he was ultimately mistaken in believing that this support would force the Senate into approving the Treaty. He was, moreover, mistaken in his belief that the 1920 election would serve as a nationwide referendum on the Treaty of Versailles. In short, the situational factors which during the crisis permitted the President to exercise the widest possible prerogatives of his office were not present in the League of Nations case.

In this chapter we have compared two important but dissimilar episodes in United States foreign policy. In seeking the answers to the two questions posed at the beginning of this chapter, we cannot overlook the facts that Wilson's personality and "political style" differed from that of Kennedy, that the international system in 1919 was quite different from that in 1962, or even that institutions for making United States foreign policy were not identical in the two periods. Each of these factors no doubt contributed to the process of decision making. But they do not account for all of the differences in the two cases. This point can be illustrated by a brief example. During the summer of 1963, the Kennedy administration negotiated a Nuclear Test Ban Treaty with the British and Soviet governments. Would we expect to find that the decision-making process on the Test Ban Treaty was more similar to that during the Cuban crisis (in which personalities, the international system, and other pertinent components were essentially the same), or would it be more like that of the League of Nations debate (in which the situation or problem was somewhat similar)? The latter answer is in fact correct. It is true that the Test Ban Treaty was ratified whereas the Treaty of Versailles was not, largely because President Kennedy avoided many of Wilson's mistakes. He actively sought the support of both Democrats and Republicans, and especially the support of leaders of both parties in the Senate, thereby assuring a wide margin of approval for the Test Ban Treaty. But the political process was basically similar to that in the League of Nations debate.

Thus, it appears that differences in the nature of the situation — the problem which called for a decision — facing United States policy makers in the League of Nations and Cuban cases were crucial to decision making. According to our definition of crisis (unanticipated situation, threat to important values, and short decision time), the Cuban confrontation was a crisis, whereas the League of Nations debate was not. And, as we have seen, the presence of these factors in the Cuban situation and their absence in the League debate contributed to the quite dissimilar political process by which a policy was formulated in the two cases.

Chapter 4

POLITICAL ELITES IN THE SOVIET UNION AND CHINA

Michael P. Gehlen
University of New Mexico

This chapter is designed to show how the study of political elites can be used to create a greater understanding of the making of foreign policy. By the term *political elite* we refer to those individuals who are most influential and most active in the making of public policy. The elite approach is one that attempts to identify those individuals and to determine how they reach and maintain their positions as well as precisely what roles they play in the system. Such an approach may be viewed as an attempt to learn how power is structured among individuals in particular communities.

Rather than discussing specific foreign-policy cases, this chapter will examine some of the factors that shaped the broad foreign-policy orientations of decision makers in the Soviet Union and the People's Republic of China in the period 1966 to 1970.

ELITES IN THE FOREIGN-POLICY PROCESSES OF NATION-STATES

Every nation-state must conduct some kind of relations with other nation-states. Often people tend to think of nations' foreign policies as those of abstract governments or of a country as a whole without bothering to examine how or why those policies came to be made. The study of elites brings the formulation and conduct of foreign policy more clearly into focus by reminding observers that people are behind those policies. Individuals and groups of individuals make the decisions that are officially carried out in the names of governments or nations.

The elite approach therefore asks the student of international affairs to focus attention on individuals in the decision-making processes. Who makes decisions? Why does someone in the elite want a particular decision to be made rather than another? How do the members of the elite interact in order to arrive at decisions? Rather than examining institutions and political processes, the elite approach focuses attention on the individuals who make the institutions work and who devise the policies that are pursued.

The particular concern of this study is to examine the political elites that are influential in the shaping of foreign policy in the USSR and China. The selection of these two communist states allows us to make comparisons of the backgrounds, roles, and values of elites in two of the largest nations in the world and the two most important that are governed by communist parties.

By *backgrounds,* we refer to such factors as education, occupation, and ethnic association. A person trained as an engineer who had a career specialization in the construction of hydroelectric plants may have developed attitudes and interests different from those developed by a man educated in philosophy who spent the bulk of his career working in the propaganda organs of the Communist Party. Education and occupation bring different special interests and attitudes to the political elite.

By *roles,* we refer to the different types of involvements or positions a person has in the course of his life. Everyone has several roles to play. The same man in the Soviet Union may be in the role of a party member when he attends a party meeting, a bureaucrat when he sits at his desk as deputy minister of transportation, a consumer when he pays for groceries, and a father when he goes home and talks with his two teenage children. The question that must be asked is to what extent one role influences another, and which role or roles are most important in shaping his general outlook.

By *values,* we refer to the personally held attitudes and goals that influence an individual's choice of objectives, the priority he gives those objectives, and the means he employs to attain them. In short, values are closely related both to the aspirations of an individual and to the way he plays the roles that are a part of his life. In the cases of the Soviet Union and China, the outside observer is usually quite interested in how the ideology of Marxism-Leninism influences a person's choices. Questions can be raised about how firmly this ideology really determines a man's choices and influences his behavior and as to what extent it merely provides a vocabulary with which to justify certain choices that he has made on other than ideological grounds.

The concepts of background, role, and values are means of helping us classify and analyze information. To say this does not imply that these factors are completely separate from one another. Instead, they should be viewed as ways of examining complex problems, ways that are interrelated and may even be contradictory. The roles a person plays may be influenced in large part by his social background and both of these factors may be expected to influence the values that a person develops.

The Soviet Political Elite

The members of the Politburo of the Central Committee of the Communist Party of the Soviet Union (CPSU)[1] are generally recognized as the principal high-level decision makers in the Soviet system. From 1966 to 1970, the Politburo consisted of eleven full members and eight candidate (nonvoting) members. In some instances, as during the Cuban missile crisis of 1962, a select group of the Politburo rather than the entire membership appears to have been responsible for decisions. This small group acted in consultation with others — namely the Minister of Foreign Affairs and the Minister of Defense — who, while they may not be members of the Politburo, do hold important party and government positions. In other circumstances, such as the unsuccessful effort to oust Khrushchev in 1957 and the removal of Khrushchev in 1964, a large group of individuals, including the entire Central Committee, participated in the resolution of the conflicts. The first situation points out that position alone may not always determine who plays an important role in the making of decisions; this determination may result in part from reputation or professional competence as particular situations require. In the second situation, where membership in the Central Committee determined participation, position is the critical factor.

For our purposes, the general political elite of the USSR can be identified by membership in the Central Committee of the Party. The Central Committee is composed of the leadership of key components of the social system. For example, the major party leaders, government officials, military officers, scientists, trade-union officials and other leaders of important groups have full or candidate membership in the Central Committee. Since the Twenty-third

---

[1] CPSU will be used hereafter for *Communist Party of the Soviet Union*.

Party Congress in March, 1966, there have been nearly 400 members of this high-level party organization. The Central Committee meets only a few times a year, however; the Politburo ordinarily meets weekly. The members of this body, therefore, rank as the "elite of the elite." They are all members of the Central Committee, but they participate much more regularly in decision making than the average member of the Committee. Consequently, the members of the Politburo are at the apex of the power structure. Who are the members of this elite? Taking the Politburo of the 1966-1970 period as the basis of our observation, the following statements can be made about their identities and backgrounds.

L. I. Brezhnev. General Secretary of the Party. Born in 1906.
  Education: Technicum[2] and the Metallurgical Institute.
  Occupation: Land engineer and a party worker specializing in agricultural and civilian-military problems.
  Regional Association: Ukrainian Party background.
  Status in the CPSU: Central Committee member since 1952; Politburo since 1957.
A. P. Kirilenko. A Secretary of the Party. Born in 1906.
  Education: The Institute of Aviation.
  Occupation: An aeronautical engineer and a party worker.
  Regional Association: Ukrainian and Russian Soviet Federated Socialist Republic party organizations.
  Status in the CPSU: Central Committee member since 1956; Politburo since 1962.
A. N. Kosygin. Prime Minister of the Government. Born in 1904.
  Education: Technicum.
  Occupation: Economic planning and government administration.
  Regional Association: The Russian Soviet Federated Socialist Republic.
  Status in the CPSU: Central Committee member since 1939; Politburo since 1960.
K. T. Mazurov. Party leader of the Belorussian Republic. Born in 1914.
  Education: Highway Construction Technicum and the Higher Party School.[3]
  Occupation: Government and party leader in Belorussia; chairman of the Belorussian Council of Ministers and First Secretary of the party in Belorussia.
  Regional Association: Belorussia.

---

[2] Technicum: A specialized technical school, similar to the last two years of high school and junior college in the United States.
[3] The Higher Party School is designed to give advanced training to a very select number of party workers. This training is primarily in the areas of party administration and in Marxist-Leninist thought.

Status in the CPSU: Central Committee member since 1956; elected to full membership in the Politburo in 1966 (previously a candidate member).

A. Yu. Pel'she. Party leader in Latvia. Born 1899.

Education: Institute of Red Professors.[4]

Occupation: Professor and corresponding member of the Latvian Academy of Sciences.

Regional Association: Latvia.

Status in the CPSU: Central Committee since 1961; Politburo since 1966.

N. V. Podgorny. President of the Presidium of the Supreme Soviet. Born in 1903.

Education: The Kiev Technological Institute.

Occupation: Engineer, a specialist in agriculture, and a Ukrainian party leader.

Regional Association: The Ukraine.

Status in the CPSU: Central Committee member since 1956; Politburo since 1960.

D. S. Polyansky. Born in 1917.

Education: Kharkov Institute of Agriculture.

Occupation: The central party apparatus and chairman of Russian Soviet Federated Socialist Republic Council of Ministers.

Regional Association: The Ukraine and the Russian Soviet Federated Socialist Republic.

Status in the CPSU: Central Committee member since 1956; Politburo since 1960.

A. N. Shelepin. A Secretary of the Party. Born 1918.

Education: The Moscow Institute of History, Philosophy, and Literature.

Occupation: The apparatus of the League of Young Communists and former director of the party security forces.

Regional Association: Russian Soviet Federated Socialist Republic.

Status in the CPSU: Central Committee member since 1952; Politburo since 1965.

P. Y. Shelest. Born 1908.

Education: Evening Metallurgical Institute.

Occupation: Worker in the Ukrainian party apparatus.

Regional Association: The Ukraine.

Status in the CPSU: Central Committee member since 1961; Politburo since 1965.

M. A. Suslov. Principal party theoretician. Born 1902.

Education: Moscow Institute of Economics and Moscow State University.

Occupation: Since 1946 in the central party apparatus.

Regional Association: Russian Soviet Federated Socialist Republic.

---

[4] The Institute of Red Professors was an institution in operation during the 1920's and 1930's designed to develop a teaching staff strongly rooted in the philosophy of Marxism.

Status in the CPSU: Central Committee member since 1941; Politburo
   since 1955.
G. I. Voronov. Born in 1910.
   Education: The Kirov Industrial Institute in Tomsk.
   Occupation: Worker in the party apparatus; former Minister of Agri-
   culture.
   Regional Association: Russian Soviet Federated Socialist Republic.
   Status in the CPSU: Central Committee member since 1952; Politburo
   since 1961.

The data presented on the eleven full members of the Politburo
enable us to make several generalizations about the characteristics of the elite decision makers. In 1966, they had an average age
of 58, while the age span was from 48 to 67. (In 1970, the average
age was 62, and the age span was from 52 to 71.) Three of the members were too young to remember the Revolution and Civil War
of 1917-1920, and all but one of the eleven men were too young to
have played a role in the politics of that period. Only Pel'she can
be considered an "old Bolshevik" in the sense that he joined the
Party before the Revolution. Indeed, it appears that he was elected
to the Politburo in 1966 largely because he fell into that category
and not because he was expected to play an important role in the
decision making. In this case, reputation indicates that the member had less political influence than others who held the same position in the party hierarchy.

Age in this case can be considered a significant factor for at least
two reasons: first, only an older member could have had genuine
revolutionary experience, and second, the younger members have
had much greater access to higher education and to modern technological training.

In regard to education, eight of the members had technical training, while only three had been educated with specialties in the
humanities and social sciences. All but one, Kosygin, had spent
the bulk of their careers in the party apparatus. Five of these had
been associated with the Ukrainian party organization. This factor
suggests that they rose to prominence primarily under the tutelage, or at least the support, of Nikita Khrushchev, who had once
headed the party organization in the Ukraine. Only two, Kosygin
and Suslov, had attained membership in the Central Committee
prior to 1952. Shelepin and Shelest had attained that status only
in 1961. Four of the Politburo members were serving concurrently
in the important party secretariat. Two of the members, Kosygin
and Podgorny, held the two most prominent positions in the government. With the exceptions of Pel'she and possibly Kosygin and
Suslov, the membership of the Politburo represented a new gen-

eration of Soviet leaders – persons with little or no memory of the
revolutionary years, who came to maturity during the harsh years
of forced industrialization and collectivization. Furthermore, the
majority of them worked their way up in the party echelons during
the postwar reconstruction period.

United States and British intelligence reports indicate that the
members of the Politburo do not share equally in all matters requiring decisions. Instead, the membership is broken down into
several committees that are organized around particular types of
policy questions. One committee, for example, is concerned with
diplomacy and trade, another with defense and intelligence, and
others with agriculture, industry, domestic party affairs, and relations with Communist parties in the other countries. Some of
the members serve on only one or two of these committees while
the more influential members serve on several, if not all of them.

Since the Soviet Union does not publish the membership of these
functional committees, it is necessary to speculate on which individual serves on which committee. In regard to the two committees that involve general foreign affairs, it could be fairly safely
assumed that Brezhnev and Kosygin were members of both the
working groups on (1) diplomacy and trade and (2) defense and
intelligence. It is difficult to identify which other Politburo members served on those committees. The committee on relations with
other Communist parties also touches on foreign relations. It appears to be especially concerned with relations with governing
Communist parties (the party-states). Brezhnev, Suslov, and Shelepin seemed to have the greatest concern with this aspect of Soviet
foreign policy.

While Brezhnev, Kosygin, Suslov, and Shelepin appeared to
exercise the greatest influence over the formulation of foreign
policy, it was clear that others were consulted by the committees
concerned with this area. The persons most frequently brought
into the committee proceedings were the Minister of Foreign Affairs, Andrei Gromyko, and the Minister of Defense, Rodion Malinovski and his successor Andrei Grechko. While they were
members of the Party Central Committee they were not in the
Politburo. In addition, periodic consultation with heads of military
and civilian intelligence organs, the general staff, and ambas-
sadors took place.

After a committee of the Politburo has deliberated a particular
policy question, it is likely that it recommends a resolution to the
full Politburo. When there is a single leader capable of exercising
great persuasion over his colleagues, the full Politburo may be
bypassed. However, no person of such dominance had emerged.

Although Brezhnev had become more influential than any other individual, his power was tempered by the influence of Kosygin, Suslov, and Shelepin. In such a situation, collective decisions are more likely to be made. Even so, however, some members carried more persuasive power than others.

Despite the claim of operating under collective leadership, it is known that the Politburo members frequently do not see eye to eye on policy and that serious conflicts have existed and in all probability continue to exist among them. In 1957, Khrushchev was almost removed by a hostile majority of the presidium (now the Politburo) and was saved only by a hastily convened session of the Central Committee. His opponents felt that he had moved too rapidly in his de-Stalinization program, and also blamed him for the unrest in Eastern Europe in 1956. In 1964 Khrushchev was removed by a coalition of moderates and conservatives in the Party hierarchy who believed that he was permitting experimentation in economic reform and party organization to be carried too far and was making too many decisions without consulting other members of the elite.

At the time of his removal, Brezhnev and Kosygin, whom Khrushchev had designated as the heirs to his two major posts, joined his old-guard opponents, Podgorny and Suslov. Brezhnev was closely associated with Khrushchev's policies of experimentation, but was much more sophisticated in approach than his mentor. However, other members of the elite, especially Suslov and Shelepin, were much less inclined to accept drastic changes in economic policies and organization. They also displayed less sympathy toward reaching a detente with the West. All of the leaders tended to agree that domestic development should have the highest priority, but they disagreed as to how a rapid economic growth could best be attained. Collective leadership during this period may be interpreted either as a genuine effort to force the various factions to learn how to compromise and to live with one another, or as merely a transitional phase during the course of which a new strong leader may be expected to emerge.

Vacancies inevitably occur in the higher party organs as a result of death, retirement, loss of favor from the majority faction, and the creation of new positions. The principal means by which the leadership replenishes its membership and draws new persons into its ranks is co-optation. Co-optation is in part an administrative device by which the existing elite elects new members into its own membership. For example, when a vacancy occurs on the Politburo, the remaining members of the Politburo actually decide who will fill the vacancy, although technically the Central Committee is responsible for formally electing him. Related to the co-opting of new members into a formally organized body is the need to draw upon expert consultants to advise those in decision-making positions. In this kind of situation the consultant is not drafted into the membership of a body, but is simply called upon for advice.

In addition, co-optation is a political device that provides an important means of assuring the stability of the decision-making processes and the system as a whole. By calling upon experts, those in decision-making positions can increase the effectiveness of their decisions. Consultation with experts enhances the ability to make effective, operational decisions. Co-optation also enables the leadership group to give formal recognition to powerful vested interests in the system. For example, if the influence of the military for some reason has been growing, and the leaders want to draw the military into its elite circle rather than risk alienating the officer corps, a prominent military officer may be co-opted into member-ship. This practice reduces the possibility of a serious opposition by an important group developing outside the leadership group and helps to assure its support of the system.

In this way the membership of the elite undergoes change. New leaders are brought in, old ones who have lost their support are dropped. The conflicts that take place among the leaders may re-sult from any one factor or combination of factors—personality, identification with competing interests, different priorities, dif-ferent understandings of national values and goals. Members of the political elite maintain themselves in power and keep the system functioning by constantly attempting to control and direct these conflicting groups and interests.

The Chinese Political Elite

It is even more difficult to get well-substantiated information on decision makers and decision making in China than it is on the Soviet Union. Nonetheless, from pieces of information gathered by a wide variety of sources, it is possible to put together a plausi-ble picture of how the Chinese leadership reaches decisions and who are the members of the political elite in the People's Republic of China.

As in the Soviet system, the key to political power in China is found in the Communist Party. Also, as in the Soviet case, it is possible to define the *general* political elite as consisting of the nearly 200 members of the Central Committee. The membership of the Central Committee includes representatives of the four most influential groups in China—leaders of the central party apparatus, party secretaries from the major geographic subdivisions of the party, the principal government officials, and the major military officers. However, unlike the Central Committee of the Soviet Party, the Central Committee of the Chinese Communist Party rarely meets as often as the rules specify (twice yearly) and then is convened only at the instigation of the Politburo. Although official reports on the proceedings of these meetings are not released, it is possible to state on the basis of communiqués released at the conclusion of each session that the Central Committee has given formal consideration to every major policy question confronting China. However, most students of the Chinese system believe that these meetings do not contain genuine debates and that perfunctory approval is given decisions already reached by the Politburo.

The characteristics of the members of the Central Committee are distinguished primarily by the length of time they have served with the top elite of the system. Donald W. Klein breaks down the Central Committee into five groups.[5] First are those who were full members in 1945, at the end of World War II and the outset of the renewed revolutionary struggle. This group consists of the "hard core" of Mao's followers, who participated in the Long March for survival in 1935. Second, there are those elected as alternates to the Central Committee in 1945, including most of those who climbed to leadership positions after the famous Long March. Third, there are those who were elected full members at the Eighth Party Congress in 1956 who did not fall into the second category. Fourth, there is the group elected to candidate membership in 1956, most of whom had their ascendancies in the party hierarchy after the beginning of World War II. Fifth and last, there are those elected to alternate membership in 1958, consisting mainly of those who rose to prominence about the time the Nationalists were defeated in 1949. The members of the first group averaged 71 years of age in 1966, and had worked and fought together for about 35 years. Those in the next two groups had an average age of slightly over 60, while those in the last two averaged between 55 and 60.

While the Central Committee contains the members of the political elite from the major factional divisions of Chinese society, the Politburo and its Standing Committee contain the most influential decision makers in the system. At the pinnacle of this constellation of power from the early 1930's until 1970 was Mao Tse-tung. Mao is venerated as the greatest military leader, the

---

[5] See Allen S. Whiting, "China," in *Modern Political Systems: Asia*, ed. Robert E. Ward and Roy C. Macridis (Englewood Cliffs: Prentice-Hall, 1963), p. 161.

greatest Marxist-Leninist theoretician, and the greatest political statesman of the Chinese People's Republic. His Chinese contemporaries attributed to him a kind of omniscience and godlike quality that was awarded to Lenin in the Soviet Union only after his death. Although ill health inhibited Mao's activities, he continued to be the center of political attention in the 1960's. However, knowledge of his illness stirred rivals to action when it became apparent that Mao would not be able to engage in personal leadership for very long.

As in the Soviet Union, the Politburo of the Chinese Communist Party stands above the Central Committee in terms of power. It is of somewhat larger size than its counterpart in the USSR, consisting of twenty full members and six alternates. Although the Politburo is near the top of the power structure, the seven men who serve on the Standing Committee are regarded as the highest-ranking political elite in Communist China.

In the spring of 1966, the members of the Politburo Standing Committee were Mao Tse-tung, Liu Shao-ch'i, Chou En-lai, Chu Teh, Ch'en Yun, Lin Piao, and Teng Hsiao-p'ing. Their backgrounds were quite similar to each other, but were in rather marked contrast to the members of the Politburo of the Soviet Party.

Mao Tse-tung. Chairman of the Party. Born in 1893 in Hunan Province.
Education: Chinese military academy.
Background: Joined the party in 1921; member of the Politburo since 1933; founded the Workers' and Peasants' Army in 1927; led the Long March for survival in 1935; strategist in guerrilla warfare; leading writer and theoretician of the party. Relinquished Chairmanship of the Government in 1959, presumably to concentrate his efforts on the work of the party.
Liu Shao-ch'i. Chairman of the Government. Born 1898.
Education: In Moscow in one of the early Communist Party Schools.
Background: Joined the party in 1921; member of the Politburo since 1931; leader in the civil war and thought to have been Mao's chosen heir until 1966.
Chou En-lai. Premier of the Government. Born 1898.
Education: Tientsin (China) and France.
Background: Joined the party in France and organized other Chinese students while there; helped found the Chinese Red Army; elected to Politburo in 1930's; former Foreign Minister and most experienced diplomat among the members of the Chinese leadership.
Chu Teh. Born in 1886.
Education: Yunnan Military Academy (China) and in Berlin.
Background: Early leader of the party and marshal in the Red Army. Apparently remains in the Standing Committee as a result of his past service.
Ch'en Yun. Born in 1900.
Education: Unknown; probably limited to primary school.

Background: Joined the party in 1924; elected to Central Committee in 1934; became Vice Chairman of Politburo in 1949. After 1958 he lost influence and was removed from Politburo in 1967.

Lin Piao. Marshal and Minister of Defense. Born 1908.

Education: Military academy.

Background: Joined Young Communists in 1925; elected to Politburo in 1956; former Director of Political Training in the Red Army; considered the leading Chinese military strategist; Chairman of the Council of National Defense.

Teng Hsiao-p'ing. Secretary-General of the Party. Born in 1902.

Education: In France.

Background: Joined the party in France; member of Politburo Standing Committee since 1956; Commissar of Eighth Army during Chinese civil war; former Minister of Finance; Vice Chairman of the Council of National Defense.

The members of the Standing Committee represent one of the oldest leadership groups of any country in the world. Although slightly younger than the Politburo as a whole, the members of this select committee had an average age of nearly 68 in 1966. The age span was 58 to 80. All seven members were first-generation communists. All had experience in the Chinese civil war, spending the greater part of their careers from 1931 until 1949 in military service to the party. Two of the members received part of their educations in Paris and one received part of his in Berlin, but even there they devoted most of their time to recruiting Chinese students into the Communist Party. One attended a university in Moscow. For the most part, however, their experience had been confined to China and their activities had been heavily oriented toward military roles. Only one person, Teng Hsiao-p'ing, occupied positions in all three of the chief party organs—Politburo, Standing Committee, and Secretariat.

Relatively little is known about the relations among the seven members of the Standing Committee and their relations with the other members of the Politburo. Mao was the only member who regularly received public acknowledgment for his role in policy making. Mao himself rarely bestowed public accolades on any of his colleagues, although he did single out Marshal Lin Piao for praise as a military strategist and in 1959 he chose Lin to be his successor as Chairman of the Government. In the aftermath of the Great Proletarian Cultural Revolution, Lin became recognized as the official heir to Mao.

In the spring of 1966, events erupted that cast greater light on the politics of the higher party organs. A campaign was launched against "rightist deviationists" and part of the intellectual community. The military newspaper controlled by the Ministry of Defense was the first to announce the campaign by attacking persons who purportedly had some misgivings about the country's hard-line foreign policy. The fact that Marshal Lin was Minister of Defense appeared to identify him as one of the leaders of the attack on intellectual circles. Apparently some members of university communities, with the tacit support of a few high-ranking party officials, had questioned the wisdom of Chinese policies toward both the Soviet Union and the United States. These persons were dubbed "rightists" and "opportunists" and came under bitter de-nunciations by the military and by others in favor of continuing the hard line against the United States and the USSR.

At the height of the campaign, editors of major newspapers and presidents of major universities were deprived of their positions for their alleged complicity in "rightist" circles. The most sur-prising development came with the announcement that Peng Chen, the mayor of Peking and a member of the Politburo, had been deprived of his posts. Peng had been considered by many to have been a potential successor to Mao. Vice Premier Lo Jui-ching, Chief of the General Staff, was forced out of his office. In addition, several members of the Ministry of Culture lost their jobs. During the course of the cultural revolution, Chu Teh and Teng lost their positions and Liu was eventually forced from both his party and government posts.

The army played a key role throughout the course of the leader-ship conflict. The military press repeatedly called for vigilance against the "anti-party, anti-Socialist intellectuals." Two out of four newly co-opted deputy ministers of culture were army officers. In addition, the supporters of Mao organized more than one hun-dred million youth of the country into the Red Guard. This massive organization reached a peak of revolutionary frenzy early in 1967, before encountering a period of decline.

Perhaps the most important aim of the cultural revolution launched by Mao was to "purify" the Chinese party by purging those who had turned some of their efforts toward stabilizing the bureaucracy and who were giving greater heed to the technocrats' desire to exercise more influence over economic decisions. Mao was apparently convinced that the Chinese revolution might be going the same route as that of the Soviet Union. He saw the Soviet leaders as traitors to their revolutionary commitment and as men who had meekly succumbed to the pressures of bureaucrats and specialists who were more interested in order and domestic eco-nomic progress than in carrying the message of their revolution to the oppressed peoples of the developing nations. Liu Shao-ch'i became the principal opponent of what he deemed to be Mao's destructive course. In the struggle that followed between these two factions of the Chinese party, many former members of the elite lost their positions and new faces assumed greater importance in Chinese politics.

Among those who rose to prominence were Ch'en Po-ta, head of the Cultural Revolution Group, and T'ao Chu and K'ang Sheng, chief advisers to the Group. All three became members of the Standing Committee of the Central Committee. All three had strong theoretical and propaganda orientations. All three were associated with the more militant wing of the Party. Ch'en Po-ta, a close associate of Mao since 1927, was editor of the theoretical journal of the Party and author of *The Thoughts of Mao*. T'ao Chu, Director of Propaganda for the Central Committee, vaulted from ninety-fifth place in the Central Committee to fourth after Mao. He had little experience in the foreign-policy area. The third member of the trio, K'ang Sheng, bore the responsibility for overseeing relations with foreign Communist parties.[6] However, in the estimation of most observers of Chinese politics, the principal beneficiary of the leadership struggle continued to be Lin Piao and his People's Liberation Army.

The 1966-1967 conflict among members of the party elite was the third and most serious leadership problem since the communists came to power in 1949. In 1954, the Central Committee denounced Kao Kang and Jao Shu-shih for engaging in "separatist" plots. Both men had been Politburo members and had been first chairmen of the Northeastern and Eastern regions of China. In 1959, Marshal Peng Tu-huai was dismissed as Minister of Defense, apparently because he opposed the use of the army in civilian projects associated with the "Great Leap Forward." The fact that Peng had just consulted with Khrushchev prior to his dismissal has led some observers to suggest that Sino-Soviet relations may have also been a factor in his removal.

These three conflicts, combined with frequent public denunciations of "rightists," indicate that there have been significant differences over policy among the members of the elite. In at least two of the purges, the army played a major role. In all cases the hard-line militantly nationalistic supporters of Mao emerged victorious.

On the basis of information concerning leadership problems and

---

[6] These three men were slightly younger than those they replaced on the Standing Committee. Ch'en Po-ta was 63, T'ao Chu was 61, and K'ang Sheng was 64. Those who lost their positions included Liu Shao-ch'i, 69; Chu Teh, 71; and Teng Hsiao-p'ing, 65. In terms of the history of the party in China, there was no significant generational change.

policy conflicts, it appears that all of the members of the Standing Committee, with the possible exception of Chu Teh, had played roles in the formulation of foreign policy. Considering the decline of Mao's health, it is not at all unlikely that Lin and Chou were the most active participants in foreign-policy problems. Chou, as Premier, was head of the State Council, and therefore was the immediate superior to the Minister of Foreign Affairs. Consequently, he was more involved in the implementation of foreign policy than the others.

VALUE ORIENTATIONS OF POLITICAL ELITES

Every individual is influenced in some way by his cultural heritage, his environment, and the belief patterns associated with them. The general goals are the kernel of any value system. Many problems arise in analyzing the value orientations of individuals, however, for subtleties exist that are not readily apparent. While the members of a particular political elite may share the same general value orientations, differences may still exist as a result of varying interpretations of the same goals, different priorities placed on goals, and differing choices on how goals can be attained. Our concern here is with the general value orientations of the Soviet and Chinese elites in foreign policy, but it should be kept in mind that variations may exist in the specific values among the members of each elite.

Value Orientations of the Soviet Elite

In order to comprehend the value system attributed to the Soviet political elite, one should keep in mind the background factors of the members of that elite. They are about a decade younger than their Chinese counterparts. Most of them grew up after the old Bolsheviks had consolidated their regime. Most of them had technological educations and were trained by education and experience to concern themselves with developing the productive capacity of the nation. They all experienced the physical hardships and mental anxieties resulting from invasion and near-conquest by Nazi Germany. They had seen their country grow from a backward one to an increasingly prosperous and productive one. Most of them were in every respect second-generation communists who had been educated and who had matured after the revolution and during the struggle to expand the Soviet economy at a rapid rate.

The foreign-policy value orientations of the Soviet leadership can be classified in three categories. First, there are those values relating to the international communist movement and to the leadership of it. Second, there are those concerned largely with domestic practices that relate to foreign affairs. And last, there are those values that affect interpretations of the non-communist world. In each of these categories there have been differences of opinion among the Soviet leaders. Marxism-Leninism by no means gives all of them the same understanding of the policy questions they must face.

Values relating to the international communist movement

One of the principal tenets of Marxist-Leninist theory is that of proletarian internationalism. This concept states that class ties are more important than national ones and that the workers of the world have a natural affinity that transcends nationalism. In other words, the working classes of different countries have more interests to fight for together than they have nationalistic reasons to fight against each other. It follows from this proposition that states governed by working-class parties should naturally be allies.[7] Also, nongoverning parties of the proletariat have common interests that bind them together in the international movement of the working class.

If these propositions are correct, there should be no serious conflicts among the parties or governments claiming to represent the interests of the workers. Practice, however, has demonstrated that such is not the case. Stalin sought to answer the problem by defining proletarian internationalism in such a way as to make support of the policies of the Soviet Union the test of whether or not a party belonged in the movement. Other parties were expected to follow the dictates of the Kremlin. If they were in power, they were expected to imitate the Soviet example as exactly as possible.

The 1950's brought a change to the practices associated with Stalinism. Proletarian internationalism was redefined so that "many roads to socialism" were deemed possible. It was no longer necessary for other parties to adopt slavish imitations of the Soviet system. Ways of acquiring political power other than by violent revolution were also endorsed. In short, there was an effort to update Leninist theory by reducing the emphasis on violence.

The problem arose, however, of how the various parties would maintain their unity once the Soviet Union ceased to be the sole authority and example of the movement. Initially it was assumed that loyalty to the tenets of Marxism-Leninism would be

---

[7] Those countries which are governed by Communist parties are called *party states* in this chapter.

sufficient to bind the different national parties together. It was soon discovered, however, that the writings of Marx and Lenin were so voluminous and could be interpreted in so many different ways that this common ideological base was not sufficient to eradicate conflicts.

The Soviet leadership then sought to bring representatives of all organized communist parties in the world together in Moscow for the purpose of drafting declarations that would set forth the essence of Marxism-Leninism. It was expected that such a declaration would clarify the meaning of communist theory in a simple, concrete fashion. All the parties would then subscribe to it and the problem of conflicting interpretations would be minimized. In 1957 and again in 1960 this method was utilized. In neither case did the declarations succeed in accomplishing their intended purpose. The Chinese and the Yugoslavs in particular continued to give interpretations to Marxism-Leninism that the Soviet elite could not accept.

Having failed in this course, the Soviet leaders attempted to assert their right as the oldest ruling communist party to give the definitive interpretation to Leninist doctrine. The right to do so was obviously important for reasons of power as well as of theory. Whoever could establish the right to interpret had power over those who had to accept their interpretations. In essence, what the Soviet leaders wanted was a uniform foreign policy for all governing parties. They were willing to allow the party states a moderate measure of freedom to make whatever domestic innovations were deemed necessary, but they wanted every communist state to follow the leadership of the USSR in foreign affairs.

The goal that the Soviet elite was attempting to obtain was recognition from the other parties as the leading voice in the communist movement. The Chinese wanted at least to share this role, if not to have it exclusively to themselves. The Yugoslavs refused to place themselves in a subordinate position for different reasons. The Soviet leaders were anxious not to read anyone out of the movement, but wanted to restore general consensus and to be recognized as the most powerful and influential party state.

In February, 1964, the Central Committee of the Soviet Party released a detailed statement prepared by Mikhail Suslov. The statement attacked the Chinese "claim to the role of 'supreme arbiters' in the socialist community" and sharply criticized their attempt to "excommunicate" Yugoslavia from the movement. "Tomorrow it may occur to the CPC [Chinese Communist Party] leadership to do as much with regard to other socialist countries."

In pursuing such policies the Chinese leaders were judged guilty of "subversive activity against the Leninist unity of the world communist movement."

The strongest language of the Suslov report indicted the Chinese leaders for "petty-bourgeois, nationalist, neo-Trotskyist deviation." It asserted that "nationalism is inexorably gaining the upper hand in the entire policy of the Chinese leaders, that it is becoming the mainspring of their actions." Having recognized the nationalistic flavor of China's position, it is quite likely that the Soviet leaders were also aware of the significance of Russian nationalism to their own interpretation of the guidelines and objectives of the international communist movement. The Soviet elite simply could not allow the Chinese to define the goals of the movement and prescribe the tactics when they were likely to upset the aspirations of the Soviet decision makers for their nation and perhaps even to threaten the security of the USSR and the entire system of party states.

The general goals of the Soviet elite in regard to the international communist movement appear to be the gaining of recognition as the prime mover, not necessarily the dictator, of all communist parties and the assurance that no party's recklessness becomes a threat or a liability to the Soviet nation. These goals are set forth in the terms of Marxism-Leninism, but are strongly colored by the interests of the Soviet nation-state as perceived by the elite.

Values concerning domestic policies

According to Marxist-Leninist theory, there are several stages to communist development. In the first stage after the revolution, the traditional ruling class must either be converted or liquidated. Following this is the stage of building a "socialist" society. This stage generally is held to include the nationalization of industry and the collectivization of agriculture. If the country is not already industrialized, then the stage also includes a period of intensive industrialization. During this period, antagonistic classes disappear. Only after the construction of socialism can the country begin the building of communism, which theoretically consists of a totally classless society in which everyone is provided with all basic needs and social conflict is completely eradicated. Since 1961, the Soviet Union has claimed to be in the early phase of constructing communism.

All of these elements of theory suggest concern for internal national affairs. They all point to the building of a prosperous society that is advanced both economically and technologically. Despite their reputations as revolutionaries with global aspirations, the

Soviet leaders have been very much concerned with domestic problems. The greatest investment of energy and resources has been devoted to domestic economic construction. The successes of this construction have had both domestic and international ramifications. They have been producing a population of increasing discrimination and growing expectations. At the same time the successes have enhanced the reputation of the USSR as the most powerful party state and the natural leader of the communist movement.

The concern of the Soviet elite with domestic economic growth, however, is coupled with a disinclination to devote any large part of the country's resources to helping the other party states. Probably the clearest example of this to the Chinese was the Soviet withdrawal of technical assistants and nuclear specialists in 1959-1960. Furthermore, the Soviet leaders recognize that their nation is much more likely to be the target of hostility from the West than the less powerful party states. Keeping uncommitted nations uncommitted and free of Western military bases became a prime objective. This situation has made the Soviet elite more willing to give economic and military aid to nonaligned nations than to party states, which, with the exception of China, are either already allies or are in no position to constitute an immediate military threat to the USSR. This concern with national security and with internal welfare has provided another source of tension in the communist movement.

The Chinese were highly critical of Soviet value orientations on these points. The Suslov report condemned the Chinese leaders for attacking the effort of the Soviet policy makers to improve the standard of living in the USSR. Suslov also criticized the contention that "the improvement of the living standard is making Soviet people 'go bourgeois,'" and sharply denounced the assertion that "the principle of material incentives 'results in people seeking personal gain and enrichment, inducing the itch for profit and a growth of bourgeois individualism, and injuring socialist economics.'" In rebuttal, the report claimed that "neither Marx nor Lenin have anywhere even remotely hinted that the rockbottom tasks of socialist construction may be realized by the methods of 'leaps' and cavalry charges, overlooking the degree to which the socio-economic and spiritual premises of the advance have matured and ignoring the task of improving the living standards of the people." The reference to "leaps" was to the Chinese assertion that they could bypass the stage of socialism and move directly into the stage of constructing communism.

In addition to concern with domestic economic advances and

protecting their image of faithfully following the stages of development established by doctrine, the Soviet elite has demonstrated
concern with protecting the territorial boundaries of the USSR.
This traditional concern of nation-states with territorial integrity
became manifest in a series of border disputes between the USSR
and China. Western sources had often indicated that tension existed over territory along the Sinkiang-USSR boundary as well
as on the Manchuria-Siberia border. However, it was not until
1964 that Soviet and Chinese statements confirmed the extent of
the dispute and the length of time in which counterclaims had been
made. The Chinese contended that in 1957 their government had
asked the Soviet government to confer on the question of "unset-
tled" boundaries. *Pravda,* on September 2, 1964, asserted that the
Chinese had made claims against Soviet-held territories as early
as 1954. The early dating of the boundary dispute suggested that
this question may have been one of the primary causes of the growing coolness between the policy makers of Moscow and Peking in
the late 1950's, long before the rift became open. The preoccupation of the Chinese with reclaiming the ancient territorial borders
of the empire and of the Russians with maintaining possession of
land already under their domain resulted in additional charges
of nationalism by spokesmen of each nation against the other.

Value orientations on war, peace, and revolution
The international objectives and methods of a country's decision
makers are inevitably influenced by the perceptions the policy
makers have of the world around them. These perceptions are part
of the value orientations of the elite.

The Soviet elite has inherited a Leninist view of the countries
where some form of capitalism prevails. According to this view,
such countries are by nature *imperialistic.* That is, the ruling
classes attempt to utilize the power of their governments in order
to enhance their opportunity to acquire wealth from weaker nations. Imperialism, to the orthodox Leninist, exploits whole nations
of people and thereby breeds war. Furthermore, the imperialist
countries were thought to be destined to confront the communist
countries in a final "inevitable war."

This thesis of the inevitability of war was officially abandoned by
the Soviet Party in 1956. Instead, the Soviet leaders contended
that a prolonged period of peaceful coexistence was possible and
that competition would take place between the "camps" of imperialism and communism largely in the economic and ideological
spheres. These modifications of Leninist doctrine are a significant
reflection of the evolutionary changes that were taking place in

the Soviet system. They appear to substantiate the view that the Soviet leadership was not inclined to take undue risks in the nuclear age and that they preferred to devote most of their resources to domestic improvement.

The more moderate, though not always openly friendly, attitude of the Soviet leaders toward the Western powers, coupled with the Soviet effort to inculcate a spirit of friendship with neutral states, tended only to deepen the rift between the elites of the USSR and China. The leaders in the Kremlin treated the nuclear capability of the West as a serious threat, necessitating peaceful coexistence between states. The Chinese expressed their differences with the USSR in ideological terms. Declaring that the sun was "rapidly" setting on the imperialist countries, Mao declared that "Imperialism and all reactionary forces, which appear strong but are actually weak, are paper tigers." This assertion was tantamount to telling the Soviet leaders that they were afraid of a paper tiger.

Moscow was as cold toward some of Peking's policies as the Chinese elite was toward those of the Soviet leadership. The Kremlin showed disapproval of the Chinese provocations along the Indian border by noting that "it would be wrong not to express regret that the incident took place." In turn, the Chinese defied the Soviet commitment to a policy of coexistence by publishing an article in their party's theoretical journal explaining the impossibility of coexistence. The Chinese contended that the policy of coexistence in fact assumed that the very nature of imperialism had changed and that the conservatism of Soviet policy was equivalent to renouncing the revolutionary purpose of the communist movement.

The Suslov report reaffirmed the disagreements of the two largest communist parties on the issues of war, peace and revolution. The report charged the Chinese with thinking that war was necessary in order to create revolutionary situations and that war provided "the only means of settling the contradictions between capitalism and socialism." Particularly strong criticism was hurled at the Chinese for extending the Sino-Indian conflict during the tense moments of the Cuban crisis and for opposing efforts to obtain disarmament. In addition, Suslov declared that the Soviet elite considered it "inexpedient" to help the Chinese produce nuclear weapons because such a course would lead to the acquisition of nuclear power by West Germany and Japan. The Chinese were also accused of organizing separate cliques in the communist parties of underdeveloped areas. In pursuing this course, the Chinese had attempted to set "the Eastern peoples apart on a nationalist and even racial basis."

All of these charges help to identify goals and priorities set by the Soviet elite as well as to cast light on reasons for dissension between the leaders of the two chief communist states. In general, it can be said that the Soviet leaders have permitted experience to influence their ideological precepts. Their educations, for example, were heavily oriented toward the technical. This type of education, especially in the USSR, emphasizes the economic requirements of the country – how to accomplish things that stimulate productivity. Their careers have reinforced this training; many of them have held or still hold positions where they are expected to help increase production – whether as party supervisors on collective farms, administrators in economic ministries, or in other posts. Age is also a factor because they reached maturity during the five-year plans of the 1930's when the emphasis was on rapid transformation of the Soviet economy into an industrial one. They have been imbued with a deep awareness of the close relationship of economics and politics and the importance of using politics as an instrument to promote the rapid growth of the country. Their desire to avoid war, to spend the bulk of their resources on economic growth, and to recognize the "practical" necessities of international politics is consonant with their educational and career backgrounds. These value orientations were the combined product of their ideological and cultural heritage, their personal background and experiences.

Value Orientations of the Chinese Elite

The Chinese leaders do not interpret all of the major tenets of Marxism-Leninism in the same manner as the Soviet elite. A number of probable reasons can be set forth for the distinctiveness of the Chinese position.

For example, the experience of many Chinese leaders in military academies and as participants in the extended revolutionary ride to power contrasted sharply with the experiences of present-day Soviet elites. The Soviet leaders were, for the most part, trained as technocrats or party cadres with great emphasis on the construction of an advanced economy, whereas the Chinese leaders were most concerned with winning a civil war and establishing the boundaries of their power. The Soviet elite came largely from the intelligentsia, but were taught to appreciate the importance of the working class in building an economy that could be competitive with that of the United States. The Chinese, on the other hand, were mostly peasant in origin and had only slight appreciation for the Soviet effort to construct an economic base similar to those of Western Europe and North America. The difference in the generations of the members of the two elites was also signifi-

cant. The older Chinese, experienced in revolution and the problems of establishing control over a vast population, disliked having
to seek the aid and advice of the younger Soviet elite, who in their
estimation were only the belated heirs to a revolutionary tradition.
The Chinese communists felt that they were the real revolutionaries. Finally, it should be noted that the USSR is more Western
than Eastern in its culture. This factor undoubtedly contributed to
the sensitivity of the Chinese elite, who view their own culture
as superior and hold great animosity for the West, based on the
period of nineteenth-century history when China was humiliated
and exploited by European powers.

Value orientations concerning the international communist movement

The Chinese leaders have been particularly sensitive to the
question of leadership in the international communist movement.
After the death of Stalin, the only old communist attracting wide
recognition for his leadership abilities and his theoretical writings
was Mao Tse-tung. As the leader of a successful revolution, especially one that occurred without much significant assistance
from the Soviet Union, Mao could legitimately expect to be recognized as the most authoritative interpreter of Marxism-Leninism.
That he should place himself second to such nontheoretical persons
as Khrushchev and Brezhnev undoubtedly would have been demanding too much. At the international party conferences of 1957
and 1960, it appears that the Chinese wanted at least equal status
with the Soviet leaders. Later, from the Soviet point of view, the
Chinese demanded more than equal status.

In response to a speech by Maurice Thorez, the former leader of
the French Communist Party, the Chinese attacked his criticism
of them for not abiding by the decisions of the Twentieth Congress
of the Soviet Communist Party. The Chinese party newspaper
declared, "No one has the right to demand that all fraternal parties should accept the theses of any one party. No resolution of any
congress of any one party can be taken as the common line of the
international Communist movement or be binding on other fraternal parties." A sense of national and racial pride crept into the
Chinese statement as it criticized the attitude of superiority held
by communists in advanced countries. "The proletarian parties
of the metropolitan imperialist countries are duty bound to heed
the voice of the revolutionary people in [underdeveloped areas],
respect their revolutionary feelings, and support their revolutionary struggles." The newspaper went on to note that the Western
communists "have no right whatsoever to flaunt their seniority

before these people, to put on lordly airs, to carp and cavil, like Comrade Thorez of France, who so arrogantly and disdainfully speaks of them as being 'young and inexperienced.'" These remarks indicate how sensitive the Chinese leaders are to being considered inferior to Western communists.

The Chinese elite clearly served notice that China did not intend to play second fiddle to anyone. Addressing the men in the Kremlin, the party press wrote: "Dear friends and comrades who claim to possess the whole truth! Since you are quite definite that our articles are wrong, why don't you publish all these erroneous articles and then refute them point by point, so as to inculcate hatred among your people against the 'heresies' you call dogmatism, sectarianism, and anti-Marxism-Leninism?" The Chinese proceeded to answer their own question. "If you are men enough, you will. But having a guilty conscience and an unjust case, being fierce in visage but faint of heart, outwardly as tough as bulls but inwardly as timid as mice, you will not dare. We are sure you will not dare. Isn't that so? Please answer!" The above passages indicate the extent to which the Chinese leaders have disagreed with the Soviet attempt at leadership of the movement and with Soviet innovations in doctrine and policy. From them it seems fair to surmise that the Chinese want not equal but superior status in the movement.

Value orientations on domestic policy

To the Chinese leaders, domestic policy has served not only as a means of making economic advances, but as an instrument to assert their leading role in the communist movement. In 1958, the Central Party Press announced the construction of a national system of communes as part of a "great leap forward" to the construction of communism. The commune scheme was widely interpreted as an effort to bypass the Soviet Union in the world of Marxism-Leninism, by asserting that China was thereby entering the stage of "building communism" while even the USSR, at that time, had made no comparable claim.

Acceptance of the Chinese claim would have placed the People's Republic of China in a more advanced stage of domestic construction than the Soviet Union and would probably have increased the prestige of the Chinese regime at the expense of the USSR. The Soviet leadership was temporarily able to persuade China to modify its stand, and *Hung ch'i*, the journal of the Central Committee of the CCP, stated that the transition from socialism to communism could not be achieved until a high level of production existed. In spite of the momentary truce, the Chinese leadership had demonstrated willingness to compete with the Soviet Union for prestige among both the ruling and nonruling communist parties of the world. Eventually the Chinese had to abandon their commune scheme. Its failure after such widespread publicity apparently discouraged the Chinese leaders from making grandiose claims for the time being. Relatively little was published in the first half of the 1960's about domestic plans and problems. From scant evidence it seems that the emphasis was shifted to agriculture and that crash industrialization programs had been postponed except in the area of nuclear and thermonuclear physics. At the same time, the elite was busy trying to establish China as the revolutionary center of the underdeveloped world, asserting that the Chinese revolution was the natural example to all oppressed peoples.

Value orientations on war, peace, and revolution

The cultural heritage and revolutionary experience of the Chinese elite have given the decision makers an appreciation of Marxism-Leninism rather different from that held by the new generation of Soviet leaders. They have taken what is generally described as a much harder position on the questions of relations with capitalist states, war, and the necessity of violent revolution.

The Chinese have held rigorously to the older and more orthodox interpretation of imperialism. In doing so, they have contended that the Soviet leaders had abandoned one of the cardinal tenets of Leninism. "The minimum demand that can be made of a communist," the party newspaper declared, "is that he should make a clear distinction between the enemy and his own comrades. He should be merciless toward the enemy and be kindly toward his own comrades." Then in a veiled reference to the Soviet leadership, the newspaper went on to say: "But there are some who do just the opposite. While being so 'accommodating' and making such 'mutual concessions' to imperialism, they treat fraternal parties and fraternal countries as implacable enemies."

In response to the Soviet contention that modern weaponry required a policy of peaceful coexistence, the Chinese elite has been adamant. "But no Marxist-Leninists or revolutionary peoples have ever been paralyzed with fear by the nuclear weapons in the hands of imperialism and given up their struggle against imperialism and its lackey." Although they claim to recognize the destructive power of thermonuclear weapons, they contend that these weapons cannot have a decisive influence on the outcome of a war and that "the revolutionary masses" will inevitably be the ultimate victors. For example, they were sharply critical of Khrushchev's with-

drawal of missiles from Cuba in 1962. "The only way to win victory
in revolution is for Marxist-Leninists and revolutionaries to com-
bat resolutely every trace of weakness and capitulation, and to
educate the masses of the people in the concept that 'imperialism
and all reactionaries are paper tigers. . . .'" In short, the Chinese
leaders discount the contemporary Soviet version of imperialism
and the noninevitability of war on two grounds. First, they charge
that the noninevitability-of-war concept implies a change in the
nature of imperialism and they refuse to accept that possibility.
Second, they contend that the capitalist countries are basically
weak and that the Soviet Union has capitulated to nuclear blackmail by the Western powers.

With these views, the Chinese reject the fundamental assumptions behind the Soviet theory of peaceful coexistence. The principle of coexistence, they assert, cannot apply "to relations between
oppressed and oppressing nations. . . . For an oppressed nation
or people the question is one of waging a revolutionary struggle to
overthrow the rule of imperialism and the reactionaries; it is not,
and cannot be, a question of peaceful coexistence with imperialism
and the reactionaries." They further charge that those who hold
such attitudes cannot claim to be Marxist-Leninists. This charge
then gives them additional justification to claim that they should
be the leaders of the international communist movement rather
than the Soviet policy makers.

The attitude of the Chinese leaders toward revolution and na-
tional-liberation movements (struggles for independence) also
takes a harder stance than has been taken in the Kremlin. They
accused the Soviet leadership of behaving like "opulent and lordly
philanthropists" rather than like revolutionaries. The Chinese
press expressed particularly harsh criticism toward the practice
of giving aid to "bourgeois" governments in countries like India
and Egypt, rather than supplying the communist-led revolutionary
forces of those nations with assistance. Leadership of the movement ought to be in the hands of persons who are not afraid of
"waging wars of resistance against oppression."

The official positions taken by the Chinese leaders on these international issues provide us with a general picture of their value
orientations and of some of the reasons for their disagreements
with the Soviet leadership. The members of the Chinese elite spent
a large part of their lives in revolutionary activity. Having won
their civil war, they do not appear to be afraid of involvement in
revolutionary struggles. In fact, they are convinced that many
similar revolutions can be won in other underdeveloped countries
if only given the proper leadership and support. The reluctance of

the Soviet leaders to give more than token support to revolutionary movements in these countries is decried by the Chinese as lack of revolutionary faith and indications of excessive concern with domestic comfort. In turn, the Soviet leaders are inclined to view their comrades in Peking as too "adventurist."

CONCLUSION

From the foregoing observations it should be clear that elite study is designed to concentrate attention on the individuals who play roles in the decision-making centers of nation-states. Ability to identify members of an elite and gain knowledge of the backgrounds and values of that elite enables us to acquire greater insight into and understanding of the problems of determining who makes national policy and why they make the choices that they do. The elite approach therefore serves as a tool of analysis that is designed to enlighten us on questions of leadership, decision making, and policy formation.

Chapter 5

INTERNAL ENVIRONMENTAL INFLUENCES AND FOREIGN POLICY

Roberta Koplin Mapp
University of Alberta

The two preceding chapters have focused primarily on the characteristics of national decision makers and certain internal political processes to see how these may be related to either specific foreign-policy decisions or broad foreign-policy orientations and directions. This chapter is concerned with a much broader class of factors in the national environment that can influence policy choices. These factors are not as neatly separate as the two discussed earlier, and for lack of a better name will be referred to as aspects of the internal environment or setting. Some of these influences are physical and can be rather easily measured, such as the geographic size and population of a nation, or its wealth and resources. The internal environment also includes factors more vague and difficult to measure, such as the morale of a nation's people, the degree of internal conflict or cohesion within the nation, and several others that might be lumped together under a concept like political culture.

Normally, those who conduct a nation's foreign policy will take these internal environmental influences into account, at least to the extent of keeping them "in the backs of their minds," when they are initiating policy or reacting to inputs from the other actors in the international system. We consider them important enough to rate separate considerations, because in many cases they impose important limitations on the courses of action open to decision makers and in some cases may actually dictate whether a foreign-policy decision is made or how leaders respond to external stimuli (or actions of other nations). The first section of the chapter will treat the physical and nonphysical internal environment in general terms. The second and third parts will consider specific cases that illustrate their impact on foreign policy.

TYPES OF INTERNAL INFLUENCES

Physical Environment

Physical internal influences are often referred to as the "capabilities" of the nation and are measured in numerical terms. Thus we read of per capita gross national product, miles of paved roads, number of telephones per thousand of population, kilowatt hours of electricity generated per annum, average daily caloric value of food per person, and the like. A glance at one of the statistical volumes published by the United Nations would provide other examples. Because they involve measurements and, inevitably, comparisons of specific quantities of this or that, physical capabilities have a deceptively solid look. In the past, such appearances have sometimes led one nation to think that another could not defend itself against a military attack because it was "weaker" as measured by some one or more of these indicators of capability. A purely physical factor that remains important is geography and climate; in the past this has often been a crucial factor and must still be taken into account in terms of "limited conventional warfare." We need only cite the cases of Napoleon and Hitler, both of whom grossly underestimated the defensive capability inherent in the Russian winter and its effect on an invading army. They also underestimated the nonphysical factor of the will of the Russian armies and people to resist. The calculations of both invaders were based on the probability of victory because of comparisons of well-trained, well-equipped armies versus the ill-trained, poorly equipped Russian armies, as well as greater industrial capacity (or national wealth, in the case of Napoleon), better transport facilities, and the like. This type of miscalculation can err in the opposite direction, as when a potential victim overestimates the capabilities of an aggressor and capitulates with undue haste. Let us turn now to a consideration of some of these capabilities and physical factors.

A basic element in the physical environment is the size and location of the nation-state. While weapons development has rendered this factor less important for the policy considerations of the larger states possessing modern weaponry systems, it remains a useful starting point for examining historical cases and for the current situation of smaller states. For example, the constricted and insular position of Great Britain has been adduced as the single most important factor enabling her to play the role of "balancer" in nineteenth-century European politics. As an island, Britain had turned to the sea for both livelihood and defense — after 1588 she had no rival as a naval power for centuries. Secure from the threat of invasion by foreign armies, Britain could throw her considerable weight as a naval power into the "balance" of European politics. The fact of insularity has also been influential in directing the attention of her enterprising citizens outward — first as pirates, then as traders and colonists, and finally as administrators of the empire acquired largely as a result of the activities of merchants and settlers.

Insularity need not have this effect, of course. It is entirely possible that an island population may become complacent and inward-oriented. Given, however, that the population of the United Kingdom was expanding, that agricultural practices of enclosure were driving the population into urban centers, that the industrial revolution started in Britain and perhaps reflected more than anything else the enterprising and innovative characteristics of the British people, it is not surprising that this energy and excess population flowed outward.

The continental location of the United States operated in the opposite direction. A vast and fertile country, isolated by oceans from the political turmoil of Europe, offered seemingly endless space and resources to absorb the energies of an increasing population. Under these conditions the population tended to be preoccupied with internal concerns and did not develop *sustained* interests in external affairs. The intermittent character of United States involvement in foreign affairs, particularly prior to World War I, may be in large part attributable to this "spatial isolation" and material abundance.

In the case of the Soviet Union, which in area is the largest nation in the world, the great land mass borders on numerous other countries and attention to foreign policy has necessarily been continuous. In addition, the northern location of most of the country means that few ports are ice-free the year around. Indeed, during most of the tsarist period, the foreign policy was directed toward pushing national borders southward in an effort to obtain warm-water ports, and, as well, to establish more defensible boundaries.

The tragic history of Poland is closely tied to its position in the midst of the sweeping Eastern European plains which offer no such natural boundaries as mountains or deep, swift rivers. A contrasting example is found in the boundary between Spain and France (the Pyrenees mountains), which has effectively limited invasions across this barrier.

In the modern world, the location of such a country as Gambia, stretching some two hundred miles into the heart of Senegal for a few miles on either side of the Gambia river, means that her foreign policy must be in accord with that of Senegal, the larger and more prosperous French-speaking nation that surrounds her. Indeed, any inland nation must remain on reasonably friendly terms with the nations that lie between her and the sea to the extent that she is dependent upon imports and exports moving across the intervening state or states. Botswana, Lesotho, and Swaziland are African-ruled states located in the midst of South Africa. Since they must rely economically upon the Republic of South Africa, they cannot denounce apartheid policies or harbor "freedom fighters," no matter what their sentiments may be on these issues.

Size and location alone are not sufficient guides to assessing capabilities. At a minimum, they must be considered in conjunction with population. Some of the largest states in Africa—Mali, Chad, the Sudan—are also among the least densely populated because of their location on the fringe of the southern Sahara, and are eclipsed in continental affairs by much smaller nations of larger population—Ghana, Guinea, the Ivory Coast. At the same time we should note that it is only in the fertile imaginations of movie producers that a country of the size of Monaco, Liechtenstein, or Gambia mounts a military attack on a great power—and wins! Rather more realistically, one might attribute the generally peaceful foreign policies of these tiny nations to the dearth of handy opponents of a beatable size. It is most useful to consider size, population, and industrialization together in assessing national capabilities. The United States and the Soviet Union in part owe their present world position to the felicitous combination of these factors plus adequate natural resources. That any one factor alone is not enough is evident when one notes India's population or Australia's size. These, however, do provide a potential for future power *if* other capabilities can be developed. Some observers of world politics suggest a minimum population of fifty million for any nation aspiring to great-power status. When a population is largely engaged in subsistence agriculture, it is extremely difficult to divert resources for foreign-policy purposes. Financing an army may be impossible; it may be difficult even to maintain diplomatic posts in all of the foreign nations where it would be advantageous to have them.

A nation's capability position may change, not only relatively as other nations surpass her or fall behind her in industrial or military strength, but even absolutely in relation to her own capabilities in the past. The costs of two world wars to Great Britain in terms of men, deteriorated or destroyed industrial plants, and financial drains have combined to dictate her relative decline from great-power status. The continuation of the internal economic strains has influenced the extent of Britain's military commitments to NATO and underlies her desire to join the European Common Market.

All of these factors suggest that one useful method of comparing national capabilities is to compare per capita income or per capita gross national product. It is equally important to make even these comparisons with the differences in internal political processes in mind, for the type of political system may influence the percentage of national resources that can be devoted to foreign-policy ends. The Soviet Union, for example, is able to divert a larger *percentage* of national resources into military establishment, space research, and perhaps even into foreign aid than is normally expended by the United States. The result is that total expenditures on these items are more nearly equal for the two countries than we might expect from gross-national-income data alone, where the United States still enjoys a sizeable competitive advantage.

Despite the drawbacks of this sort of quantitative analysis to discover physical influences on foreign policy, the use of such gross data is a useful starting point for analysis. If national economic development is an announced domestic policy of an "underdeveloped" nation, we can generally assume that it will endeavor to stay on good diplomatic terms with at least some possible sources of financial and technical assistance.

Certainly one of the great dilemmas confronting the newly independent and economically underdeveloped nations is the need to maintain good relations with aid-giving nations and still retain their sense of being free from foreign domination. The annual debate in the United States Congress over the foreign-aid bill, with its emphasis on trying to ensure that the money is not wasted or used for "socialistic" projects, is duplicated in *reverse* in the parliaments of the aid-receiving countries. They object strongly to the conditions attached to aid that limit their freedom of action, to the "advisers" who may try to manipulate them, and to the implicit assumption that their vote in the United Nations can be bought. Even Canada, a relatively wealthy nation, keeps a wary eye on the "colossus to the south." There is a general feeling that too large a percentage of Canadian resources and industry is owned by United States nationals, thereby restricting Canada's choices of foreign policy to those acceptable to the United States.

We also expect that small nations will keep a wary eye on large neighbors and to avoid antagonizing them unduly, and that exporting nations will keep in mind the necessity of retaining existing markets and finding new ones. The expanding economies of Western European nations have led industrialists to look to Eastern Europe for new markets and, not surprisingly, diplomatic relations between the two halves of Europe have improved significantly. As a final example, the rather high level of diplomatic exchange between Zambia in Central Africa and Chile in western South America makes sense only if we recall that these two countries account for the majority of the world's copper, and that it is in their mutual interest to achieve a more stable world price for copper to avoid the wide fluctuation in national income that results from price movements.

The politics of the Cold War have introduced an interesting paradox into national-capability analysis. We find that the smaller and weaker nations seem to enjoy greater freedom of action in foreign policy than the great powers. They change alliances without being penalized, accept aid and advisers from both East and West, and can criticize the actions of larger nations, particularly the United States, with a high degree of impunity.

Nonphysical Internal Influences

We use the term nonphysical rather than psychological or some other term because many of the aspects of internal influences are neither purely psychological nor physical. Political scientists refer to this potpourri as "political culture." The political culture of a nation is the sum total of the particular ways its citizens have of looking at politics, of feeling about politicians, the national flag, and the constitution; of what they think should be their duties to the nation and what they expect in return; of what presidents or kings may properly do and what a fellow citizen may do before they call it treason. Students in the United States, for example, have had their political culture shaped by what they have been taught, by their experiences at home and at school. It will continue to be shaped and perhaps radically changed by their future experiences in work and dealings with fellow citizens.

Attitudes and Political Behavior

This set of collective attitudes that we term political culture is learned, as are all attitudes — an infant is born with little in the way of culture, political or otherwise. There are two primary sources for learning political attitudes: one is by learning from nonpolitical experiences, and the other is from experience with politics directly. The first includes the particular information *about* (this is quite different from experience *with*) the political system which begins in the earliest years in school and is supplemented by what parents may teach or inadvertently demonstrate by actions or spontaneous remarks. It also includes attitudes toward other people and toward authority in general that may later be transferred and applied in a political situation.

Perception of strangers

For example, an individual may learn from the family that "outsiders" cannot be trusted and in later life continue to be suspicious of the motives and trustworthiness of all who are not relatives or close friends. When this general attitude is applied to the political arena it can contribute to violent forms of politics. One set of politicians will be loath to turn over office to another if they are firmly convinced the other party is not to be trusted. For the average citizen, this attitude may mean that he will not attempt to find a political solution to his problems — unemployment, poor schools, no roads — unless the politicians to whom he would apply for this relief happen to be friends or relatives. All unknown politicians will be suspected of being knaves, thieves, or worse. The political culture of Italy has been characterized as being dominated by distrust, antagonism, and hostility resulting in long-festering social problems that are beyond the capacity of the political system to handle. Thus, while Italian children may read in their school books that Italy is a democracy, that one elects representatives to serve the people, and the like, the contrary attitudes that they learn in the family may prove more important.

Authority

A second general attitude that has important political implications concerns the general nature of authority. Are children taught to give unquestioning obedience to parents, to teachers, and perhaps to certain other groups as well — the village elders, the local aristocracy, the tribal chief, or the tax collector? Or are they encouraged to think for themselves, to give respect only to those who have earned it by their actions in the past and retain it by continuing accomplishment rather than to those whom the accident of birth has placed in a certain family? These are the extremes of this attitude about authority; generally we discover a mix of varying proportions of the two. The general attitudes toward authority will be reflected in the structures of authority, as they tend toward a hierarchy of authority or toward equality. A hierarchical structure is one in which each person has a specific role and knows to whom he must give obedience and from whom he may receive it. Examples of this are armies, feudal kingdoms, and bureaucracies. The equalitarian structure implies an opposite type, in which all have equal claims and obligations. Examples of this are harder to cite, since in practical life the division of labor that makes politics practicable means that we must delegate some of our claims to equal authority if we would find time to do our own work and devote time to family and personal pursuits. Quaker meetings, the New England town meeting, or Athenian democracy in its ideal form would be examples of equalitarian social and political structures. To return, however, to societal attitudes toward authority and their implications for modern political culture, it is useful to point out some of the striking contrasts found in various countries. The Ethiopian child is taught to defer to authority; the American child is expected to temper his deference with critical questions about limits, proper exercise and appropriateness; the Italian or French child does not learn to temper his distrust with much deference.

Fate
A third important attitude deals with how people feel about their ability to change their environment. Does the culture stress accepting "what is" because it cannot be changed – perhaps because "it always has been" – or is the accent on "doing something about it"? Does the society seem to accept disease, poverty, flood, famine and taxes as unpleasant but unavoidable facts of life, or are these viewed as within the control of man, particularly of his concerted effort through government? This type of attitude is especially interesting to political science when it is in the process of change, particularly when part of a society begins to view the environment as manipulable while the rest retains what we think of as the traditional attitude of nonmanipulability. This attitude difference is one of the main problems besetting the developing nations. The

young government official sent out to the villages to introduce basic public-health measures or improved agricultural practices may run into difficulties because he is trying to change ingrained habits and attitudes that are hallowed by time and ancestors. In some cases people will defer to his authority, allowing the changes to be made easily, but he may return in several months to find that the pump for the new unpolluted water supply has been allowed to rust and that the women are once again drawing water from the stream that serves also as communal bathing facility, laundry, and sewage system. India's attempt to curb population increase is in part stymied by the traditional attitude that large families represent wealth. Many developing countries find it very difficult to rid government and civil service of graft because the traditional culture dictates that one gives a gift when asking a favor or when a benefit is received. The military leaders who engineered the coup d'état against Nkrumah in Ghana found themselves deluged with gifts of chickens, cows, jams, cloth, and money as the tribesmen expressed their gratitude in the traditional manner.

Level of individual loyalty

A fourth type of attitude that is crucial for a functioning political system is loyalty or commitment of the citizens. By this we do not refer to national patriotism, for the nation is only one object to which loyalty may be directed. There are other levels that an individual may well consider more important — his family, kin, tribe, religion, district, or region. In cases in which loyalties are predominantly directed to one of these nonnational levels, it is difficult to speak of a national political culture at all, for there are usually a number of subcultures coexisting uneasily within the confines of the state. In the Biafran crisis, for an instance, tribal loyalties proved more important than any idea of Nigeria as a nation; in India before independence, religious loyalty proved stronger than national loyalty and the colonial entity had to be partitioned; in the United States during the Civil War, regional loyalty had to be reconciled by force. These are examples of the extreme tensions that can arise when subnational loyalties are stronger than national. The last example will serve to point up that the political problems created may persist for generations after the primacy of national loyalty is established by force.

Political Experiences

The source of the attitudes we have discussed thus far stem largely from *other than* national political experiences. A second kind of relevant experiences that mold political culture is those which people have directly with the political system itself. One must inquire how the government affects the lives of its citizens and how its agents treat them. For some developing countries, at least for many groups within them, the significant question might be: Does the citizen know that the goverment exists? He may know that it exists, but not feel that it has anything to do with his own life – his area of awareness may not extend beyond the confines of the tribal area. Experience may be limited to the tax collector, the military recruiters, or a glimpse of the national leaders sweeping past in a magnificent but incomprehensible political tour. When experiences are all negative ones like exaction of men or money, the individual is not likely to think of government as a solution to his problems and he will tend to ignore it as much as possible. If we are considering a more sophisticated citizen, it would be relevant to inquire about different political experiences he may have had. Are his petitions to government attended to respectfully; does his vote count or are ballot boxes stuffed; is his street paved, or does it remain a muddy morass while the local politicos have four lanes leading to their abode; is his child getting a good education from public schools, or can only the rich afford to educate their children? These need not be his personal experiences – the things that happen to his brother or neighbor will be substituted. The important thing is that these direct or indirect political experiences are combined with the general attitudes toward authority, change, the nation, and other people. The experiences may change the attitudes, reinforce them, or neutralize them.

History as a Source of Political Culture

There is yet a third source of political culture: the total history of the nation. The political culture is not built anew by each individual or each generation, although it may undergo fantastic change. Historical legacy is passed on to and absorbed by each new generation. The political culture of Britain is made up of the Magna Carta, Oliver Cromwell, and Queen Victoria, as well as of the Battle of Britain and the welfare state. That of the Soviet Union is compounded of a curious mix of Ivan the Terrible, Lenin, the Battle of Stalingrad, sputniks, and purges, to mention only a few of the more striking ingredients. It should be noted that the history that is passed on is often subject to reinterpretation (the blatant rewriting of Soviet history books is a case in point) both by the political elites and by the mass of the population. Defeats may be forgotten as quickly as possible, or somehow converted into partial victories.

It may be possible to create a history where none existed. One of the cases that we will consider later involves the former British "Colony and Protectorate of the Gold Coast." The name "Ghana" was adopted at independence in a deliberate attempt to borrow for the new nation some of the historical luster of the ancient Saharan Empire of Ghana. The factual basis was slight, for the old Empire had been a thousand miles to the north, but it offered a tie with past greatness that might help to create a sense of unity among the diverse tribes of the new nation.

A major crisis (economic, political, or even religious) in the past may continue to influence political culture long after it is over. The reactions of various governments to the worldwide economic depression of the 1930's offer an example. Positive, if belated, efforts by the United States government to relieve the economic suffering served to reinforce the existing elements in the political culture that predisposed toward faith in the political system, while at the same time they expanded the arena in which political action was seen as relevant. Thus, the political culture itself changed somewhat as a result of the crisis. A more radical change took place in Weimar Germany during the same period. The feeble and ineffective efforts of the democratic government resulted in a wholesale rejection of the experiment in parliamentary democracy and the swift descent into the Nazi period.

The way in which the political system has responded in the past can thus become an important factor in the *expectation* of how it will respond in the present or future. This point is clearer if we look at the contrasting history of France and Britain. France will be considered in more detail later, but we can summarize briefly by saying that its history appears to be a chronicle of radical changes in the form of its government – monarchy to republic to empire to republic, and on through these and other types again. The whole Fourth Republic period (1946-1958) was one of the weak governments that fell in succession because they could not handle recurring crises. The average Frenchman came to expect that his government could not cope; thus he persisted in voting for parties that could not win majorities, or threw up his hands and allowed the constitution to be scrapped. The British, on the other hand, with the exception of the Cromwell period, have managed to solve quite critical problems within the framework of continuing constitutional adaptation without violence or major political upheaval. Because the government has always coped in the past, the Briton expects it will somehow "muddle through" the next crisis as well. Because of this rather wry faith of the citizenry, the government is more able to apply its attention to the problem at hand.

The newer nations have been shaped by the nature of their struggle for independence. In some cases it was a hard-fought battle (either political or military) that, at the outset, welded diverse peoples into a unified nation in the process. In other instances, as literally happened in the former Belgian Congo, independence was thrust upon them almost before they asked for it, and certainly before there was an effective political system that could govern.

For older nations, the comparable political experience may be the way in which new demands to share in the political process were met by the old elite. Did the old regime give way gracefully, as the aristocracy did in Britain, co-opting first the rising business class into its ranks, later labor, thus setting and continuing a tradition of peaceful settlement of political demands? Or did it clutch tenaciously to its power and privilege, ignoring claims from business or labor, and thus suffer the violent transfers of power that have scarred French history – the Revolution of 1789 and the Communes of 1848 and 1870?

The types of political crises that affect internal politics and thus political culture in the modern world may be related to the redistribution of wealth (taxation, social security, poverty programs), or to the provision of goods and services (schools, flood-control projects), or they may involve interaction with other nations. Winning or losing a war, negotiating an extension of territorial waters to keep out foreign fishing fleets, surviving a crisis of confidence in the pound, getting World Bank financing for a dam, and riding out a missile crisis are examples of bits of history that accumulate to form a political culture. Whatever the size or nature of the crisis, the way in which each one is solved, the mood of chaos or business-as-usual that surrounds it, is in large part derived from the way the last crisis was handled and will in turn influence the way the next one is handled.

To sum up what we have said about political culture so far, (1) it is the general set of people's attitudes and beliefs relating to politics, and (2) the major sources of political culture are non-political attitudes and experiences, direct experience with a political system, and the political history of the nation. It should be noted, however, that citizens of a given country may not share the same set of attitudes and beliefs. There may be several political cultures present and none of them dominant; we will later discuss France from this perspective. Alternatively, the mass of the citizens may share a common political culture that is quite different from the one held by the governing political elite, as appears to be the case in colonial situations. A third possibility is that a general political culture may be shared by people living in different countries. This common culture certainly appears to be an important factor responsible for the peaceful cooperation among the so-called "Anglo-American democracies" of Britain, Canada, Australia, and the United States.

Before turning to two cases which illustrate the effect of internal influences, a final caveat is in order. It is rarely possible to single out "internal influences" as the most important factor — most foreign policies are a mix of these and the political processes and the characteristics of the people making foreign-policy decisions. As a moment's reflection will indicate, the three factors interact and change constantly. Just as the personality of a Winston Churchill or a Joseph Stalin will leave its mark on the political culture and/or the political processes, so too these latter factors can constrain the influence of a larger-than-life personality. Our cases will examine instances in which some aspect of "internal influences" appears to have been crucial in defining foreign-policy choices. This aspect is more likely to be in the realm of political culture than of geographic or physical factors, if only because the latter types of cases tend to be more cut and dried and less interesting than those involving nonphysical factors.

The first case study involves the foreign-policy response of Ghana to the Congo crisis, particularly during the first months. This reaction to the results of a basically internal political crisis in the Congo will be analyzed in terms of problems of political integration or nation building. Most African states, including both the Congo and Ghana, are experiencing difficulty in developing national identity and internal cohesion.

The second case involves the national emotional crisis of decolonialization for France as the Indo-Chinese possessions demanded independence. Again, political culture seems to be an important explanatory factor if we are to understand the reaction of France to this demand.

COLONIAL LEGACIES AND THE CONGO CRISIS

To state that Africa presents diversity is to understate the obvious. We can reduce some of the differences by considering only the states of tropical Africa which have attained independence since 1956. This group of some two dozen states has enough in common that we can draw useful generalizations that would not be possible if we included the white oligarchies of southern Africa, the feudal kingdom of Ethiopia, or the Arab nations to the north.

The most striking feature of tropical Africa is the incohesive and nonintegrated nature of national societies. Most nations seem to represent a collection of smaller societies, each existing rather independently of the others much as they did fifty or one hundred years ago. Neither Kenya nor Tanzania has had much luck in convincing the Masai to settle down as farmers and stop raiding neighboring tribes' cattle herds. There is a small segment of the population, the new elites, who have had a modern (Western) education, live in urban centers, travel abroad, and think and act in terms of the nation. Even a Western education, however, does not guarantee national orientations, and many politicians have been quick to use tribal sentiments as a basis for political support. Between the new elite and the wandering tribesmen is a numerically larger group who are in the process of moving from the traditional ways of life to the modern. The change is easiest in economic pursuits, but even here it is not uncommon to find an urban worker quitting his job as bus conductor in order to go home to the tribal area during the growing season to plant and tend his share of land, or to find a school teacher sending his adolescent son back to the tribe to undergo initiation rites with his age group. The subgroups of the nation to whom men give their first loyalty are not necessarily tribes, although they often are. The unit may be smaller (a clan or lineage) or larger (a cultural group, a linguistic group, a religion, or even a region of the country). Whatever the focus of loyalty, it is common to discover that men's loyalties do not extend above it to the nation, or beyond it to another comparable unit within the nation. A man thinks of himself as a Hausa, a Baganda or an Ewe, and does not see that he has much in common with an Ibo or a Fra-Fra. "National" boundaries in almost all African countries include several of these diverse cultural groups.

Part of this problem dates from the past. Colonial boundaries were established with little regard for tribal realities and a tribe might find itself divided between two colonies, thrown together with ancient enemies, or cut off from ancient allies. It is doubtful however, that it was ever possible to draw boundaries in Africa (assuming one wanted something larger than petty tribal kingdoms) that did not divide one ethnic group in the attempt to encompass another. The nature of colonialism, however, had an additional aspect that contributed to the problem of parochial versus national loyalties. The colonial administrations neither expected nor particularly wanted loyalty or allegiance — they were content with acquiescence. Of the European powers involved in Africa, only the British dimly foresaw a day when their dependencies would be independent, and thus made a start toward developing democratic processes; and until World War II they were thinking in terms of independence being fifty or eighty years in the future. Some slight beginnings had been made toward establishing native political institutions at the local, usually urban, level to give practice in participation through jurisdiction over minor matters. In contrast, French policy proceeded as if they were convinced that no rational human being could aspire to be anything but a Frenchman, as if they could not envisage any political demands other than for greater participation in the metropolitan French National Assembly and for incorporation into French culture. This option, however, was open to only a few Africans at the time the independence movements suddenly blossomed after World War II. The great majority of Africans had not developed the concept of a nation toward which they could direct their aspirations and loyalties. In some cases there was considerable doubt as to the future boundaries of the new national units, especially in the large units of French West and Equatorial Africa. Some new African leaders who took over the reins of government were not much better off than the average citizen. Their political experience had been limited more to opposition to the colonial power in contrast to effective participation, and they often found themselves elevated overnight into the positions of power but with little useful knowledge of how to make a government run properly.

To the lack of political experience must be added the overwhelming nature of the problems that had to be confronted: disease, illiteracy, tribal animosity, subsistence peasant economies that had to be modernized, lack of transportation facilities, and commerce largely in the hands of foreigners. In short, there is a host of problems that would tax the resources and ingenuity of any nation and which form a background of social and physical factors against which foreign policy is played out.

There is an additional physical factor in these tropical nations — the glaring contrast between the modern capital cities and the mud hut out in the "bush." The naked painted tribesman may appear picturesque in the pages of the *National Geographic Magazine,* but he is an affront to the sensibilities of his fellow national who is the accredited Ambassador to the Court of St. James, or heads his country's delegation to the United Nations.[1] Almost all of the heads of government in Africa (and other leading politicians as well) have had their education in Europe or the United States, and their conception of what a nation should look like is based on the modern industrial model, not the backward peasant model that is all too visible at home. Too, in the heat of the independence movement, rash promises about the future may have been made that the people refuse to forget.

Thus, we have situations in which the modern political elite wishes to drag the population (some of which is more than willing to make the transition) into the twentieth century, but cannot because the problems are simply too immense, the country too poor and backward. Yet the cinema and cheap magazines portray life as one in which the ordinary man has a motor car, a house with wooden floors and running water, a television set, and probably two six-shooters. (The Hollywood productions that are popular in Africa leave much to be desired in terms of the image of Western civilization they present. However, the physical amenities are strikingly in contrast to even the urban African's life.) On top of this, the elites have promised to *do something* about these conditions which had been blamed on colonialism.

Foreign Policy and Domestic Unity

In these circumstances, foreign policy offers one method of diverting attention from domestic problems, of explaining nonfulfillment of announced national goals and of building a sense of nationhood among the diverse groups who lack it. Two basic themes that recur constantly in African foreign policy—nonalignment and neocolonialism—are largely responses to these internal circumstances. It should be noted that many African statesmen (Nyerere of Tanzania and Baunda of Malawi are two striking examples) have chosen to deemphasize the neocolonialism theme and stress the need for sacrifice and hard work if their nation is to develop by its own efforts.

To some extent these policies are a continuation of the revolt against colonial rule. Although political independence has been gained, economic and technical independence are far in the future. The lack of trained personnel and capital means continued de-

---

[1] The Tanzanian government, for example, has recently undertaken a concerted campaign to get the Masai tribesmen to wear clothes and to stop posing for tourists in various fierce stances (with a set price scale for the possible degree of menace portrayed).

pendence on the former metropole (colonial power) for teachers, technicians, money, equipment, and the like, who may remain as expatriates, or else the transfer of this dependence to one or more other sources of aid if minimal government service and civil order are to be maintained. The absolute amount of external aid usually increases after independence as ambitious new programs are initiated, hence dependence in these areas increases. But the expatriates and their projects are very visible; therefore one's political independence from the sources of aid must somehow be established. A policy of neutrality or nonalignment must be announced, reiterated, and if possible demonstrated. One method of demonstration, other than to diversify sources of external aid as much as possible, is to differ with the former colonial mentor in order to underscore one's new status of independence. The foreign policy of the old metropole is fair game for this purpose, particularly as it relates to one's own country or to other underdeveloped nations. Here "neocolonialism" is the magic word; everything can be interpreted as a devious attempt to reestablish the imperial relationship in new forms.

The concept of opposition to neocolonialism contains a fairly complete world view. One of its major tenets is pseudoindependence or, as Kwame Nkrumah termed it, "clientele sovereignty." This accounts for the fact of continued economic and technical dependence. The colonial power is felt to have only granted political freedom with the concealed intention of continuing to pull the strings by nonpolitical means. A basic strategy of the imperialists to accomplish their aims is "Balkanization," which is the second theme of neocolonialism – fragmenting a state into smaller units, none of them viable, which thus must remain dependent on the former metropole. The tactic is also seen as being used at the regional and continental levels to forestall pan-African movements toward unity, for the neocolonialists would rather deal with small, weak states than with one or several larger and stronger ones. The African leader who had more experience with a fragmented state than anyone else, Patrice Lumumba of the Congo, stated the African case thus: "We know the objectives of the West. Yesterday it divided us at the level of tribes, clans and chiefs. Today – because Africa is freeing itself – it wishes to divide us on the level of states. It wishes to create antagonistic blocs and satellites and from that state of cold war accentuate the divisions with a view to maintaining its eternal trusteeship."[2] The underlying unity that

---

[2]Quoted in Robert C. Good, "Four African Views of the Congo Crisis," *Africa Report,* VI:6 (June, 1961), p. 3.

is assumed to exist in Africa is prevented from developing by the tactics of the colonial powers, or so the African leaders believe. These solidarity-sabotaging tactics are carried out by stooges or accomplices recruited from within the African population. Thus the third tenet of the neocolonialist concern revolves around the enemy within, who may be serving the interests of the colonial power without knowing it because he, or they, have been so thoroughly corrupted by the colonial mentality that they act against the best interests of their own state and of Africa as a whole. The political opposition within a state is often branded as "colonial stooges" because the mere fact of political opposition is preventing total national unity. The charge may also be brought against the head of another state who maintains too-close ties with the former metropole.

Leaving aside the question of the amount of truth or fact in these charges, we shall consider the usefulness of nonalignment and of opposing neocolonialism to the nation itself. Most of the utility is related to the fragmented nature of the national society. Nationhood is not an internal reality, and the new leadership may find it very difficult to create any immediate sense of nationality by its domestic policies; the leaders are generally well aware of the semifictional nature of their claims to "lead a nation." In the international sphere, however, even the weakest and most disorganized nation can express its integrity and uniqueness. In the exchange of diplomats, particularly with major powers, the new state can assert its identity in the larger community of nations as an equal member. Even more satisfying, and constructive in building a sense of national unity, is the role it can play within the United Nations organization. Almost its first independent action will be to apply for membership in the United Nations where its vote will count equally with that of any one of the great powers.

It should be stressed that there is much more than the national ego involved in United Nations membership. The African states are quite sincere in the vocal support they give this organization. Much more than the big powers, they value it as a place where their voices can be heard, where smaller nations can work together and achieve an impact on the international scene that would be impossible if this forum did not exist. It offers a continuing arena where nonalignment can be demonstrated through voting and speeches on major international issues. They will voice strong criticisms of the United Nations when it does not take as strong a position on Angola, Rhodesia, or South Africa as the more militant states would prefer. The normal attitude, however, is expressed by the following editorial from an African news-paper:

. . . in the 17 years of existence, the U.N. has clearly established itself as mankind's last refuge in a world riddled by nuclear weapons and war-mongering politicians.
We may disagree with some of its methods. Certainly we detest its in-capacity to resist the manipulations of the so-called big powers. But our faith in the U.N. as the last resort of the oppressed and exploited, of the weak and the bullied, of the suffering and the cheated, has never been shaken – and we hope never will be.[3]

Other devices for asserting the uniqueness of the nation are available. Diplomacy tends to be at the head-of-state level and the comings and goings of presidents and prime ministers are given full coverage in the mass media. Attendance at the numerous re-gional and continental meetings emphasizes the substance and reality of the new states. Not only does all this give the leader-ship a chance to be heard and to play an independent role, but it also diverts attention from insoluble domestic problems.

The opposition to neocolonialism serves an internal political function by identifying an external enemy against whom the coun-try must unite, and upon whose head the responsibility for domes-tic ills may be heaped. The functionality of an "enemy" for creating unity cannot be overestimated. Particularly when the designated culprit *was* responsible for colonial mismanagement in the past, the credibility of guilt continues into the present. (The politics of the Cold War have yielded an unexpected dividend to the new states by increasing the number of potential neocolonialists from which to choose.) This rally against "enemies" is only one possible solution, of course, and its choice may be dependent on the per-sonality of decision makers. Other leaders confronted with similar problems will stress hard work and cooperation, and never mention "enemies" at all. Jomo Kenyatta is a striking example of this more pragmatic political style. In the process of winning inde-pendence, some degree of national unity is created by the very fact of opposition to the metropole, but there is no assurance that this unity will persist and be available for "nation building" once the immediate enemy is defeated by the acquisition of indepen-dence. It may be, and certainly appears to some African leaders to be, essential to discover a substitute enemy if revolutionary fervor is to be maintained. The process of discovery is not as cold-blooded and hypocritical as this cursory analysis might suggest

---

[3] *The Ghanaian Times,* October 25, 1962.

—the weakness of the new state and its vulnerability to external influence are quite real. Because the foreign policy is so closely related to internal domestic problems, it is sometimes difficult to determine where domestic policy leaves off and foreign policy begins. In new nations the two are much more interrelated than in the United States or other long-established nations. That is, the need to establish national identity and to distract attention from pressing development problems (both domestic-policy areas) can be partly resolved through foreign policies that cause national decision makers to appear important and usurp the headlines that might otherwise focus on internal events and problems.

The Congo Crisis

The former Belgian Congo became independent on June 30, 1960, and almost immediately became the focus of a United Nations crisis. It is generally agreed that no colony had ever been as poorly prepared for self-government as the Congo. A disastrous combination of a misguided colonial policy, strong tribal distinctions and animosities, and the fact that economic development was localized in only a few areas led to a collapse of the new nation into tribal war, army mutiny, provincial secession, and external intervention. In short, the Congo presented a magnified picture of the many ills that beset other African nations in more modified forms, and it seemed to have all possible acute ills at the same time.

The development of political consciousness among Congolese Africans had been severely repressed by the Belgians until just prior to independence. The multitude of political parties were little more than tribal political associations which had been deprived of the unifying experience of a fight for independence when the Belgians yielded to almost the first demands. The new Prime Minister, Patrice Lumumba, headed the closest approximation to a national political party, but he was viewed with considerable suspicion by other politicians, including President Joseph Kasavubu, with whom he cooperated uneasily.

Independence celebrations degenerated rapidly into tribal disorders in the main cities. Against this backdrop, the immediate cause of the crisis was the mutiny of the Armée Nationale Congolaise (the ANC hereafter) against its Belgian officers. The mutiny spread rapidly and offers by the Belgian government to use its troops still stationed in the Congo for the restoration of order were rejected by Lumumba. When the mutiny reached the rich mining province of Katanga, the provincial government under Moise Tshombe appealed to the Belgian army for help. The response was immediate—in fact, Belgian troops were being reinforced from Europe even before the appeal was made. Lumumba, of course, protested, although he was unable to bring military pressure to bear on Tshombe. Encouraged by the Belgian residents of Katanga, Tshombe decided to take the province out of the nation, and announced its secession. Lumumba denounced the "Belgian aggression" and dispatched frantic cables to the United Nations, the United States, and other countries, seeking aid.

There were actually two sets of requests for aid dispatched by the Lumumba government: the first was at the initial stages of the ANC mutiny, the second after the Belgian intervention. The wording reflects not only the fact of Belgian intervention, but also points up the two ways of looking at the Congo crisis—a difference that persistently divided interested states and precipitated both constitutional and financial crises within the United Nations. The first requests were in terms of the unreliability of the ANC and the inability of the central government to restore civil order. The second requests were phrased in terms of "external aggression" and "colonialist machinations." Of interest to us is the reaction of other African states to the second set of requests, a reaction based on their own internal circumstances. Given the potentialities for either tribalism or secession or both in most of the other African states, the United Nations military operation was a particularly sensitive one. There were two divergent views of the crisis and the military operation. The view adopted by a nation depended on its answers to a number of interrelated questions: (1) Who was the enemy—the mutinous Congolese soldier or the Belgian para-trooper? (2) Was the case one of internal disorder or of external aggression? (3) Was there a Congolese state, or was the fictional entity that existed momentarily at the instant of independence better forgotten and allowed to sort itself out into a number of smaller states? (4) What was the proper role of the United Nations, both military and political?

The actual crisis dragged on four years, but we are concerned here only with initial reactions during the first months. The answers to the above questions were eventually hashed out in General Assembly and Security Council debates, as well as by the pragmatic responses to events by the United Nations mission on the scene. Although the African states initially managed to present a united front in the General Assembly, it often concealed basic disagreements on significant issues. We will examine the reaction of the more militantly radical states, as led by Kwame Nkrumah of Ghana, for they exemplify the influence of internal factors on a foreign-policy response.

The Ghanaian Reaction

Ghana, formerly the Gold Coast, was the first tropical African state to gain independence (in 1957) and this slight chronological lead gave some weight to Nkrumah's claim to speak for Africa as well as for Ghana.

Although Ghana is a relatively small state, it has its share of internal diversity – tribal, religious, linguistic, and economic. This diversity is, to some extent, concentrated according to geographic areas. The northern third of the country is dry sub-Saharan fringe, its people Moslem or pagan, largely illiterate, and economically backward compared to those in the more Westernized coastal belt. At the time of the Congo crisis, the Convention Peoples' Party (CPP), Nkrumah's personal vehicle to power, was firmly in control of the country and still tolerated the existence of a weak opposition party. Opposition to the CPP had been largely from small tribally based parties, which were eventually driven into uneasy coalition in an attempt to augment their several small bases of support. Among these, the major tribe providing consistent opposition was the Ashanti, a proud people with still vivid memories of their former power and prestige in the precolonial period. They had not relished being submerged in a state composed of their former vassals or enemies, who seemed certain to dominate the country numerically. The Ashanti attempt to obtain more autonomy during the constitutional negotiations preceding independence had been defeated by Nkrumah, but the fight had left bitter memories on both sides.

The last election supervised by the British, in 1956, had demonstrated the continuing importance of local, as opposed to national, interests. Immediately after independence there had been armed rebellion in the eastern part of the country by dissident Ewe tribesmen who wished to be united with their fellow Ewe in neighboring Togo. The army had restored order, but the opposition Congress Party had appealed to the United Nations to intervene, an appeal that strengthened Nkrumah's view of the Congress Party as the "enemy within." Within months there were further tribal disorders in Accra itself that later spread north into Ashanti and the Northern Territories and necessitated the declaration of states of emergency, arrests, deportations, and the purging of traditional tribal groups (such as regional Houses of Chiefs).

The possibilities for internal conflict remained in 1960, and domestic policies reflected Nkrumah's firm conviction that national economic and social development was impossible without a firm basis of national political unity developed through the agency of the mobilizing single party. Nkrumah felt that "the luxury of political competition" was one that a developing country could not afford. Progress required unity and the devotion of energy to the tasks at hand. Any diversion of talent or resources to political competition was a net subtraction from what was available for purposes of nation building. Efforts were undertaken to bring all organizations under the wing of the CPP, whether youth groups, women's clubs, farmers, or labor unions, to give factual support to the claim that the CPP represented all of Ghana.

This preoccupation with internal unity, based both on the ideological tenets of "Nkrumahism" and on the pre-independence experiences, was carried over into foreign policy. When domestic politics are defined in the unity-disunity framework, it is easy to view the internal politics of other countries, and one's relations with them, in much the same terms.

The basic goal of unity was extended into international policy as well. All of Africa must be united, said Nkrumah, for the continent was only as strong as its weakest members. If the task of national reconstruction was delayed by the imperialist stooges within Ghana, the larger task of reconstructing all Africa was retarded by the same Balkanizing, neocolonialist tactics. The major difference was the greater success of the new imperialists on the continental scale than on the national. A basic postulate of the pan-African faith was the underlying unity of Africa. There was an almost mystical sense of organic unity, and a favorite analogy was that "when one finger is hurt, the whole body feels pain." At this point in time, Nkrumah was still basically pro-Western. His ideological swing toward the East did not become apparent until after his extended tour of the Soviet bloc the following summer. He shared the view of the United Nations held by most developing countries—that it provided a forum and a defense for the smaller, weaker new nations.

What, then, was the reaction of Ghana and the African states to the Congo crisis? It was immediate and intense, particularly among the militantly radical states. They were quick to identify with the struggles of other emerging nations, and to oppose any policy of the major or colonial powers that looked even faintly like neocolonial intervention. Their strong support of the United Nations has been mentioned earlier. Thus when the crisis broke, the one African state on the Security Council, Tunisia, was able to consult with the informal "African caucus" that had grown up, and to present *the* unified African view in the first debates. Although few of these states had taken an active interest in the Congo before the crisis, they identified their interests with those of the Lumumba government as soon as the threat appeared to be

the reimposition of Belgian rule. When the additional danger of
Balkanization appeared in the secession of Katanga, the reaction
again was in support of the central government. It has been said
that every African state has its Katanga or its Biafra, and the
possible contagion of a successful separatist movement is a constant danger to all. Reactions were more than verbal — the United
Nations military forces were largely composed of African and
Asian troops. Providing these forces was not an entirely disin-
terested action — the operation offered the chance to give national
armies some actual field experience, and there was a certain element of prestige involved. But it must be emphasized that these
motives were minor. The African commitment to the United
Nations as an organization was and is very strong.

In effect, the African answer to the questions posed earlier was
that the enemy was the Belgian paratrooper; it was a case of external aggression; the Congolese state must be the one formerly
enclosed by colonial boundaries; and the role of the United Nations was clear. As the protector of the weak against the strong,
the United Nations Force (UNF) must remove the Belgian threat
to the integrity of the fragile new nation, and must support the
central government by restoring order and stability. Above all,
the new state must not be allowed to disintegrate, for that course
was the very essence of Balkanization and would represent a victory for the reactionary forces of neocolonialism.

The role of Ghana was more significant[4] than that of most other
African states, largely because of the personal and ideological
ties between Lumumba and Nkrumah, and because of Nkrumah's
self-defined role as *the* spokesman for African unity. Thus, this is
not purely a case of internal influences on foreign policy, but of
one in which these influences were considerably modified by the
personality of the nation's decision maker, Kwame Nkrumah.
They did, however, serve to define the nature of the crisis in very
clear-cut terms, terms that had as their reference point similar
crises in Ghana in the immediate past.

There is considerable evidence that Nkrumah felt he stood in
the role of mentor to the younger and inexperienced Lumumba.
Of the numerous Congolese politicians only Lumumba was clearly
associated with the aim of a strong, unified central government
and nation and seemed to have the leadership qualities that could
unite the nation behind him. In June of 1960, Nkrumah had established an office in Leopoldville and his personal representative,
Andrew Djin, served as the link between the two men and, in addi-

---

[4]Ghana's military contribution of almost one-third of its national army was also
the largest, proportionately, of any African nation.

tion, as unofficial adviser to Lumumba. When Lumumba traveled to New York at the end of July to appear before the United Nations General Assembly, Djin accompanied him as an adviser. The official Ghanaian ambassador to Leopoldville, N. A. Welbeck, served in much the same capacity to the fledgling government.

In the first few weeks of the crisis, the African nations presented a fairly unified approach. The divisions within the radical group (Mali, Ghana, Guinea, Morocco, and the United Arab Republic), as well as those between radicals and moderates, had not yet appeared. The Congo crisis already had the characteristics of a test case on the machinations of neocolonialism versus the new nation, but it still appeared that it could be handled by the United Nations. The first doubts were being created by what the African states considered the weak handling of the Katanga secession. In August Ghana warned that it would take "independent action" if the United Nations continued to deal with those [Tshombe] "who base their authority to negotiate on a repudiation of the authority of the Congolese government. . . . It would be entirely contrary to the mandate of the United Nations to allow the puppet regime in Katanga to continue."[5] The growing division between Lumumba and Kasavubu, which eventually ended in the tragic farce of each simultaneously dismissing the other from the government, kept the Ghanaian agents in Leopoldville fully occupied. The façade of unified government had to be maintained to support the claim for action against Katanga, and the energies and diplomatic talents of Welbeck and Djin were directed toward papering over the deep differences between the two leading Congolese politicians. It is doubtful if Nkrumah saw the actions of his representatives as constituting "interference in the affairs of another state," but it created difficulties for the United Nations commission. As one report understated the problem, "The task of United Nations officials in the first few months was complicated by having to deal both with the disorganized Congolese administration and with the Ghanaians who appeared to be a key influence."[6]

Other activities and advice of both the Ghana and the Guinea representatives to Lumumba centered around the need for greater United Nations action against the Katanga rebels and contributed materially to the growing rift between Lumumba and the Secretary General of the United Nations, Dag Hammarskjöld. It is somewhat difficult to assess the Ghanaian position because of the striking difference between its official policy statements (which

---

[5] Quoted in Ernest W. Lefever and Wynfred Joshua, *United Nations Peace-Keeping in the Congo: 1960-1964* (Washington: Brookings Institution, 1966), vol. II, p. 226.
[6] Lefever and Joshua, p. 266.

also varied from week to week) coupled with general support of
the United Nations, and the unofficial, undocumented activities
and advice of Welbeck and Djin in Leopoldville.

The question of "intervention" was brought up by the radical
states' offers and threats of military forces to the Lumumba government outside the United Nations context, and by their obvious
advisory roles and machinations behind the scenes in Leopoldville.
Were these not unwarranted interventions as much as were the
unilateral Belgian troop movements? The logic of the answer is
fascinating. It was not intervention for the simple reason that the
Leopoldville government was not yet an independent regime! It
had merely pseudoindependence as long as the Belgian intervention continued. The African states were not intervening, or
threatening to do so, but rather assisting the revolutionary nationalists in their continuing struggle for true independence. It
is also possible that some of the more militant pronouncements
were not so much declarations of actual intent as attempts to convince Hammarskjöld of the seriousness of the Katanga situation.
With the ANC still rebellious and of little use to the central government, the Africans doubtless realized the futility of any attempt
by Lumumba to subdue Tshombe by force or arms. Thus they also
devoted their persuasive talents to advising Lumumba to arrive
at a negotiated settlement with the Katanga regime, however
odious the prospect was to him.

The events of September sorely tried the conflicting Ghanaian
commitments of support to Lumumba and to the United Nations.
The constitutional crisis between Lumumba and Kasavubu culminated in the ouster of the former on September 5. When Lumumba and his bodyguard attempted to force an entry to the
Leopoldville radio station in order to broadcast an appeal to the
nation, their way was blocked by the Ghanaian United Nations
contingent. Understandably, Lumumba lodged a strong complaint
with Nkrumah through Djin. Nkrumah's reply is revealing. "It
was an unfortunate affair, but I think the troops behaved like
that because they are for the moment under the orders of the
United Nations."[7] However distasteful keeping hands off may at
times have been, none of the militant African leaders tried to interfere with the actions of their national troops committed to the
United Nations Force (UNF). Certainly, they often threatened to
issue direct orders to their troops, but there is no evidence that
they did so. The more normal course was to withdraw the national
troop commitment when disaffection with the UNF operation be-

---

[7] Lefever and Joshua, p. 278.

came unbearable (and it must be added that they all paid their assessed financial share of the operation, even those who had withdrawn military forces in protest). It was obviously painful for Nkrumah to acquiesce in the UNF decision on this and other occasions, but his behavior demonstrates a stronger commitment to the United Nations than that displayed by some European nations.

The Ghanaian diplomats in Leopoldville continued to intrigue on behalf of Lumumba with such vigor that in October they were declared *persona non grata* by the Kasavubu regime and in late November were finally expelled.

In the meantime, the major scene of action had shifted to the United Nations headquarters in New York with the arrival of rival delegations from Kasavubu and Lumumba, each insisting that it was *the* official Congolese delegation.

The end of African unity and of the common front the African states had heretofore presented in the General Assembly was marked by the issue of which Congolese delegation should be seated. The radical states, of whom Ghana was the foremost spokesman, continued to urge that the United Nations should place its resources at the disposal of the Lumumba faction by recognizing his delegation, and by participating actively and forcefully to aid him in suppressing the Katanga rebels. (Their contention that Lumumba was the true government leader was not purely wishful thinking because of their ideological identification with his interests. The Congolese Parliament had met in joint session on September 13, had endorsed Lumumba, and had conferred full powers on him. Kasavubu had responded by dissolving Parliament. Then the commander of the ANC, Joseph D. Mobutu, topped the bids of both politicians by seizing control in order to "neutralize" them. It was apparent, however, that he was in sympathy with Kasavubu, and that the neutralizing operation was directed only against Lumumba.) The delegation credential fight continued through October and was not settled until November 22, when the General Assembly finally voted to seat the Kasavubu delegation. Alone among the radical states, Ghana did not respond by withdrawing her troops from the Congo, and later argued during the course of the Casablanca conference (a meeting in January, 1961, of the radical states and Libya) that the United Nations should be given another chance.

The death of Lumumba in February, 1961, resulted in a decrease of interest in the Congo by the radical states. Ghana's military contribution continued, and her policy pronouncements were now directed toward the Katanga secession. This continued to be de-

fined in somewhat strident terms as unwarranted Belgian interference, and resolutions were introduced in the General Assembly
calling for the removal of Belgian military and paramilitary
personnel and political advisers. The Katanga situation was
never defined as a genuine internal dispute, ". . . as it was clear
from the beginning that the Katanga secession was engineered
and maintained by foreign mercenaries and financial interests.
The secession of Katanga is indeed a clean and unequivocal
manifestation of Belgian and other interference in the domestic
affairs of the Republic of the Congo . . . and should have been
brought to an end promptly through the mandate of law and order
given by the Security Council."[8]

Even aside from the Belgian role, it was in the interests of the
African states, including Ghana, to prevent the establishment of
any precedents for separatist movements. The Ewe in the Volta
region, and the Ashanti, still represented potential areas of disaffection with the Ghanaian central government. Other African
states had similar internal problems of varying degrees of im-
mediacy and intensity. Once the disunity of the central government
was settled and the United Nations Force could act in support of
it (rather than having to choose between various claimants to the
role), more effective policies could be focused on the Katanga issue,
and on restoring order in the ANC. Ghana could again give unequivocal support to the United Nations operation, however much
it might mourn the passing of the more compatible Lumumba
regime.

The role of the African states in the Congo crisis was crucial
for the eventual success of the United Nations operation. As
significant as their military contribution was their political support of Hammarskjöld during the troika[9] controversy; indeed it
cannot be underestimated at that stage of the United Nations
constitutional crisis. At other points the Secretary General was
insulated from East-West pressures because he had the support
and cooperation of the African states. It was politically inexpedient
for either East or West to veto Security Council resolutions that
were presented with the united backing of the "African caucus."
We have seen that the role of Ghana was often pivotal, either in
deterring the other radical states from withdrawing their support,
or, when this was no longer possible, of continuing its own support
and thus lessening the political impact of actions or speeches of
others. We have also seen that Ghana played something of a two-

---

[8] Resolution presented by Ethiopia on November 13, 1961.
[9] The Soviet proposal for a three-man secretariat (representing East, West, and
Third World views) that would have replaced Hammarskjöld.

faced role until the Lumumba question became moot. Both of these roles stemmed from Nkrumah's ideological positions based on his own political experiences and internal political problems.

To summarize the foregoing discussion: We have viewed the reaction of the Ghanaian government to the Congo crisis as being partly conditioned by the domestic political problems in Ghana. A major internal problem in Ghana had been to create a loyalty among citizens directed toward the nation-state rather than toward tribe or region. Competitive politics before independence had tended to reinforce tribal loyalties, even though the CPP managed to gain majorities in all elections. The drive to establish a one-party state derived in part from the need to create unity and in part from the unique personality characteristics of Kwame Nkrumah. The problem, if stated in terms of political culture, would be that basically there was not a common political culture. Ghanaian politics can be seen as focusing on two aspects of this problem: (1) to create a political culture via the one-party state, and (2) to distract attention from pressing internal problems (that could create even more divisive forces) by an exaggerated emphasis on external affairs. This latter aspect included, as we have seen, much stress on the role of external "enemies" who seek to keep underdeveloped nations divided and weak. That Ghana was an underdeveloped nation, with a significant percentage of the population illiterate, dependent on agriculture rather than industry, was a physical internal factor compounding the problem of developing popular loyalty to a single political system.

Nkrumah's slogans for unity and socialism and against neo-colonialism were understandable in the context of Ghana's internal circumstances and were readily transferable to define policy in an international situation. Nkrumah, in 1960, was midway in his career as political leader and roughly midway in his ideological progression toward radical authoritarianism. The Congo crisis may well have been a factor in his increasingly anti-West, anti-neocolonial foreign policy and in his domestic efforts to root out the political opposition and establish the one-party state in the name of national unity. Thus we may have a doubly interesting case of internal circumstances influencing foreign policy and of the foreign-policy experience in turn influencing subsequent domestic policy.

FRANCE AND THE INDO-CHINA WAR

France is one of the most industrialized, prosperous, and established of the world's nations. At the height of her period of glory, her colonial empire included one hundred million people and was second in size only to the British Empire. In the years since 1945, France has undergone a painful and protracted process of "decolonization" that has been in marked contrast to the fairly dignified withdrawal of the British. The French approach to demands for independence has ranged from the prolonged bloodbath of Algeria to the precipitous departure from Guinea – in a towering fit of pique when that country voted *non* in the 1958 French Union election, carrying away the phones ripped from the walls of government offices. The Indo-Chinese case is instructive, not only because it was the first, but because it contained all the elements that reappear in the French attitudes toward decolonization in later cases.

France usually appears as somewhat of a paradox to the non-Frenchman. Her contribution to "Western civilization" in terms of literature, art, philosophy and even of political ideas is probably unsurpassed by any other nation. Yet the best description of French politics is that they are unstable, going from one extreme to the other. Under the Fourth Republic, politics became nearly stalemated; France could not cope with the growing crisis of decolonization since no government could stay in office long enough to formulate a policy on the problem. It often appeared that one of the most civilized peoples of Europe had devised a system of government that could not govern. The sources of the paradox of French politics are to be found in the French political culture. As much as any developing nation, France is divided by competing loyalties. Unlike new nations, however, these competing loyalties exist within the framework of a strong feeling of national unity, of great pride in being French. Perhaps because of this fact, and because they are deeply rooted in the history of the country, the cleavages within French society are deeper and stronger than the ethnic or tribal divisions of Africa.

Since the 1789 Revolution, France has had sixteen different constitutions that have included various sorts of Republican, Monarchical, and Bonapartist solutions. The French bookseller in 1848 who could not supply a copy of the Constitution because "I do not deal in periodical literature" was perhaps exaggerating the extent of instability, but the story is believable, whether or not it is true. These radical constitutional changes have not been purely capricious; they result from the inability of competing groups to compromise, wherefore the solution of the strongest group must be imposed. The radical shifts in form, then, reflect *changes* in the relative strength of social groups or shifts in ideological orientations. Basically, the French cannot agree on the form of government they wish to have. They occasionally experiment with a new form, but usually end up trying a slightly different version of an old one when a given constitution becomes manifestly unworkable. As a consequence, "the constitution" is not viewed with the respectful veneration accorded the Constitution of the United States. The French political tradition includes a strong measure of disrespect toward and violence against both political authority and constitution. The generalized aura of instability extends to the working level of politics as well. The Fourth Republic had twenty different cabinets and seventeen prime ministers during its short life.

The factors making for the nonintegrated African nation were reasonably easy to define: poverty, tribal norms, the colonial experience, and the like. Since few of these factors are operative in French society, we must look elsewhere for the causes of societal and political cleavages. The first and perhaps main source is to be found in history. France was one of the first European nations to emerge from feudalism into nationalism under the tutelage of the strong Bourbon monarchs, reaching its peak during the seventeenth century under Richelieu and Mazarin. A legacy that remains from this period, besides the occasional royal pretender, is the strong and efficient central administrative service which was given the finishing touches by Napoleon. The eighteenth-century claims of the rising commercial urban bourgeoisie for a share in political power were resisted by the entrenched aristocracy until the Revolution temporarily resulted in a radical transfer of power. Thus began the republican tradition of the right of the citizen to have a part in the government processes. The ideals of *liberté, égalité, fraternité* took deep root in some sections of society, but have been required to coexist with the conflicting claims of the nobility, clergy, and the centralized administrative state. Napoleon added the third major constitutional concept — Bonapartism, the rule of the strong man who steps in to save France when others have reduced it to chaos. The rapid vacillation among the three constitutional forms during the nineteenth century did not result in any one of them lasting long enough to prove its superiority. As a consequence, as urbanization and industrialization progressed, the people of Paris resorted to civil rebellion in 1830, 1848, and 1870 to press their claims for the right to participate. Each change of constitution served to convince the dissatisfied segments of society that it was unwise to trust the others.

The final event of history that shaped French political culture was World War II — a catastrophe of humiliation. Only a generation earlier France had been one of the strongest nations in Europe, yet for her World War II lasted only a few months before the touted Maginot Line was turned and she sued for peace. The armistice signed with Germany was not only humiliating in itself, but also represented a serious breach of faith with Britain, with whom France had signed an agreement not to make a separate armistice or peace. And if defeat had revealed the glaring weaknesses of France, the occupation added new sources of division. Not only did it divide France between "occupied" and Vichy, but it also divided Frenchmen in terms of their attitude toward the occupying power. This was by far the most divisive element, for the postwar "spirit of the Resistance" was limited to the minority who had resisted. The occupation also involved objective economic loss: the payment of an occupation indemnity of 400 million francs per day (later raised to 500 million), and the drafting of French workers, many of whom were sent to Germany. The final element of humiliation was the slight share in the final Allied victory. Charles de Gaulle was unknown in France before 1940, and he was widely regarded as a "mercenary" in the service of England. The United States and British leaders, on the other hand, tended to view him as an incipient dictator and a sorcerer's apprentice, and gave him little concrete support. Even after the liberation of France, de Gaulle complained of the "little drops" of aid from the United States that did not allow him to play a major role in the final battles or in the postwar negotiations. The mood of the country was to get back to normal as quickly as possible. For the average Frenchman this meant preoccupation with shortages of food and consumer goods and the dangers of inflation. For de Gaulle, a return to normal meant a revival of France's past greatness. The adoption of the constitution of the Fourth Republic in October, 1946, meant a political return to normal — a revival of the party strife, weak executives at the mercy of strong but irresponsible parliaments — for it was a blurred copy of the Third Republic and represented a reaction against the strong executive of the Pétain regime of the war years. It was not a constitution that appealed to General de Gaulle, and he withdrew to brood and await his "moment of history."

When historical events form part of the common memory of a people, they can be a uniting force. When certain groups remember one set of historical events, and other groups recall quite different ones, however, the effect is not unity but disunity. Such is largely the case in contemporary France, where historical memories are reinforced by ideological differences. We can identify at least eight distinct historical-ideological groupings. The *traditionalists* harken back to times when the privileged orders — monarchy, church, army — ran the political system on the basis of their superior knowledge and claims to authority. The Count of Paris is their quiet hero. *Liberalism* is the nineteenth-century variant; this being France, liberals would limit the activities of the state severely in favor of the laissez-faire economy and individual freedom. The parliamentary democracy of the Third Republic period represents the preferred constitution for liberals. *Christian democracy* is in favor of active social-welfare programs and to this end would use economic controls on business and income redistribution combined with active participation by the church to solve social problems. *Industrialism* would apply rational techniques and defer to experts and administrators to solve problems; it has a strong tendency toward authoritarian solutions. *Socialism* is an ancient and honorable ideological tradition in France: the control of the means of production by the state, but within a political context of the representative institutions of a republican form of government. *Communism* is still a strong force in France, due to the popular-front governments of the 1930's and their role in the resistance forces during the war. Its aims are classical — the overthrow of government and expropriation of private property. *Radicalism* dates back at least to 1789. It distrusts the government (particularly the executive branch), the church, the civil service, and the army. Rather than advocating any particular economic policy, radicalism pins its hopes on government *by* the people and the strong legislatures of the last two republics. Finally, *Gaullism* is the modern version of Bonapartism, which sees the contradictions of the political system and believes they can be circumvented only by the personal rule of a strong leader.

A striking feature of these diverse ideologies is the intensity with which they are held. Differences are more than political slogans to be waved at election time and reconciled afterward; they tend to create irreconcilable breaches. It is therefore in the interest of all ideological groups to have a weak and ineffectual government, for each fears that one of the others might get control of a strong government if such were to be allowed. In order to make the system work at all, the political debates in the National Assembly tended to avoid the major issues, for to talk about them would expose the deep national cleavages to view. Thus, cabinets were frequently overthrown on minor issues in order to preserve a working majority coalition that could be reunited behind the next government. Under the Fourth Republic there was a great deal of continuity in the personnel of the cabinets and a defeated prime minister was fairly sure to find a place in the cabinet of his successor. The tendency of the Assembly to avoid debating major

issues, coupled with the weak executive written into the Third
and Fourth Republics, meant that a consistent and directed policy
was impossible to achieve. A prime minister who attempted to
cut through this tangle and impose the necessity of unwelcome
choice soon discovered that he had violated the rules of the game
and had committed a supreme affront to his sovereign parliamentary colleagues.

Behavior (or lack of it) of the central government reinforced
a general attitude of hostility toward the state among French
citizens. Their experience of central government has been either of
ineffectual attempts to solve pressing domestic and international
problems, or else the periodic degeneration of republics into
authoritarian forms of government which, while they may solve
problems, further alienate a large proportion of the population.
Democracy has come to mean suspicion, distrust, resistance, and
hostility to all forms of government. Additionally, the small scale
of commerce, particularly in the retail trades and in agriculture,
has reinforced the basic individualism derived from the diversity
of incompatible political beliefs. Unlike the British subject or
United States citizen, but like the African tribesman, the Frenchman has had little experience in running local government, the
classic "primary school of democratic participation." We mentioned
earlier the strong centralized administrative machinery of the
Bourbon monarchy; this has survived the various constitutional
changes of the past two hundred years, even being strengthened
in the process. The *départements*[10] of France are administered
directly from Paris and the civil service is as inexorably pervasive
and efficient as the central governments have been unstable and
weak. The recourse of the citizen was to discover devices to protect
himself against the state bureaucracy while withdrawing further
from identification with the constitutional arrangement of the
moment.

The situation in French politics in the second half of the 1940's,
then, was typically French: a multitude of political parties playing
the political game in Paris while the citizenry largely turned its
attention inward, to cope with the economic problems resulting
from wartime dislocations. New to the political scene, however,
was the general feeling of humiliation resulting from the war,
and an uncommon consensus among most of the parties concerning
the necessity to "recapture the grandeur that is France." And

---

[10]*Départements* are regional administrative units of the central state which have
no political autonomy.

the average citizen would have concurred, for he shared with the politicians a great pride in France and its culture. To recapture, however, required holding onto what was left of past grandeur and building on it. At this point the great villain of the Fourth Republic comes on stage: decolonization.

Generations of Frenchmen had been taught that French power was related to the size of the colonial empire. It was also widely believed that the French were better colonizers than other nations, for they were liked by their Arab, African, and Asian colonials. How else could one explain the wartime heroism of the colonial troops? It is ironic that the process of painful decolonization started in Indo-China, since this was the one colony that the French government hadn't wanted in the beginning. The Prime Minister of the day (1862), Jules Ferry, had presented it to an outraged parliament as a *fait accompli*, the result of the quiet but efficient action of naval officers and missionaries on the scene during the Second Empire. France had soon reconciled herself to the acquisition and Indo-China became the "jewel" of the French Empire: a beautiful land of prosperous and docile people who could be administered with only a minimum of military and civil effort. The war changed that, as it changed so many other things. Indo-China fell to the Japanese and the myth that Asiatics were the natural colonies of European nations was demolished. French military weakness at the close of the Pacific war meant that reoccupation of Indo-China was carried out by the British and Chinese, and the French administrators reappeared only later. In the meantime Ho Chi Minh had established a national government directed toward independence. The French were able to come to terms with Laos and Cambodia, the other components of Indo-China, but despite an initial period of uneasy recognition of the Vietminh government, by late 1946 the French had decided the Vietminh demand for total independence could not be tolerated because of the danger that the example would present to the African territories. The Emperor Bao Dai was established instead, for although the French had little confidence in his abilities, he was docile and ready to accept a position within the framework of a French Community (as yet undefined). Once the guerrilla warfare was underway, it rapidly became impossible to shift French policy out of the status-quo stalemate.

Opposition to the Indo-China war had, from the beginning, come from the Communists in France. They had moved from urging negotiations with Ho Chi Minh to outright demands that France get out of Vietnam immediately. By 1950 they were supplementing slogans with a campaign to obstruct the shipment of men and war materials through French ports. Verbal opposition also came from prominent intellectuals, noncommunist left-wing newspapers, and from liberal Catholic sources. The Socialists also favored negotiations with Ho Chi Minh, but their position was complicated because they were often part of the governments that were conducting the war. They did add a new option with the suggestion that it be referred to the United Nations Security Council.

Support for the Indo-China war came largely from the center parties and from the far right, which criticized the government for doing too little. Earlier the government had been shaken by the revelations of the "scandal of the generals." The army chief of staff had been sent to Indo-China to make a report on the situation there. His report, emphasizing the low army morale and weakness of French territorial control and administration, was leaked to the Vietminh. The suspicion that the generals themselves had done it added fuel to widespread distrust of the army.

By 1951 it was becoming apparent that the military operation was going badly for the French. Their political operation, based upon reliance on Emperor Bao Dai, was not going much better, but there seemed to be no alternative. The French people were as divided over the proper course to follow as were the political parties: they were torn between the desire to avoid another blow to national pride and growing dissatisfaction with the increasing costs of the effort to hold the colony. The term of military conscription had to be increased, casualties were mounting, and so were financial costs. At the same time, economic conditions at home were improving and the proposals for a common European Defense Force proved that France was once again regaining her proper role in Europe. An active minority of voters could not accept the contrast between growing domestic strength and the deteriorating colonial situation, for by now the first rumblings of discontent from the North African colonies had appeared. The result of this "psychological crisis" was an assertive nationalism.

In the National Assembly, a majority could not be put together in support either of a push for military victory at any price or of peace by negotiation. The result was ineffective compromise whenever the issue was debated. Often it was not even debated. Because the deputies could not accept the discipline necessary to make the multiparty system work, their attention was distracted to minor matters. When the assembly recessed in the summer of 1953, for instance, they had not debated policy in North Africa, Europe, or Indo-China for over a year, despite the pressing importance of all of these areas.

Given the situation in Vietnam, the problem was to get out of the conflict while still preserving the "national honor." The Socialist solution, to internationalize the conflict by turning it over to the United Nations, was resisted as being an acknowledgment of defeat even after independence had been granted to the Bao Dai regime on July 3, 1953, thus taking the conflict out of the category of colonial war.

Standing apart from the processes of stalemate and ineffectual compromise during this period was Pierre Mendès-France, a leading Radical who had not participated in any of the governments since 1945. Of unquestionable integrity, he had, for a Frenchman, a rare gift for posing clear answers to political problems. He had almost become Prime Minister on July 3, 1953, but failed by 13 votes, perhaps because in his declaration of investiture he had exposed too many areas in which choices had to be made and because he favored direct negotiations to end the Indo-Chinese war. Popular discontent with the government failure to end the war had increased since 1953, and the right-wing government of the period could not bring itself to act. The fall of the Laniel cabinet provided a unique opportunity to Mendès-France, who was invested as Prime Minister on June 17, 1954, largely because of his promise to bring the war to an end. His initial vote was overwhelming — 419 out of 627 — particularly since. he made no attempt to temper his speech to attract votes. He promised to resign if the war were not ended by July 20. He entered into negotiations immediately both with the Chinese and with Ho Chi Minh, and brought into the settlement as arbiter the Convention of Geneva, then meeting to discuss Asian problems. The cease-fire that actually terminated French authority in Vietnam was arranged on the deadline Mendès-France had set for himself. Such unusual decisiveness was too much for the Fourth Republic to tolerate for very long; in another four months his cabinet was overthrown, and the Republic reverted to stalemate and the much worse decolonization crisis of Algeria.

The conflicting forces in French society had been accurately reflected in the constitutional arrangements of the Fourth Republic. Unable to reconcile ideological differences through compromise, the National Assembly had no option other than to stalemate on major issues. As the situation in Indo-China dragged on, it became impossible to decide either to withdraw or to win. As so often before in French history, "the man in the wings" was called upon to step in to solve the insoluble. Parliament, however, soon reasserted its sovereign right to return to the previous state of political indecision once the immediate crisis was past. In the end it demonstrated its supreme inability to function as a decision-making political institution and in 1958 was replaced by the Fifth Republic.

The Fifth Republic was the personal instrument of de Gaulle. The strengthened executive power of the Presidency, which he held, and the weakened parliament were his solutions to the basic ills of the political culture. The solution continued to work while he remained in office because of his overwhelming personal popularity among the voters — his tendency to appeal directly to the country through referenda was indicative not only of this but also of his disdain for the continuing multiparty debate in parliament. In the first years of the Fifth Republic, it seemed that the presence of de Gaulle would force the development of a two-party system that might allow the growth of responsible party behavior in parliament. The hope has proved illusory as the basic societal divisions continue to be reflected in the party system; they were only suspended on the appeal of de Gaulle.

De Gaulle saw himself as "custodian of the national unity" and in this respect he represented the Monarchical as well as the Bonapartist strain in the French political culture. Quite in keeping with the ideologies of both of these strains, de Gaulle took the policy initiative in all matters involving France's position in the world: defense, relations with the former colonies, and foreign policy. At least since 1940, de Gaulle had had a vision of a renovated and revitalized France, a France that would have some role of world leadership and whose weight would be felt in the contemporary balance of forces. To this end he had directed policies aimed at making France the leading power in Europe: a necessary partnership with West Germany, the famous "force de frappe," freezing of Great Britain out of the Common Market because of her continuing ties with the United States, withdrawal from NATO because of hegemony of the United States in its councils, and a leading role in the European Common Market. Although this foreign policy reflected above all de Gaulle's own vision for France, it also touched a responsive chord of Frenchmen's pride in their nation.

CONCLUSION

The case involving France is instructive because it provides an instance in which policy — stalemated indecision *is* a policy — was largely dictated by internal influences. An examination of French political culture revealed that deep societal cleavages often resulted in governments that were unable to act on or to resolve pressing political problems. The historical solution had often been recourse to a strong leader when this "immobilism" became intolerable. This was demonstrated in the Indo-China crisis by the emergence of a strong political leader, Pierre Mendès-France. His loss of office shortly after he resolved the conflict was characteristic of the frequent change of prime ministers under the constitution of the Fourth Republic. That Republic limped on to an even worse decolonization crisis in Algeria a few years later. This time the strong-leader solution was a "package deal" including the adoption of a new constitution, the Fifth Republic, which was designed to de Gaulle's specifications — a directly elected and powerful presidency.

As opposite as they may seem, both the Fourth and Fifth Republics are "typically" French. The former was a reflection of the political culture that distrusts political power; the latter reflected the political culture that sees power in the hands of a strong man as the solution to political crises. These two strains coexist but seem unable to combine or coalesce. It would seem that no matter what type of government France adopts, it will be basically unacceptable to significant portions of the population, even if temporarily tolerable. The source or basis of political pride and accomplishment must be sought in French interaction with the external world.

Ghanaian politics were also dominated by the larger-than-life personality of one man, Kwame Nkrumah. Internal environment was not as totally dictating of the foreign-policy decision as in the Indo-China example, for it was mediated by Nkrumah's interpretation of the nature of internal and external problems. Ghana, however, is illustrative of the general type of internal problems that beset the new African nations: poverty, illiteracy, tribalism, economic underdevelopment. In addition, the possibility of dissident tribes or regions demanding a separate national state, as Biafra in Nigeria, is a spectre that haunts almost every African state. Nation building under these circumstances is a difficult process at best. Nkrumah's interpretation of internal and external problems in terms of neocolonialism was parsimonious, if not entirely rational. It provided at once an explanation of internal problems, a course of action to solve them (the one-party state), and a framework into which the Congo crisis could be neatly placed. Both Nkrumah's reaction to the crisis and the foreign policy adopted were highly predictable given these factors.

The generally high degree of support for the United Nations by the African states is also related to their internal conditions. The orientation that would be expected from that set of factors is reinforced by their relative power position, vis-à-vis the other nations of the world. For Ghana as for the other small nations, the United Nations is a bulwark against the possible machinations of much more powerful nations – perhaps the only such bulwark. In a world dominated by nuclear superpowers, the General Assembly is a forum where small nations have both a voice and a vote that counts. In addition, the United Nations is a source of technical aid, through such organizations as UNESCO and WHO, that is untainted by the threat of neocolonialism. The long-range interests of African states are more likely to be served by a strong United Nations. Although Nkrumah had an immediate personal interest in supporting Patrice Lumumba, when this interest conflicted with the broader interest (the incident at the radio station), it was the broader long-range interest that prevailed. Despite the fact that Nkrumah dominated Ghanaian politics, his continuing and important support of the United Nations and the Secretary General was due to his perception of internal Ghanaian conditions rather than to his own desire to support a fellow ideologue, Lumumba.

It is interesting to note that since the coup d'état in Ghana which overthrew Nkrumah in 1966, the personalistic element has nearly vanished from Ghanaian foreign policy. While Nkrumah's ideological drive to create unity may have succeeded, it did so at the cost of economic bankruptcy for the nation. The new rulers are faced with overwhelming problems of economic reconstruction that demand immediate and almost total attention. The foreign-policy adventures of the Nkrumah era have been scrapped, strident charges of neocolonialism replaced by attempts to obtain assistance from Western nations. At this time, the search for enemies has been largely forgotten as policy emphasizes domestic growth and the older "sloganized" anticolonial style is only a memory.

The possible internal influences that may affect foreign policy are many. The earlier part of this chapter tried to indicate the range of factors – from size of country to child-rearing practices – that might be considered. The impact of quantifiable ones (that is, those that can be measured, such as numbers of men available for military service, levels of industrialization, and quantities of mineral resources) was suggested but not dealt with in great depth. Far more interesting are the qualitative factors of mood or morale. We have considered political culture in two rather different contexts: France, where the problem is too many political cultures; and Ghana, where there is not yet a basis for a well-defined national one.

It must be emphasized again that the study of internal environmental influences does not yield a total answer to the question of why nations behave the way they do. It is, however, a useful way to define some of the limits within which foreign policy will be formulated and may provide hints about probable directions of policy. In conjunction with other analytic tools, it adds to our ability to understand and ultimately to predict.

Part II

Additional Reading

Abel, Elie. *The Missile Crisis.* New York: Harper, 1965.

Almond, Gabriel, and Sidney Verba. *The Civic Culture.* Princeton University Press, 1963.

Apter, David E. *Ghana in Transition.* New York: Atheneum, 1963.

Aspaturian, Vernon. *The Soviet Union in the World Communist System.* Stanford: The Hoover Institution, 1969.

Austin, Dennis. *Politics in Ghana, 1946-1960.* London: Oxford University Press, 1964.

Bailey, Thomas A. *A Diplomatic History of the American People,* 4th ed. New York: Appleton-Century-Crofts, 1950.

Bailey, Thomas A. *The American Pageant.* Boston: Little, Brown, 1956.

Bailey, Thomas A. *Woodrow Wilson and the Great Betrayal.* New York: Macmillan, 1945.

Barnett, A. Doak. *China After Mao.* Princeton University Press, 1969.

Brzezinski, Zbigniew K., and Samuel P. Huntington. *Political Power USA/USSR.* New York: Viking, 1965.

Brzezinski, Zbigniew K. *The Soviet Bloc, Unity and Conflict,* 2nd rev. ed. New York: Praeger, 1963.

Burns, Arthur Lee, and Nina Heathcote. *Peacekeeping by United Nations Forces, From the Suez to The Congo.* New York: Published for the Center of International Studies, Princeton University, by Praeger, 1963.

China After the Cultural Revolution. Prepared by *The Bulletin of Atomic Scientists.* New York: Vintage Books, 1969.

Cohen, Bernard Cecil. *The Political Process and Foreign Policy; The Making of the Japanese Peace Settlement.* Princeton University Press, 1957.

Crankshaw, Edward. *Khrushchev: A Career.* New York: Vintage Books, 1967.

Furniss, Edgar Stephenson. *France, Troubled Ally; De Gaulle's Heritage and Prospects,* 1st ed. New York: Published for the

Council on Foreign Relations by Harper, 1960.

Gehlen, Michael. *The Politics of Coexistence.* Bloomington: Indiana University Press, 1967.

Grosser, Alfred. *French Foreign Policy under De Gaulle.* Boston: Little, Brown, 1965.

Hermann, Charles F. "Some Consequences of Crisis Which Limit the Viability of Organizations." *Administrative Science Quarterly,* VIII, 1963.

Hermann, Charles F. (ed.) *Contemporary Research in International Crisis.* New York: Free Press, 1971 (forthcoming).

Hermann, Charles F. (ed.) *Crises in Foreign Policy.* Indianapolis: Bobbs-Merrill, 1969.

Jacobs, Dan (ed.) *The New Communisms.* New York: Harper, 1969.

Lefever, Ernest W. *Uncertain Mandate.* Baltimore: Johns Hopkins Press, 1967.

Legum, Colin. *Pan-Africanism, A Short Political Guide,* rev. ed. New York: Praeger, 1963.

Linden, Carl. *Soviet Leadership Under Khrushchev, 1957-1964.* Baltimore: Johns Hopkins Press, 1967.

Link, Arthur S. *American Epoch.* New York: Knopf, 1955.

Luethy, Herbert. *France against Herself.* New York: Meridian, 1957.

McKay, Vernon (ed.) *African Diplomacy.* New York: Praeger, 1966.

Morgenthau, Hans J. "The American Tradition in Foreign Policy," in Roy C. Macridis, ed., *Foreign Policy in World Politics,* 2nd ed. Englewood Cliffs: Prentice-Hall, 1962.

Morison, Samuel E. *The Oxford History of the American People.* New York: Oxford University Press, 1965.

Pachter, Henry H. *Collision Course: The Cuban Missile Crisis and Co-Existence.* New York: Praeger, 1963.

Pye, Lucien W., and Sidney Verba. *Political Culture and Political Development.* Princeton University Press, 1966.

Rosenau, James (ed.) *Domestic Sources of Foreign Policy.* New York: Free Press, 1967. (*Conference on Public Opinion and Foreign Policy,* Princeton, N.J., 1967.)

Salisbury, Harrison. *War between Russia and China.* New York: Bantam Books, 1970.

Sigmund, Paul (ed.) *Ideologies of the Developing Nations.* New York: Praeger, 1962.

Snyder, Richard C., H. W. Brauck, and Burton Sapin (eds.) *Foreign*

Policy Decision Making; An Approach to the Study of International Politics. New York: Free Press, 1962.

Sorensen, Theodore. *Decision Making in the White House.* New York: Columbia University Press, 1963.

Sorensen, Theodore. *Kennedy.* New York: Harper, 1963.

Spanier, John. *American Foreign Policy Since World War II,* 3rd rev. ed. New York: Praeger, 1968.

Thompson, Scott W. *Ghana's Foreign Policy, 1957-1966.* Princeton University Press, 1969.

Thomson, David. *Democracy in France Since 1870,* 4th ed. New York and London: Oxford University Press, 1964.

Ulam, Adam. *Expansion and Coexistence.* New York: Praeger, 1969.

von der Mehden, Fred R. *Politics of the Developing Nations,* 2nd ed. Englewood Cliffs: Prentice-Hall, 1969.

Wallerstein, Immanuel. *The Politics of Unity.* New York: Vintage Books, 1969.

Woddis, Jack. *Introduction to Neo-Colonialism.* New York: International Publishers, 1967.

Young, Crawford. *Politics in the Congo.* Princeton University Press, 1965.

Zagoria, Donald, *Vietnam Triangle: Moscow/Peking/Hanoi.* New York: Pegasus, 1967.

Part III

CONCLUSION

Chapter 6

THE SEARCH FOR PATTERNS AND TRENDS

LeRoy Graymer
University of California, Berkeley

Parts I and II of this book have been devoted to an examination of patterns of relations between nations and some of the factors that influence the behavior of the entities engaged in interaction. The value of studying patterns of international relations that have functioned historically lies in the ability to learn the critical questions that can be asked to determine what patterns of relations exist currently and may develop in the future. It may be possible to ascertain or predict conditions which will lead to instability or stability or substantially alter relations between entities functioning in the international system.

The major factors that appear to play a key role in shaping the patterns of international relations are the number and characteristics of the actors (nation-states in most cases), their relative capabilities, and the rules that have been generally followed by the foreign-policy decision makers in each of the participating units. Rules in this case are not legal or enforceable but rather are types of actions and responses required to allow the system to function. We have sought to discover what appear to be regular patterns of interaction between certain kinds of actors. These systems can be more or less stable and are subject to transformations.

We have been most interested in the conditions that affect stability and change in these systems. In this chapter we will concentrate on those factors and conditions which give some evidence of having a major impact on the current international system. In doing so we will draw extensively from the materials in Parts I and II of this discussion, though they may not be specifically cited.

Specifically, this chapter will focus on national cohesion, orientation and values of leaders, technological and economic developments, and the future viability of the nation-state, and will conclude with some analysis of what future events may alter the international system.

NATIONAL COHESION AND FOREIGN POLICY

In the nearly 140 independent political entities in the world today, one can find very diverse political systems. We use many different kinds of labels to characterize these political systems, such as democratic, authoritarian, communist, socialist, or nationalist. For our purposes, these labels are not very useful. What is most helpful for our purposes is to determine the degree to which these societies are socially and politically cohesive units and what factors in the society are likely to become articulated in ways that influence foreign policy. Which individuals will become political leaders and in what degree national leaders can pursue certain foreign-policy objectives will depend on the extent to which they can maintain or gain the support of the population or certain constituencies for those policies.

To some extent, the stability of a political system is influenced by the degree of shared community on the part of its citizens. If people speak the same language, share a common set of values, and feel themselves part of a social system that rewards more often than it punishes, one might expect a relatively stable political system. Every political system has a set of national symbols that reinforce the psychological dimensions of identity. Flags, emblems, common history (as taught in school), and anthems are a part of the shared experience and views held by the people. The presence or lack of shared values and symbols of identity can be important factors in the stability of political systems. National identity is sometimes reinforced by an in-group out-group perception. Certain other groups or nations may be perceived as the "common enemy."

However, we can find many examples of nation-states which have survived, even though they do not share some important social values. Many of the well-established and stable European countries have populations which speak different languages, are of different religious orientation, and have groups who have successfully resisted efforts to be "nationalized." For example, the USSR contains many diverse nationalities; Belgium has two sharply contrasted linguistic and cultural groups; and Switzerland is a confederation of distinct groups that speak French, German, Italian, and Romansch. In these cases, the political system is built around areas of agreement and interdependence, leaving out of the political arena as much as possible those issues on which sharp differences exist. In other societies these differences are part of the political process and constitute a genuine threat to the maintenance of the political unit; Malaysia, Indonesia, and Nigeria are examples.

It may be useful to employ a set of concepts such as *power*, *legitimacy*, and *exchange* when examining the political viability of national units. Some political entities persist by virtue of the overwhelming *power* possessed by the political leader. The power may be measured by the degree of monopoly he has over force and by the degree to which he can manipulate divided political opponents. Also, mass popular appeal is used by leaders to neutralize opposing political organizations – particularly if the leaders can maintain a monopoly over mass communications. For this conceptualization, it suffices to say that political leaders can use coercion and manipulation to exercise their will.

Another concept which is important to the maintenance of the political system is *exchange*. The government sees to it that the economic system functions to meet people's material needs, that the trains run on time, that people feel protected from external threats, that their children have access to education, and that other expectations are satisfied. In turn, people are prepared to pay taxes, they submit to conscription, and they don't challenge the authority of the government.

A third concept which is closely related to power and exchange is *legitimacy*. In this case people need not necessarily agree with every act taken by the government, but they consider the system to be one which deserves their support. Legitimacy is related to how effectively the government protects and preserves the major values shared by most of the people in the system. In some cases it may be based on how effectively the government functions without encroaching on individual liberties. Another important factor is how much the government avoids becoming the tool of special interests and consistently excludes other groups from access and rewards in the system. In the United States, evidence of legitimacy might be reflected in the willingness of opposing candidates and the electorate in general to accept the president as their national leader even though he may have just won an election by a narrow margin over his opponent. Kennedy in 1960 and Nixon in 1968 won by very slight margins over their opponents, yet polls, shortly after the elections, showed overwhelming popular support for both presidents. Even in authoritarian societies a great emphasis is placed on generating popular enthusiasm for the government.

In this formulation, one could anticipate that where government enjoys legitimacy it is based on an effective exchange system plus a sufficiently large set of shared values, where the population generally sees the government as the custodian of these values. The more fragmented the society, in terms both of interdependence and shared values, the more the political leaders will need to rely on the exercise of force and manipulation to maintain their leadership. One could not hold out much promise for the political viability of any political system where political leaders could not rely on the presence of some mixture of these three factors. While democracies presumably must rely on a great degree of legitimacy and exchange, all modern political systems attempt to maintain the "support" of their population. In fact, all modern nation-states have built elaborate systems of propaganda, education, and organization to mobilize the support of their populations. National leaders have attempted to set the values of society and "educate" their populations to these values. The effort to establish national identity often depends on defining who is *not* a member of the group. Nationalism spills over into chauvinism as people identify other groups and nations as enemies against whom aggression is justified.

There are undoubtedly some "countries" that exist as territorial states only because the political leaderships have not had to face a serious challenge. This may be the case when the society is so fragmented and groups so self-sufficient that government is not called on to perform any significant function. Another reason for the existence of a state may be historical accident – such as having been a colonial territory. In some newly independent states, the basis for identity may have been a shared desire by several groups to rid themselves of colonialism. As was indicated in Chapter 5, many of the African states, once they have passed through the first phase of anticolonialism, have been taken over by military coup. As the demands on these governments increase, they become very hard pressed to reconcile critical value differences without resorting to military rule. In fact, many military governments came into being because they alone possessed the required monopoly on force. Other political parties or groups are overwhelmed because they cannot find support for their leadership beyond their own subgroup within the total population.

The number of sovereign political entities has greatly expanded in the last ten years, largely in consequence of the decolonization of Africa and Asia. While most of these entities do not share the common history, values, and interdependence that provide the basis for national identity, they do function with some type of central government that acts on foreign-policy matters.

For our purposes, the reason for learning something about the level of cohesiveness in these countries is to determine the stability of their leadership and actions in foreign-policy matters. These leaders are likely to be preoccupied with maintaining their own leadership and with internal political stability. Their reactions to issues in international politics will be greatly influenced by their domestic concerns. They are particularly sensitive to any foreign power's intrusion into their domestic affairs. The Biafran revolt in Nigeria was seen by many African leaders as a phenomenon which could occur in their own countries. For this reason, very few African states actively supported Biafra's fight for independence.

Conditions contributing to political instability in newly independent states are not limited to questions of diverse social backgrounds and lack of common cultural values. Severe economic problems place great burdens on the exchange role of the state. Shortages of capital and skilled manpower, lack of diversity in resources and products, and overdependence on external economic conditions are only a few of the almost uncontrollable problems confronting the beleaguered leaders of these countries. Expectations for the "good life" after independence place a great burden on weak economies. Under these circumstances, the degree of dependence on other major powers in the world is very substantial. Foreign aid, loans, and investments are sources of some of the scarce capital and direct assistance required for development. On many occasions survival depends on such aid.

Since aid is afforded almost always with some political or economic motivations on the part of the contributor, serious problems arise for political leaders who wish to build political identity on the basis of "national independence." Some national leaders have had the good fortune and astuteness to gain assistance from both of two major powers who were seeking to gain allies or at least neutralize the influence of the other. Thus India has been aided by both the Soviet Union and the United States. Under these circumstances aid is less likely to compromise independence. In other cases, support has been forthcoming only when both domestic and foreign policy have been compatible with the "interests" of the contributing nations.

The effort by smaller countries to gain increased latitude in their relations with major powers is explainable not only in terms of anticolonial ideology, for it is most often advantageous for these countries to seek multiple sources of foreign aid. Also the greater the market opportunities, the less dependent they are on one power. World markets for the single crops and commodities of small countries are very unstable. Most underdeveloped countries are extremely dependent on the modern industrial nations for purchase of their commodities. Increasing their market options helps to stabilize their economies.

The emergence of a large number of "nonaligned" nations who act in the international system to maximize their options is a reasonable outgrowth of the several internal considerations discussed here and in Part II. To be sure, there are several cases where geographic proximity, interdependent economies, and the dependence of political leaders on external support prevent the movement toward a nonaligned position for some countries. Certain Eastern European leaders have depended on Soviet military and economic support to maintain their political leadership within their countries. North Korean leaders – for historical, ideological, and geographic reasons – are not likely to look to the United States. However, even in these cases they have had some options between the Soviet Union and China.

While newly independent countries are having difficulties with domestic stability, their leaders are rather consistent in certain general foreign-policy directions. They seek to open their options for trade and external support without becoming dependent. They try to avoid getting involved in ways that will cause the major powers to fight over their terrains. "When the elephants fight, the grass gets trampled." Neutrality and nonalignment are positions espoused by many leaders of these countries on matters of conflict between major powers.

On the general philosophy of decolonization and the need for economic aid to developing countries the new countries speak together. However, this consensus does not carry over into specific matters of relations between themselves on a host of other political issues in international politics. There are sharp disagreements between these countries on almost all other issues, as is made evident by efforts to organize among themselves – no attempt to create unity and organization between these countries has succeeded. They find that beyond the very generalized interests discussed above, they have nothing in common that provides a basis for economic and political cooperation.

The discussion of internal stability has, so far, focused on problems of newly independent and smaller powers. Major industrial and traditionally well-established nations are also confronting major problems of stability. Challenges to political authority and even to the legitimacy of the political systems are being dramatically raised in most industrial nations today. The United States, with a long history of assimilating national minorities and dissonant groups into the "mainstream," has recently experienced substantial unrest evidenced by the eruption of violence in its cities and on campuses. Racial tension, the urban crush, radical youth movements, the tragedy and frustration of the Vietnam war, the pollution of the environment, all are problems which have provided impetus to some serious challenges to authority that go beyond the normal "bread-and-butter issues" that United States politicians are used to confronting. Very fundamental value questions related to national ideals, challenges to the basis for authority in society, and concern over the "quality of life" are being raised by an increasingly articulate and educated population. Social phenomena such as alienation and privatization have accompanied the decline in the effectiveness of traditional institutions in American society. The communications media have overdrawn the dramatic event, but there is at least evidence of noisy and possibly widespread disaffection among many groups in the society today. When major government policies create a crisis over certain basic values in society, political activity is likely to go beyond the use of regular channels for effecting policy changes. The legitimacy of the system may even be challenged. Also when certain groups who see themselves as being consistently on the short end of the *exchange system* become politically active, they may express opposition to the system rather than seek "a piece of the action." There is very little basis for claiming that these attitudes are shared by large segments of the population.

The long-run relationship of this phenomenon to foreign policy will depend on how pervasive it is. In the shorter run, we can clearly see that the opportunity for the leaders of the United States to pursue another war like Vietnam will be very constrained, at least for the near future. Between the dissatisfaction of those who felt we should not have "fought with our hands tied" and those who could find no justification for United States military involvement in Vietnam, there has been a real loss of support for government policy. The electorate in the United States seldom votes on anything so clear-cut as a specific foreign-policy issue; but general attitudes and feelings, coupled with the effects of foreign policy on domestic issues like inflation and poverty programs, can set the stage for foreign-policy change and even effect a change in political leadership.

The ability of any modern nation to hold up a credible threat to any other has depended greatly on the ability to mobilize its population. Wars are no longer comparable to chess games in which national leaders could skillfully outmaneuver the opponent by gaining good field position; nations must now conscript citizens into mass armies equipped with weapons that can devastate the domestic population and economy of the opponent. "Victors" and losers can expect to suffer significant casualties if they engage in risky ventures. Even limited wars, localized as was the Vietnam war, can prove to be chancy for domestic stability.

The level of national cohesion and the legitimacy of the government have an important impact on the latitude of decision makers in foreign policy. The credibility of a threat to use force against another nation can depend on whether the leaders have the support of their populations. The recent developments in industrial societies very greatly influence the capabilities of leaders to use force or threaten to use it in foreign policy. If states have sufficiently large-scale disaffection and fighting within their countries these will have significant impact on foreign-policy choices.

ORIENTATION AND VALUES OF POLITICAL LEADERS

While many of the internal factors we have discussed emphasize the social, economic, and political pressures on leaders, we must recognize that, in foreign-policy matters, a great deal of latitude is usually available to national leaders. Domestic affairs place constraints on policy choices, but they seldom dictate specific foreign-policy decisions. Also, leaders have at their command many resources to manipulate attitudes on foreign-policy issues. The degree to which the government is regarded as legitimate greatly affects the amount of influence leaders can exercise in gaining popular support for their foreign policy.

Since leaders interpret the events and information related to foreign policy, their perspectives define the situation. When the balance of power functioned in eighteenth-century Europe, the effectiveness resulted in large part from the relatively similar backgrounds and orientation of leaders. No crusading spirit or ideological fervor existed which would dictate that the enemy must be annihilated. Other states were regarded as opponents in a process where each was vying for comparative advantage with others. An actor would not seek to destroy a potential alliance partner. In contrast, when a national leader has aspirations for world domination by a "superior race of men" who have previously suffered disgrace at the hands of their enemies, he is not likely to respond to any set of appeals premised on "gentle-men's agreements." The British effort to appease Hitler in 1938 is an example of two sets of national leaders engaged in a "game" with each following a different set of rules.

One of the most fundamental differences in opinion over current United States foreign policy revolves around disagreement over whether Soviet leaders are promoters of a revolutionary movement designed to subvert Western democracy by any and all means or whether the USSR is governed by leaders who are most concerned about Soviet domestic development and the expansion of Soviet influence in the world only so long as the risks for the Soviet Union are low. That is, they will be cautious enough to see that no great imbalances occur which might risk a nuclear holocaust. Meeting domestic pressures and long-range development goals might take precedence over promoting communist revolutions around the world. As Chapter 4 revealed, there are substantial differences on these priorities among leadership groups within the Soviet Union. The trend has been toward gains in influence and power by those leaders whose orientation is more technical and managerial and less ideological. Soviet foreign policy appears to have been more calculating and cautious than the revolutionary doctrines of Marxism-Leninism would dictate.

Even Chinese leaders whose rhetoric would lead one to expect "reckless" behavior have been quite constrained in actual foreign-policy behavior. In other words, their relative capability to engage in direct hostile acts against larger powers is taken into account. They "speak loudly but carry a small stick" in their relations with major powers.

The fact that the threat of overwhelming destruction can be a powerful deterrent to unmeasured action should not lead us to underestimate the significance of ideology in foreign-policy de-cision making. Any highly articulated set of beliefs reinforced by the symbols and the paraphernalia of nationalism can be a very powerful influence on behavior. People with these "lenses" before their eyes will interpret events and "information" in the light of their expectations. The difficulties in negotiating an end to hostil-ities among people who have these fundamental value differences are evidenced repeatedly in history. Even an end to fighting seldom leads to settling any fundamental problems. Truce lines become borders because no accommodation with "imperialist aggressors" or "communist revolutionaries" is acceptable. The difficulties in negotiating an end to the war in Vietnam illustrate this point.

The discussions in all three chapters of Part II provide evidence that the general orientation and attitudes of leaders are critical in foreign-policy choices. For purposes of trying to predict general patterns of behavior, the key is to assess how likely foreign-policy decision makers are to follow the "rational" rules of the system.

TECHNOLOGICAL AND ECONOMIC DEVELOPMENTS AND SYSTEM CHANGE

Major technological developments can have a profound effect on the relative capability of actors in the international system. A major break-through in weapons technology is the most obvious example. If Nazi Germany had developed nuclear weapons by 1943, the international system would be much different today. The fact that the Soviet Union developed a nuclear capacity by 1950 contributed greatly to the bipolarization of international politics in the subsequent decade. What will happen to the international system if it becomes possible for several nations to build nuclear weapons and delivery systems? Anticipating the "destabilizing" possibilities of the spread of nuclear weapons, the United States and the Soviet Union have signed and are promoting a nuclear nonproliferation treaty.

Those nations which are already the most powerful usually have the greatest capacity to develop the new technology. Research and development involve great initial investments. Furthermore, a nation must have an economy capable of tolerating rapid obsolescence associated with a high rate of technological innovation. These capacities are part of the self-feeding arms-race process that consumes vast resources in the United States and the Soviet Union. The costs of this process, particularly in a runaway race, can become overwhelming even to very wealthy nations.

The mounting costs can create domestic problems that threaten the stability of nations which also have very great domestic needs and demands. Moreover, it is hard to maintain a monopoly on the broader technology out of which particular weapons systems grow. Therefore, other nations who have not paid the high price of initial development can apply the new technology at lower costs to their own industries. While the United States and the Soviet Union will no doubt hold a very significant margin in nuclear weapons, it is certainly possible for other nations to develop weapons that could make them a credible threat. While either of the major powers could obliterate almost any other power ten times over, she would not be able to do so without serious consequences to herself. Furthermore, even a small nuclear power could constitute something of a threat if her leaders could convince those of a major power they did not care about "the consequences."

Nuclear power is not the only significant technological development that can influence the international system. Any nation with scientific and industrial capacity in the modern world can alter the balance in international politics by either a dramatic breakthrough in some special weapons area or by becoming a genuine competitor in economic terms. For example, Japan has developed into the third-largest steel producer in the world. Her rate of economic growth is such that if all national growth rates in the world remained constant until the year 2000, Japan would have a greater gross national product than any other world power, including the United States and the USSR. Such a projection is completely speculative and most unlikely, but it does help to illustrate the potential for major changes in relative capability.

While Japan is a dramatic example, there are other countries with the potential to score a break-through in technology and economic development that could alter the loose bipolar system. The larger members of the European Common Market—France, West Germany, and Italy—have experienced very rapid growth since the late 1950's. China, with all its problems, has many of the resources which could be developed to make her a major contender in the international arena. As was suggested earlier, there are some internal factors that could cause the two major world powers to experience a decline in power. Domestic problems, the strains of an escalating arms race, and depleting resources could prove to be a significant drain over time.

While no country is currently in a position to militarily challenge the United States and the USSR, there are already indications that the loose bipolar system is getting looser. Expanding industrial countries provide alternative markets for raw materials. Japan, with its rapid industrial expansion, needs a vast quantity of raw materials. While the world markets are in most cases controlled by a few powers, competition could break or, at least, loosen these monopolies. For example, Chile and Peru may be less threatened by a United States boycott on copper purchasing if Japan were a potential alternative market. Japan's need for raw materials may force her to expand her military and use the threat of force to gain access to sources of raw materials in Southeast Asia. This motivation was involved in the Japanese military expansion in the 1930's and 1940's. There is currently evidence of Japan's desire to play a somewhat expanded role in Asia through such activities as foreign aid and investments.

Markets are as important as raw materials for a producing and exporting economy. The search for new markets can have a dramatic influence on the stability of international systems. In addition to markets for consumer goods, there are countries who wish to sell military equipment. France is an example of an "exporter" of military supplies. French military aircraft are a part of the political picture in the Middle East today.

The relative capability of existing entities in the international system can change. If several countries with more equal capability were to emerge, the loose bipolar system might be replaced by a multipolar system.

WILL THE NATION-STATE BE THE PRIMARY ACTOR?

In any discussion of the dynamics of international systems, one of the basic questions is what kinds of entities are going to be interacting. The very word "international" indicates that we regard nations as the principal actors in the system. In this discussion we will want to examine how pervasive the nation-state is and what developments, if any, are suggestive of possible changes which may occur.

What indicators do we have that can tell us how likely it is that nation-states will continue to be the primary actors in the international arena? We have addressed the question of how cohesive these units might be, how that measure might affect their continued existence, and what internal instability might imply. However, we should not overlook the pervasiveness of these institutions and their impact on international politics.

One of the most significant events in the twentieth century has been the emergence of a powerful revolutionary movement under the communist banner. In 1918, the movement gained a base in the Soviet Union. The expectation by the communist leaders was that this revolution could be spread by organizing people into international workers' parties that would receive their support, inspiration, and leadership from the Soviet-based movement. International communism would replace nation-state systems. The contention was that Lenin was *not* a "Russian" leader but the leader of all oppressed workers. This view was reflected in the slogan "Workers of the world, arise! You have nothing to lose but your chains." How did events, subsequent to the revolution, bear out these statements of intention? To begin, spontaneous revolutions did not break out in the rest of the world. While the Moscow leaders still gave voice to the sentiment, they did not consistently pursue such a policy. In a few years, Joseph Stalin began building socialism in one country. In fact, the Soviets have frequently sacrificed the workers' parties of other countries in the interests of Soviet foreign policy. In recent years, the Soviet Union has given foreign aid to many countries while these countries were suppressing indigenous communist parties (Egypt, India, and Ghana, among others). The USSR has given aid and support to India while she was engaged in a border war with another communist country (China). They have agreed to a nuclear nonproliferation treaty with the United States, while China has been attempting to build nuclear weapons (in fact, the USSR withdrew support for China's nuclear effort in the early 1960's). These are only a few examples from many that provide evidence that Soviet leaders over three generations have opted to strengthen the Soviet Union at the expense of communist parties and leaders in other countries. This course has been justified by explaining the necessity to build communism in one country in order to establish a better base for extending communism throughout the world. However, the fact remains that the behavior evidenced over fifty years has been highly nationalistic. Chapter 4 quite clearly revealed that the leaders of the Soviet Union have pursued foreign and domestic policies which have been designed to build and sustain the Soviet Union as a powerful and coherent political entity. She has played the role of a major bloc power throughout the bipolar era. In the Cuban missile crisis, Khrushchev was concerned with the basic question of the survival of the Soviet Union in a nuclear-threat situation. Cuban communist leaders were barely consulted in these negotiations.

To further illustrate the staying power of the nation-state as the primary actor in international politics, let us examine events in Western Europe after World War II. The European Common Market (European Economic Community or EEC) involves some efforts at political cooperation extending beyond economic agreements. Some early leaders in the EEC envisaged a political confederation between several of these states being built on top of the economic agreements. The EEC did entail a number of internal adjustments within each country, including pricing, tax policy, movement of laborers between countries, and standardization in areas such as social security. Beyond these, the structure for greater political cooperation was provided in the institutional arrangements. Through the early years, there was much discussion about a political confederation. However, in spite of the miraculous success in the economic sphere, significant differences remained in political and military policy. Particularly France under de Gaulle's leadership was concerned with reestablishing the French position internationally. The Gaullist position, discussed in Chapter 5, was incompatible with the development of a supranational institution in which French sovereignty might be even slightly subordinated to some larger political entity. In the area of relations with the United States and United Kingdom, the French leader took a position which was highly independent and not indicative of any desire to lessen national sovereignty.

In the United Nations the French consistently chose the position which reinforced the line of national self-determination. Article 2, Section 7 of the United Nations Charter states that:

Nothing contained in the present Charter shall authorize the United Nations to intervene in matters which are essentially within the domestic jurisdiction of any state or shall require the Members to submit such matters to settlement under the present Charter. . . .

This clause was consistently employed by France to demonstrate that French foreign policy was based on a French definition of her national interests.

While the French example under de Gaulle may provide us with a classical statement for national independence, there is no substantial evidence that de Gaulle's successors will act to seriously alter this stance. From what we can learn of French political culture and observe of French foreign policy, they are not apt to support supranational organizations in the near future.

This discussion could continue with an examination of foreign policies of almost all nations in the world today. While we would find substantial evidence of cooperation between nations, we see little or no evidence of self-conscious policy designed to alter the system by creating institutional arrangements that will supplant the nation-state. United States policy in Western Europe and Japan after World War II has been considered by many as very enlightened. The United States did not pursue a policy of repression against the defeated nations. In fact, the United States helped to facilitate the restoration of the economy of two former enemy nations – Germany and Japan – and also entered military alliances with both of these powers. In Western Europe, United States initiative created the North Atlantic Treaty Organization (NATO), an alliance that committed the participants to mutual defense. It does not take a very sophisticated analysis to see that the aid and the military alliances were *not* steps in the creation of new supranational entities. In the cases of Germany and Japan, national actors were restored to positions of power to strengthen an alliance in opposition to a major threat from a strong USSR. The United States retained its autonomy while seeking to strengthen other nations who might help oppose expansion of Soviet power and influence.

The evidence shows that political leaders in nations function in ways to preserve the continued existence of the nation-state. Other factors could interfere with these efforts, but we are not likely to see the political leaders responding to facilitate these changes. However, this fact does not preclude the possibility that the nation-state could be replaced. Many of the major developments in man's history have been culminations of several individual policies which, taken in their entirety, led to unforeseen consequences. The Industrial Revolution was not a design developed by some master planner. What clues can we find which would suggest that there may be another kind of political unit emerging which would supersede, subsume, or develop alongside the nation-state? First, we can find growth in the number of exchanges and communications that take place outside the official actions of governments. People travel internationally at an increasing rate; transactions by other than government agencies are increasing; communications in all forms are multiplying. It is hard for governments to maintain control over what their populations know about other countries and how they interact in "nonofficial" ways. Writers, scholars, scientists, businessmen all have associations and regular contacts in other countries and frequently belong to international associations. These affiliations and interdependencies are already sufficient to constitute problems for governments trying to control certain activities and communications.

Some of these exchanges can be costly to a nation's relative capability. Comparative standards of living become more visible and create demands on governments who would prefer to put higher priorities on industries that are not consumer-oriented. High salaries in some nations have created "brain-drain" problems for others. Scientific knowledge is communicated between scholars and technological advances are sold, in the form of services and commodities, by businessmen. Skilled laborers seek higher pay and sometimes a freer society. The Berlin wall is a demonstration of how serious the problem can become for the country losing such people.

Beyond these considerations, there is a real question as to what this high level of exchange does to nationalism. People may find they have more in common with their occupational or artistic counterparts in other countries than they have with people of other "classes" in their own society. At minimum, fairly large parts of an industrialized society have information and sometimes direct experiences that shape their impressions of people in other countries. Governments may find it is harder to successfully employ propaganda for manipulating public attitudes toward other people.

This phenomenon is not so widespread that we can say very

much about how deeply these effects have penetrated. Furthermore, the consequences do not all lead to decrease national identity. For some people, experiences with the foreignness of other people can help to reinforce loyalty to their own culture or group. This penetration does not go very deeply into the population, at this point. However, it is a growing phenomenon and has such important potential consequences, that it should be kept in mind in thinking about trends.

Aside from this nongovernmental activity, there is a wide range of official activities that should also be studied for their impact on changes in the actors and patterns in international relations. Nations do enter into arrangements which have an impact on how autonomously they can behave subsequently. Every treaty consists of a pledge by its signers to restrain their actions in accord with the provisions set forth. Such international arrangements have been most successful when there is no history of emotion-laden conflicts involved, and when the settlement results in all gaining more than they could get by failing to agree. Fishing restrictions in the North Pacific were successfully negotiated when it was demonstrated that the yields would be greater for all if they respected the spawning behavior of the fish.

The Common Market is a much more elaborate scheme involving negotiations between six nations including some rather delicate and involved economic arrangements. As has been mentioned, this scheme involved decreasing tariffs among the members, creating common external tariffs, agreeing to certain price-support subsidies, opening travel and movement of laborers between countries, changing social-security laws, and other accommodations. To administer this elaborate enterprise required the establishment of institutions to be staffed by people from these different countries. They have to be empowered in some restricted way to "regulate" certain economic activities within and among these nations. They have even created some potentially supranational political institutions with representation based on political parties within each of the countries.

The Common Market is one of the most interesting experiments involving sovereign states voluntarily entering into highly interdependent relationships with such great potential for political integration. The economic success of the Common Market is without a doubt spectacular; the development of political integration to date is not. While the commission's authority in areas of economic adjustment is impressive, each nation retains its sovereignty and right to veto measures which could commit these nations to major economic-policy decisions. Since the creation of EEC in 1957, no significant steps toward genuine political integration have occurred.

Several other examples of regional economic integration can be studied. Some of these also demonstrate an impressive capacity to deal with problems of economic cooperation. So far, they too remain economic groups without developing a real political organization independent of the sovereign members.

In long-range terms, what should be studied is the extent to which economic interdependence creates the foundation for future political integration. Short of political integration, we should look for the amount of agreement on a range of broader international political questions. At this time there is some evidence to suggest that nations act on these broader questions in such a way as not to jeopardize their shared economic stakes.

The United Nations is a very different type of international organization. It was created to provide the institutional framework for cooperation between the victors in World War II and to prevent the occurrence of a similar war. The basic concept of the organization was the idea that if an aggressor were to threaten any member, all others would be prepared to unite and take action against the aggressor.

The five major allied powers, who had defeated Germany and Japan, were given veto power in the Security Council, which was to deliberate on all cases of aggression. Since events following World War II quickly led to the two major powers on the Security Council becoming habitual antagonists, this body was deadlocked on all significant matters pertaining to threats to the peace and security of the world.

The large number of newly independent countries that emerged after 1960 became the numerical majority in the United Nations. Since their influence could be felt only in the General Assembly, where all member nations have representation, this body became the platform for nonmajor powers. They have attempted to use the General Assembly as a place to wield some influence over the behavior of major powers. In matters of greatest common interest to them, the new nations did experience some modest success in influencing major powers. Colonialism was one such common concern. Since neither the United States nor the USSR had a direct stake in maintaining the old colonial empires, the United Nations became a base of operations for speeding the process of decolonization. In areas such as aid for economic development, there is a reasonably unified stance among the underdeveloped nations. But in this area they have been less successful in using the United Nations to exert pressure on the major developed powers. Major powers have attempted to use bilateral aid to influence the political behavior of developing nations.

The Congo crisis illustrates how the African caucus, acting in coordination, effectively pressured the major powers into allowing the United Nations to act. While no great stakes were involved for either the United States or the USSR, there were times when United Nations actions in the Congo did not satisfy one of the major powers. Yet rather than losing the favor of unified African states, the major powers did not interfere with the United Nations operations. However, this case is the exception rather than the rule.

The United Nations is clearly not a supranational organization. It has no independent capacity to take direct political or military action against a member state. Its role is limited to providing channels for nations to use when they wish to act on matters of peace and security. This limited role is particularly true when one of the major powers is a party to a dispute. The United Nations is an arena in which disputes can be discussed and a national actor can "yield to world opinion" if this provides a face-saving way to give in. Khrushchev could be a hero who acted to preserve the world peace by responding to appeals from the United Nations in the Cuban missile crisis rather than a coward who backed down in the face of a United States threat.

National governments have not given up part of their sovereignty or power to act independently by entering into treaties and participating in international organizations. However, what may become important is the consequences that flow from getting involved. Arrangements which lead to greater interdependence may provide the basis for the growth of institutions that could be "influential" in future foreign-policy decision making. The most obvious case would be something like the Common Market. Entering into a common external-tariff arrangement, which is intertwined with a set of delicate adjustments on the internal-market situation of six nations, does constrict the individual discretion of each member. To handle these negotiations and adjustments requires experts and joint commissions who then either make real decisions or constitute an important source of information and lobbying on "related" matters. Eventually, if the enterprise is successful, a member cannot afford to disentangle. A veto loses its importance when a nation must maintain a "give and take" relationship, on specific issues, for the sake of preserving the overall arrangement. If this trend develops, these organizations take on increasing significance for the broader international systems.

Such organizations at this stage are still very fragile. A decline in the success of the enterprise could check the integrative development and possibly bring about the dismantling of the organization. The United Nations provides a good example of how "international" organizations reflect the existing actors and their relationships rather than making much of an impact on the system.

At this time, there has not been a sufficient development in international organizations to threaten the primary role of nation-states in the international system. The developments in the area of common markets, however, could be significant, if they succeed.

WHAT CAN WE PREDICT ABOUT THE FUTURE?

Predicting, particularly beyond the five- to ten-year range, is clearly beyond the competence of social science at this time. Even in this time frame all predictions must be guarded by stipulating that they are really projections based on the assumption that key factors will remain constant. So many variables are involved, including individual human idiosyncrasies, that we cannot expect to say what will definitely happen. In a nuclear age, one individual by a capricious act could destroy what we know as civilization. The fact that this potential has been kept in check for twenty-five years does afford some basis for confidence in looking for "rational" rules that influence behavior.

While recognizing these problems with predictions, the conclusion of a book dedicated to a search for some patterns and trends should summarize the discussion in those terms. Based on much of what has been discussed in this book, the following predictions seem in order.

Independent political entities, which we have loosely termed "nation-states," will continue for some time to dominate the political arena. The greater levels of exchange between many of these units are creating increased levels of interdependence between them. In more and more cases, we can expect to see efforts to build institutions like common markets as efforts to satisfy the demands for economic growth and development. These are not likely to develop bases for political integration, but they will provide an impetus toward stable relationships between the actors in these subsystems.

The trends indicate that major powers will be less likely than in the past to see the total globe as an arena in which they have vital stakes. True bipolarity is neither a reality nor a goal for the two major powers. While each will seek to expand its influence, they will recognize limitations on their capability to spread their power everywhere. Each will likely single out areas where it has comparative advantage for furthering its influence. National leaders will continue, however, to look for ways to expand their relative power and influence.

Industrial nations other than the two superpowers will become more important actors in the international system. As they seek to expand their markets and political influence, their intrusion into this arena will be more in the form of economic thrusts than in the form of military threats. Whether or not their expansion threatens world stability will depend greatly on how much it begins to cut into the economies of other major powers. If markets and resources are expanding, there may be enough pie for all; if not, there will be great potential for larger conflicts.

Domestic instability in industrial nations may turn more of their attention and resources to internal affairs. It will be harder to use "external threats" as a means to unify the populations. Therefore, they may prefer to keep the international front stable. Limited wars are not helpful for unifying the home front and big wars are too costly.

If internal strife continues and becomes more widespread, the nation-state system may deteriorate. In the longer span, if this change is combined with higher levels of penetration across borders, the nation-state may genuinely be threatened. If some states disintegrate and others remain cohesive, then there will be a great degree of instability in the system and one nation may emerge to dominate the whole system. This expectation is highly speculative, representing more of a projection of what *could* happen *if* certain events develop. We have no basis at present for predicting that internal strife will reach this proportion.

Some other visible considerations that have the potentiality for affecting major change in the international system are population growth, undersea exploration and exploitation, and environmental pollution and its control. Each of these raises a host of social, economic, and political issues that will not respect national boundaries. In fact, there are no real boundaries on and under the sea, beyond a narrow fringe along the coast.

The consequences of these problems are not predictable, but the fact that they will place significant burdens on existing arrangements between nations is predictable. This type of problem can provide a basis for the development of effective working relations between nations. Failing these, there will be great potential for new conflicts.

The challenge to man's ingenuity is to develop working relationships and institutions that can deal with the scope of these developments. In a time when he possesses the power to destroy his civilization, this challenge will require an inventiveness in social arrangements that equals his advances in the field of technology.

Part III

Additional Reading

Aron, Raymond. *The Great Debate: Theories of Nuclear Strategy.* Garden City: Doubleday, 1965.

Deutsch, Karl W. *The Analysis of International Relations.* Englewood Cliffs: Prentice-Hall, 1968.

Deutsch, Karl W., *et al. Political Community and the North Atlantic Area: International Organization in the Light of Historical Experience.* Princeton University Press, 1957.

Etzioni, Amitai Werner. *Political Unification: A Comparative Study of Leaders and Forces.* New York: Holt, 1965.

Etzioni, Amitai Werner. *Winning without War.* Garden City: Doubleday, 1965.

Fairbank, John K. *China: The People's Middle Kingdom and the U.S.A.* Cambridge: Belknap Press of Harvard University Press, 1967.

Friedman, Julian R., Steven Rosen, and Christopher Bladen. *Alliances in International Politics.* Boston: Allyn and Bacon, 1970.

Haas, Ernst B. *Beyond the Nation State: Functionalism and International Organization.* Stanford University Press, 1964.

Haas, Ernst B. *Tangle of Hopes: American Commitments and World Order.* Englewood Cliffs: Prentice-Hall, 1969.

Haas, Ernst B. *The Uniting of Europe: Political, Social, and Economic Forces, 1950-1957.* Stanford University Press, 1958.

Herz, John. *International Politics in the Atomic Age.* New York: Columbia University Press, 1959.

Hilsman, Roger. *To Move a Nation: The Politics of Foreign Policy in the Administration of John F. Kennedy.* Garden City: Doubleday, 1967.

Hoffman, Stanley. *Gulliver's Troubles: or, The Setting of American Foreign Policy.* New York: Published for Council on Foreign Relations by McGraw-Hill, 1968.

Holsti, K. J. *International Politics: A Framework for Analysis.* Englewood Cliffs: Prentice-Hall, 1967.

Hovet, Thomas. *Bloc Politics in the United Nations.* Cambridge: Harvard University Press, 1960.

International Political Communities; An Anthology. Garden City: Anchor Books, 1966.

Kahin, George, and John W. Lewis. *The United States in Vietnam.* New York: Dial Press, 1967.

Kennan, George F. *Realities of American Foreign Policy.* Princeton University Press, 1954.

Kissinger, Henry A. *Nuclear Weapons and Foreign Policy.* New York: Published for the Council on Foreign Relations by Harper, 1957.

Kissinger, Henry A. *The Troubled Partnership: A Reappraisal of the Atlantic Alliance.* Garden City: Anchor Books, 1966.

Kissinger, Henry A., ed. *Problems of National Strategy.* New York: Praeger, 1965.

Lowenthal, Richard. *World Communism: The Disintegration of a Secular Faith.* New York: Oxford University Press, 1964.

Morgenthau, Hans J. *Politics among Nations: The Struggle for Power and Peace.* 1st ed., 1951; 2nd ed., 1954; 3rd ed., 1966; 4th ed., 1967. New York: Knopf.

Reischauer, Edwin O. *Beyond Vietnam: The United States and Asia.* New York: Knopf, 1967.

Russett, Bruce M. *Trends in World Politics.* New York: Macmillan, 1965.

Schelling, Thomas C. *The Strategy of Conflict.* Cambridge: Harvard University Press, 1960.

Seabury, Paul, and Aaron Wildavsky, eds. *U.S. Foreign Policy: Perspectives and Proposals for the 1970's.* New York: McGraw-Hill, 1969.

Seabury, Paul. *Balance of Power.* Scranton: Chandler Publishing Company, 1965.

Singer, Joel David. *Deterrence, Arms Control and Disarmament: Toward a Synthesis in National Security Policy.* Columbus: Ohio State University Press, 1962.

Stoessinger, John G. *The United Nations and the Superpowers; United States–Soviet Interaction at the United Nations.* New York: Random House, 1965.

Tuchman, Barbara. *The Guns of August.* New York: Macmillan, 1962.

Waltz, Kenneth N. *Man, The State and War: A Theoretical Analysis.* New York: Columbia University Press, 1959.

Whiting, Allen S. *China Crosses the Yalu: The Decision to Enter the Korean War.* New York: Macmillan, 1960.

Wolfers, Arnold, ed. *Alliance Policy in the Cold War.* Baltimore: Johns Hopkins Press, 1959.

INDEX